[At] Bow Falls one fine sunset ... I found a man named Hughie.... I said, "It's a beautiful evening." He straightened himself, looked towards the west and said, "It's a beautiful world."

Elizabeth Parker, *Canadian Alpine Journal, 1928*

"Beautiful! Why, sir, I had to come to Banff to learn that there was a God...."
It was the old story of a man who in the successful pursuit of wealth and success had found himself drifting through the various stages of doubts and indifference to wind up in absolute unbelief. The relation drove home to me as never before, a realization of that subtle influence which the mountains so powerfully exert in the way of uplift and purification and moral and mental, as well as physical re-moulding upon all who come within their domain.

J. B. Harkin *Canadian Alpine Journal, 1918*

Banff has no critics because no one wishes it different.

Charles W. Stokes, *Round About the Rockies*

For the past twenty summers I have taken my family into the mountains surrounding Banff. On each trip we have tried to reach places we have not seen before, but vast stretches of untried country still beckon us on.

Belmore Browne, *American Alpine Journal 1941*

A land surveyor in his field notes ... wrote: "Land good for nothing except a fine view from the top of the hill."

A. O. Wheeler, *The Sky Line Trail, October, 1941*

The beauties of Nature retain their glory for the longest period when they are situated in such a place that they are comparatively inaccessible to man, or, at any rate, when they are placed under such conditions and possessed of such a formation that it is practically impossible for man to change their appearance to any great extent....
Surely it is in the mountains that nature achieves the greatest degree of inaccessibility, and therefore preserves the greatest quantity of glory, grandeur and splendor.

A. O. Wheeler, *Our Mountain Heritage*

No insuperable obstacles to travel exist in these mountains. Many of the passes and trails are open and easily traversed, and the field for mountain climbing and exploration is unlimited.... If fine scenery, combined with adventure of the less hazardous kind ... will compensate for the minor discomforts attending such an expedition, I can promise that the enterprising traveller will not be disappointed.

G. M. Dawson, *Read before The British Association, Birmingham, 1886*

Banff—Assiniboine: A Beautiful World

a guide to the trails
and the rich history of
Banff National Park
from Palliser Pass to Vermilion Pass
plus the core area of
Mount Assiniboine Provincial Park

by Don Beers

Unless otherwise noted, mountains, lakes and people in all photographs in this book are identified left to right in the captions.

Front Cover: *Mounts Magog, Assiniboine, Strom, Wedgwood and Lake Magog*
Back Cover: *Egypt Lake*
Page 1: *From the summit of Mount Aylmer, looking east at sunrise*
Pages 2-3: *Sunset from a knoll above Burstall Pass: Mounts Currie, Assiniboine, Strom, Magog and two peaks of Mount Byng*
Pages 4-5: *Shadow Lake, Mount Ball and the peaks of Storm Mountain from the ridge north of Pharaoh Peaks*
Pages 6-7: *Mounts Magog, Assiniboine, Strom and Wedgwood from Lake Magog*

Printed and bound in Canada by Friesen Printers, Manitoba
Separations by Colour Four Graphic Services Ltd., Calgary

Canadian Parks and Wilderness Society, Henderson Book Series No. 20
The Henderson Book Series honours the kind and generous support of Mrs. Arthur T. Henderson who made this series possible.
The Canadian Parks and Wilderness Society is a non-profit volunteer organization dedicated to preserving ecosystems, parks and wilderness in Canada. Membership in the society includes a subscription to *Borealis Magazine*. To enrol as a member, enclose payment of $35.00 by cheque, Visa or Mastercard to:
The Canadian Parks and Wilderness Society
Suite 1335, 160 Bloor Street East
Toronto, Ontario M4W 1B9

Canadian Cataloguing in Publication Data
Beers, Don, 1934-
Banff--Assiniboine : A Beautiful World

Includes Index.
ISBN 0-9695088-2-4 (bound). --ISBN 0-9695088-3-2 (pbk.)

1. Trails--Alberta--Banff National Park--Guidebooks.* 2. Trails--British Columbia--Mount Assiniboine Provincial Park--Guidebooks.* 3. Banff National Park (Alta.)--Guidebooks.* 4. Mount Assiniboine Provincial Park (B. C.)--Guidebooks.* I. Title.
FC3664.B3B43 1993 917.123'32 C93-091172-5
F1079.B5B43 1993

Published by Highline Publishing
7220 Bow Crescent NW
Calgary, Alberta T3B 2B9
Phone 403-288-9005

Contents

ACKNOWLEDGEMENTS

I thank the Alberta Foundation for the Literary Arts for its generous support in awarding a grant to provide time to research and write this book.

I gratefully acknowledge the assistance of the Alpine Club of Canada through a grant from the Endowment Fund.

Also, my thanks to:

Wynn Kline for advice on the cover design.

Nick Morant, Cy Hampson, the late Leonard Leacock, Lance Camp, Bill Vroom, Henry Ness, Bob Hind, Jim Sime, Kelly Smith, Tim Nokes, Bill Cherak, Mary Betts, the Whyte Museum of the Canadian Rockies, the Glenbow Archives Calgary, the Canadian Parks Service, Harvard University, National Archives of Canada, Hudson's Bay Company Archives, Beaver Magazine, and B. C. Archives and Records Service for providing photographs. Pictures with no source credited in the caption are by the author.

The Federal Department of Energy, Mines and Resources for permission to reproduce topographic maps. National Archives of Canada for permission to quote from H. J. Warre's Journal, Volume I.

The late Leonard Leacock, Fred Leacock, Henry Ness, Nick Morant, Ken Jones, Moe and Bill Vroom, Lance Camp, Jim Deegan, Bruno Engler, Bob Hind, Hans Gmoser, Maryalice Stewart, Ole Hermanrude, Cliff White, Brian Patton and the late Jon Whyte for sharing a rich treasure of historic anecdotes.

Hugh Dempsey and Ian Getty for helpful answers about natives. Grant MacEwan for permission to quote from *Fifty Mighty Men*.

In addition to those mentioned above:

Bill Cherak, the late Lud Kamenka, Ken Boucher, Tim Auger, Don Gardner, Jean Gill, Peter Vallance, Mary Betts, Jeanette Manry, Keir MacGougan, Stan Larsen and Mary Clitheroe for stories of Lawrence Grassi; Barb and Sepp Renner for details about Erling Strom and Lizzie Rummel plus comments on the Assiniboine area. Vic La Vica for memories of Lizzie Rummel.

For information on Bob Hind, I am indebted to his wife Marj, Bruce Fraser, Jim Tarrant, Ken Boucher and Bob himself.

Bud Brewster and Allison Brewster for anecdotes and material on the Shadow Lake area and permission to photograph the Stew Cameron cartoon at Shadow Lake Lodge. Ian Mackie for information on Lake Minnewanka.

Canadian Parks Service for permission to quote from an interview Maryalice Stewart taped with Ole Hermanrude as part of a project to compile a history of the National Park Warden Service in Canada. Bill Yeo for information on place names. Perry Davis for trail information and for making available a measuring wheel.

Glenn Boles for contributing his expertise to the section on mountaineering.

Jon Dudley for his authoritative notes on geology. Dr. Stephen Evans of the Geological Survey of Canada for information on the Valley of the Rocks landslide.

Mike Potter for permission to quote his article in Banff's *Crag and Canyon* on the bear attack at Stony Creek. Dr. Brian Horejsi for his informed comments on bears.

The helpful staffs of the Whyte Museum of the Canadian Rockies and of the Glenbow Library for assistance in going through their extensive files.

Gillean Daffern, whose artistic layout for my book *The Wonder of Yoho* has served as a model for this guidebook as well as my earlier *The World of Lake Louise*. Tony Daffern for advice about business details of publishing.

My daughters, Cathleen and Christine, who shared so many happy trips with me.

My wife, Keitha, my favorite hiking companion, for her encouragement, and for the hours she spent proofreading and revising this manuscript.

The Banff—Assiniboine area is rich in story, unsurpassed in beauty. From a network of trails you see turquoise lakes, colossal peaks, shining glaciers, tumbling creeks, ancient forests, floral meadows, mammals large and small. It is a world of beauty for everyone who loves mountains.

Hiking the Cory Pass Trail. Looking to the Sundance Range.

"My mother, unduly anxious as are many mothers, got the idea that I was somewhat of a weakling and did everything possible to overcome this failing. At five years old I must needs take a daily walk of a mile or two and increase this amount one mile for each year of my age. I finally got the record up to 35 miles in a day, which I thought enough at the time, and do so yet." Walter Wilcox, *American Alpine Journal, 1946*

INTRODUCTION

"Banff the Beautiful" was an epithet already in common use when James Outram quoted it in 1903. The area surrounding Banff is rich in splendor, and much of it can be reached by trail.

About 1895, Elizabeth Parker met a friendly workman named Hughie at Bow Falls, who responded to her casual remark, "It's a beautiful evening," with, "It's a *beautiful world*." In cold print, she could only use italics to hint at his ecstatic tone of voice.

Years later, when she published this anecdote, Elizabeth Parker used the pen name *A. L. O. W.* Though she normally wrote under a nom de plume, this is the only time she used this abbreviation; she was 72, and perhaps thought of herself as *A Lonely Old Woman*. If that was her intent, she nonetheless guarded happy memories, such as Hughie's perception of the universality of true beauty which a mountain scene can inspire.

Pioneer explorer Mary Schäffer Warren emphasized the abundant scenery near Banff. "The incoming stranger has often been heard to say, 'I think I can do Banff in three days.' He counts upon one little climb, one pony trip and one motor drive, and he can just about *do* it in that time. But he has not seen Banff. He has a whole summer's enjoyment ahead if, perchance, someone who loves Banff, and who knows her hidden secrets, takes him in hand."

This guide describes trails in Banff Park from Vermilion Pass south to Palliser Pass plus hikes in the adjacent core area of Mt. Assiniboine Park. May you find hiking enjoyment for many summers, and enough stories to whet your appetite to search out more of the area's rich history.

Bow Falls and Mount Brewster

VISITOR INFORMATION

Access

The Banff area is usually reached by the Trans-Canada (#1) Highway from the east or west. You also can join this road at the Radium Junction. Regular bus service is provided by Greyhound Lines of Canada and Pacific Western. From late May to the end of September, Brewster Transportation and Tours schedules buses from Calgary and Jasper.

Passenger train service to Banff was discontinued in 1989. Great Canadian Railtour Company offers Vancouver to Calgary weekend runs from late May to early October. It is possible to quit the tour at Banff.

Regulations

Some regulations you should be aware of are:

~ Dogs must be kept on leash. They are not permitted overnight in the backcountry.

~ It is illegal to pick plants or to remove objects such as rocks or even deadfall.

~ It is against the law to feed wild animals.

~ Fishermen require National Park fishing licenses. Information about fishing seasons can be obtained from the Information Centre at Banff.

~ Climbers may register at the Banff Warden Office or the Banff Information Centre. If you use this service, you must return the registration slip after the climb, or make known your return by telephone (403-762-4506, 24 hours).

~ If you stay overnight in the backcountry, you require a Park Use Permit which is available free at the Banff Information Centre or by writing The Superintendent, Banff National Park, P. O. Box 900, Banff, Alberta, T0L 0C0. Permits can also be obtained from Canadian Parks Service, Western Regional Office, Room 520, 220 4th Ave. S.E., Calgary (mailing address, P. O. Box 2989, Station M, Calgary, Alberta, T2P 3H8). You must pack out all your garbage. Free litter bags are available at the Information Centre. The maximum length of stay at any backcountry campground is three consecutive nights.

~ Bicycles, allowed on all roads, are permitted only on designated trails.

~ In 1993, the maximum penalty for most park infractions (poaching carries stiffer penalties) is a fine of 2,000 dollars.

Environmental Concerns

The popularity of Banff's trails demands everyone's help to protect our natural environment. You are asked to minimize the impact of your stay. Keep on established trails; don't step off the trail to avoid wet or mud and don't shortcut between switchbacks. In the alpine and subalpine zones, plants are most fragile and take longest to recover from trampling. The meadows are especially vulnerable when wet or snow covered.

Don't litter: carry out what you bring in. Don't pick flowers or other natural objects.

Pets must be on leash everywhere in the park. Dogs are not permitted overnight in the backcountry. Most hikers would prefer you to leave your pet at home because even friendly dogs disturb wildlife and bother other hikers. They spread contamination, including Giardia. Also, some bear attacks have been precipitated by dogs.

Observe sensible hygiene to limit the spread of contaminants. Don't use soap or toothpaste near water. If you must dispose of waste where there is no outhouse, choose a spot well away from any stream or trail, dig a small hole, and cover the matter (including toilet paper) to restore the spot as close as possible to its original state.

Build fires only in designated places and keep them small. Use only wood provided; if none is supplied, burn only fallen wood. Better yet, use a portable cookstove.

Accommodation

In the Banff area, Tunnel Mountain, Two Jack Lake, Johnston Canyon and Castle Mountain campgrounds can be reached by vehicle. The Banff Information Centre, 224 Banff Avenue (phone 403-762-1550) can provide current information on available accommodation (hotels, hostel, bed and breakfast, approved accommodation, YWCA and campgrounds).

Backcountry Camping

In Mount Assiniboine Park, backcountry campgrounds are on a first come first served basis. A fee is charged at the core area campgrounds.

A free Park Use Permit is required to camp in the backcountry in Banff Park. It may be obtained from the Information Centre at Banff, 224 Banff Avenue (open daily, Mid-June to early September 8:00 am to 10:00 pm; 10:00 am to 6:00 pm off season); or at Canadian Parks Service Regional Office, Room 520, 220 4th Ave. S. E., Calgary (open weekdays 8:00 am to 4:30 pm); or the Information Centre at Field, B. C. (open daily, in summer 7:00 am to 9:00 pm, off season 8:00 am to 4:30 pm).

Park use permits are also available at Warden Offices; the Banff Warden office is located at the Government Compound north of town. Up to three weeks in advance, you can reserve a site at two heavily used campgrounds (but only these two in the Banff area: Lm 8 at Lake Minnewanka, and Sp 6 on the Lower Spray River). You can make a reservation at the Banff Information Centre, or at the Calgary Regional Office or by writing The Superintendent, Banff National Park, P. O. Box 900, Banff, Alberta, T0L 0C0. The maximum stay at any backcountry campsite is three nights.

Backcountry campgrounds are designated by a letter abbreviation plus the distance, to the nearest kilometre, from the most obvious trailhead. Thus, Us 18 is in the Upper Spray River Valley, 18 km from the Mount Shark Parking Lot.

Maps

In Banff, maps may be purchased at the Park Information Centre, at The Book and Art Den, at Monod Sports, and at Mountain Magic Equipment.

Trail Conditions

A recorded description of current trail conditions is available in Banff by phoning 762-1460 or Calgary, 292-6600. This information may also be obtained at Park Information Centres.

SAFETY

Although hiking and camping experiences are usually safe, all activities in the mountain parks carry a real element of risk. If you do have an accident, the precautions you take will reduce your discomfort and may save your life.

Some things to keep in mind for your own safety are:

~ It is safer to travel with company. If you travel alone, let someone know when you expect to return. If appropriate, make use of the voluntary safety registration service offered by the park at the Information centres. The registration must be returned when the trip is completed; otherwise, you could be billed for an unnecessary search.

~ Observe the weather signs.

~ Take extra warm clothing and rain gear.

~ Wear adequate footwear. Break in new boots before you go hiking.

~ Observe trail signs with care. There are important intersections on many of these trails.

~ Bring all the items you might need: first aid kit, sunscreen and hat, insect repellent, sun glasses, extra food, etc.

~ Allow ample time to return before dark. Bring a flashlight, especially in the autumn when the days become shorter.

~ Don't bring a dog. It will increase the risk of a bear attack.

~ Take precautions with all wild animals, especially bears. Read the bear information pamphlet you were given when you entered the park

Map of the area covered by this book.

Full size map segments on the following pages.

This map is based on information taken from map sheet number MCR 220, Edition 1, copyright 1985. Her Majesty the Queen in Right of Canada, with the permission of Energy, Mines and Resources, Canada.

Corrections for trail locations, road changes and features missing on the original map have been made by the author. Public campgrounds are shown with vermilion colored teepee symbols (∧). Private campsites (Holiday on Horseback) are indicated by dark green teepees.

Scale: Distance between each set of blue grid lines is 10 km.

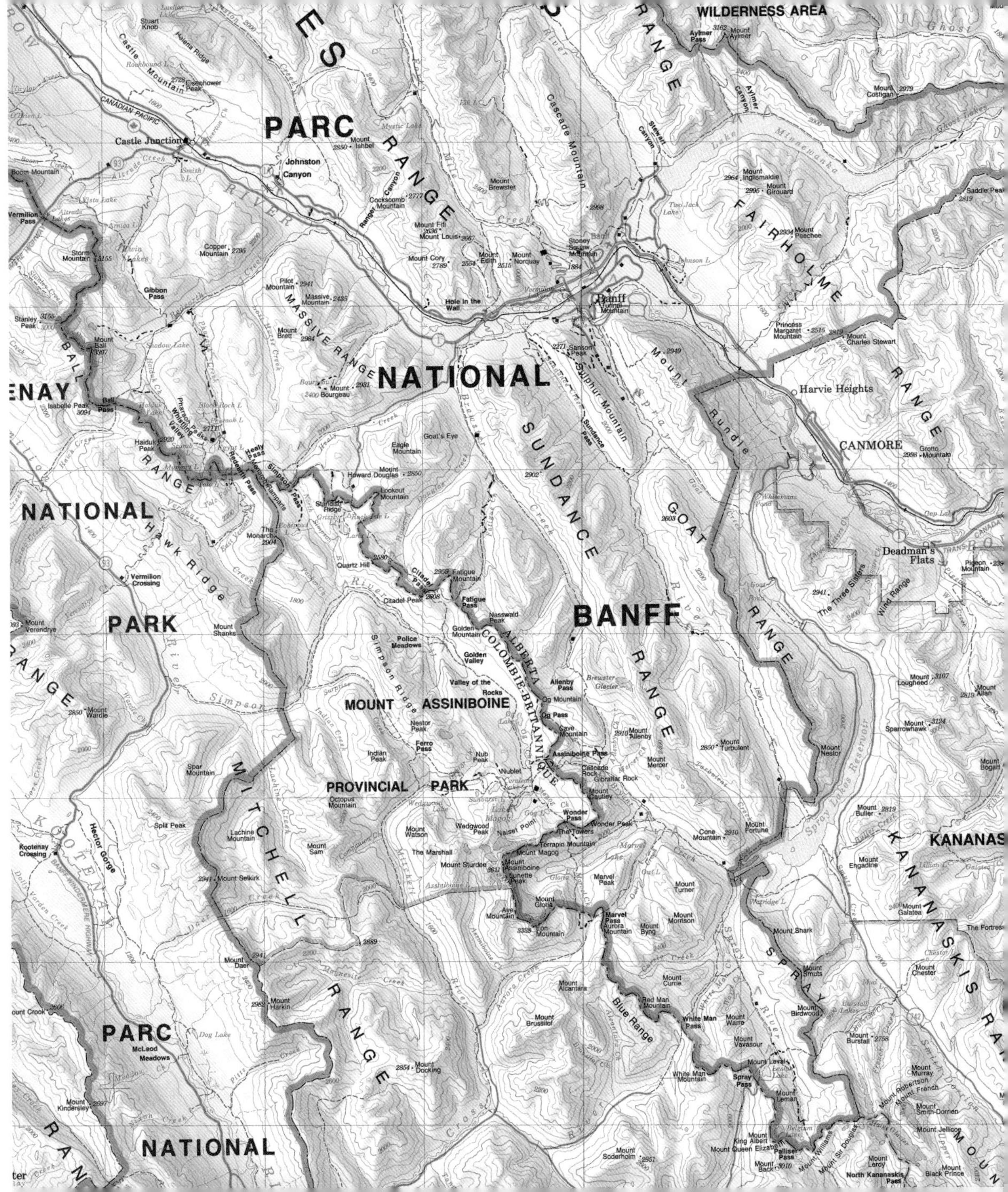

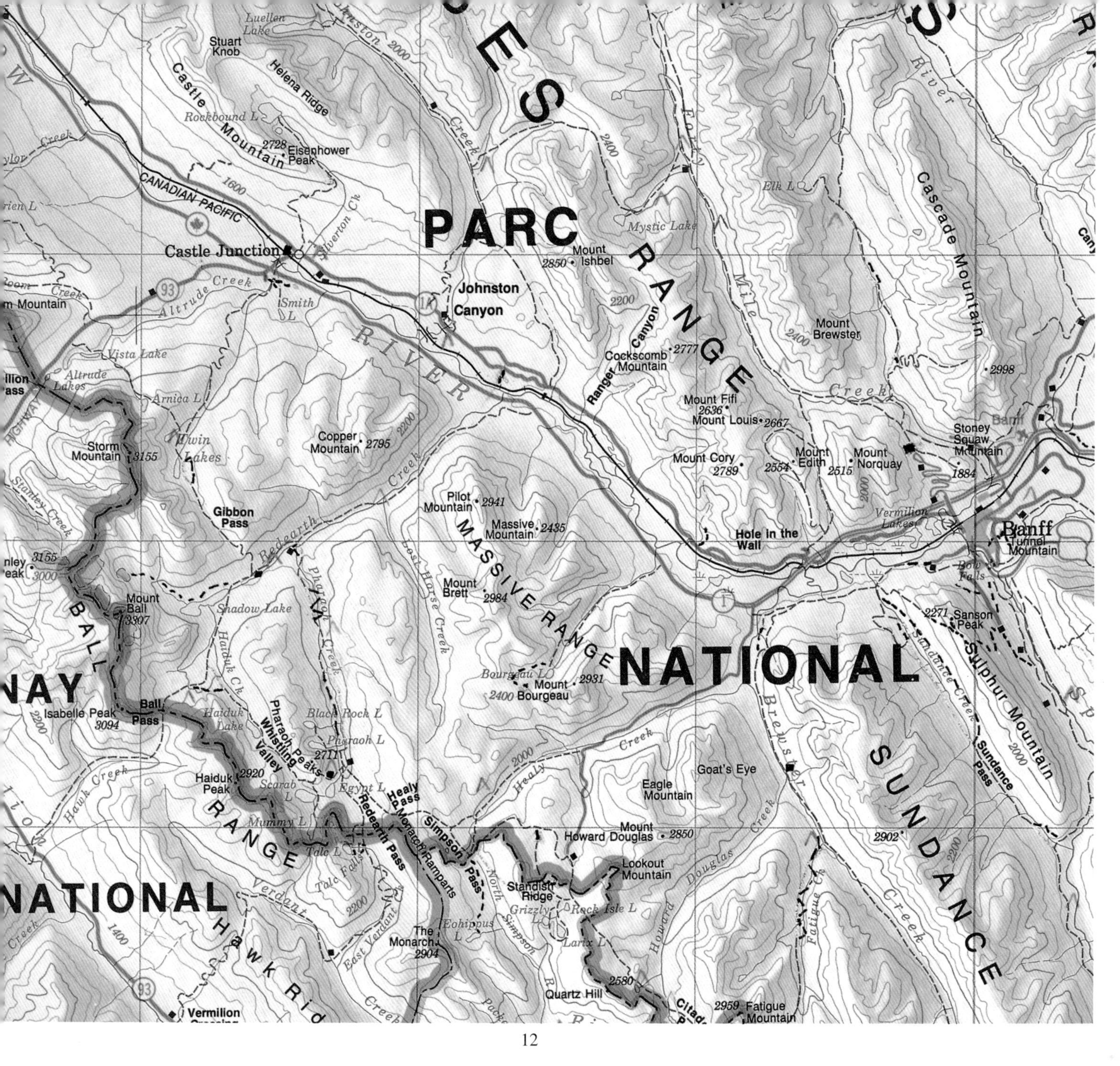
PARC
NATIONAL
RANGE
MASSIVE RANGE
SUNDANCE
BALL
RANGE
NATIONAL
Castle Junction
Johnston Canyon
Castle Mountain
Helena Ridge
Stuart Knob
Luellen Lake
Rockbound L
2728 Eisenhower Peak
CANADIAN PACIFIC
Mystic Lake
2850 Mount Ishbel
Cockscomb Mountain 2777
Ranger Canyon
Mount Brewster
Cascade Mountain
Elk L
2998
Mount Fifi 2636
Mount Louis 2667
Mount Cory 2789
Mount Edith 2554
Mount Norquay 2515
Stoney Squaw Mountain 1884
Vermilion Lakes
Banff
Tunnel Mountain
Bow Falls
2271 Sanson Peak
Sulphur Mountain
Sundance Pass
Sundance Creek
Hole in the Wall
Storm Mountain 3155
Copper Mountain 2795
Pilot Mountain 2941
Massive Mountain 2435
Mount Brett 2984
Mount Bourgeau 2931
Bourgeau L
Gibbon Pass
Twin Lakes
Arnica L
Vista Lake
Altrude Lakes
Altrude Creek
Smith L
Shadow Lake
Redearth Creek
Pharaoh Creek
Lost Horse Creek
Haiduk Ch
Haiduk Lake
Black Rock L
Pharaoh L
Pharaoh Peaks 2711
Whistling Valley
Scarab L
Egypt L
Mummy L
Talc L
Talc Falls
Healy Pass
Healy Creek
Redearth Pass
Monarch Ramparts
Simpson Pass
Goat's Eye
Eagle Mountain
Brewster Creek
Mount Howard Douglas 2850
Lookout Mountain
Standish Ridge
Rock Isle L
Grizzly L
Larix L
Eohippus L
The Monarch 2904
Quartz Hill
2580
2959 Fatigue Mountain
Fatigue Cr
Howard Douglas Creek
2902
Mount Ball 3307
Ball Pass
Isabelle Peak 3094
Haiduk Peak 2920
Hawk Creek
Hawk Ridge
Verdant Creek
East Verdant Creek
Vermilion Crossing
Stanley Creek
Stanley Peak 3155
93
1A
1
RIVER
Forty Mile Creek
River
Johnston Creek
Silverton Ck
2000
2200
2400
1600
1400

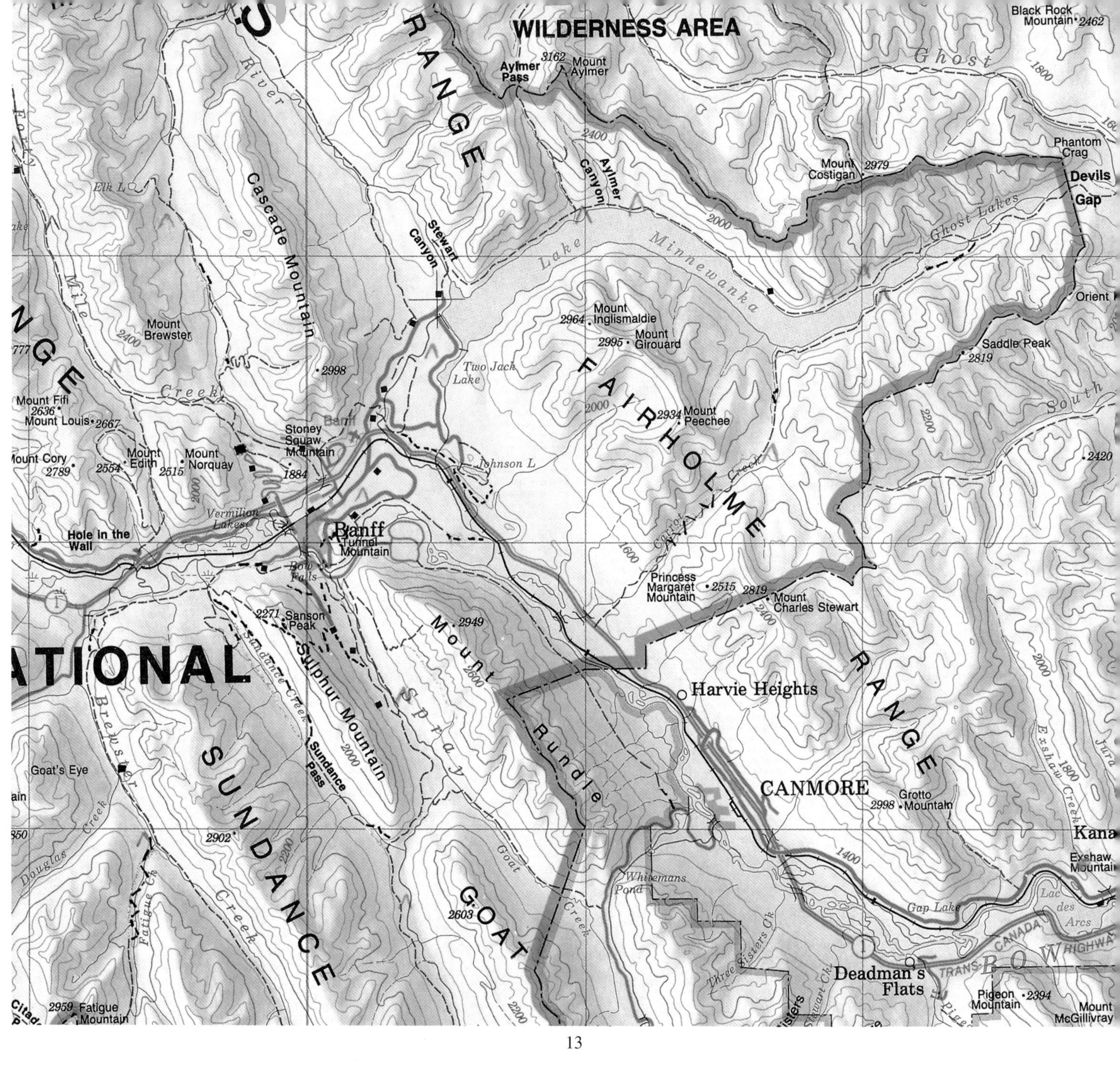

WILDERNESS AREA
Black Rock Mountain 2462
Ghost
Aylmer Pass
3162 Mount Aylmer
RANGE
River
Cascade Mountain
Aylmer Canyon
Stewart Canyon
Phantom Crag
Mount Costigan 2979
Devils Gap
Ghost Lakes
Lake Minnewanka
Elk L
Mile
Creek
Mount Brewster
2998
Two Jack Lake
2964 Mount Inglismaldie
2995 Mount Girouard
FAIRHOLME
Saddle Peak 2819
Orient Pt
Mount Fifi 2636
Mount Louis 2667
Mount Cory 2789
Mount Edith 2554
Mount Norquay 2515
Stoney Squaw Mountain 1884
2934 Mount Peechee
Johnson L
Carrot Creek
2420
Vermilion Lakes
Hole in the Wall
Banff
Tunnel Mountain
Bow Falls
Princess Margaret Mountain 2515
2819 Mount Charles Stewart
2271 Sanson Peak
Mount 2949
ATIONAL
Sulphur Mountain
Sundance Creek
Spray
Harvie Heights
RANGE
Brewster
Goat's Eye
SUNDANCE
Sundance Pass
Rundle
CANMORE
Grotto Mountain 2998
Exshaw Creek
Kana
Douglas Creek
2902
Goat
Whitemans Pond
Gap Lake
Exshaw Mountain
Lac des Arcs
GOAT
2603
Fatigue Ck
Creek
Three Sisters Ck
TRANS-CANADA HIGHWAY
BOW
Deadman's Flats
Pigeon Mountain 2394
Mount McGillivray
2959 Fatigue Mountain

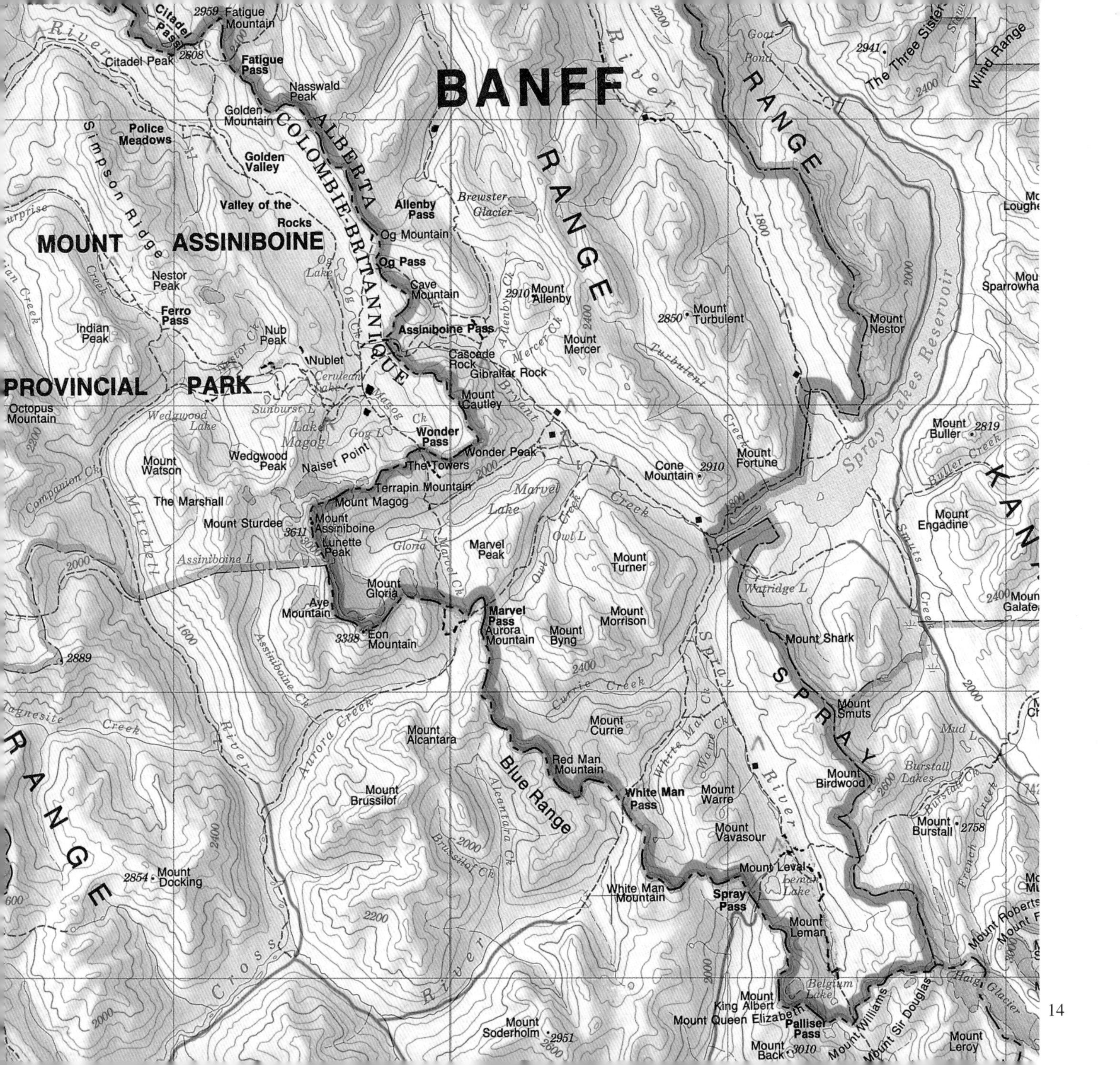
BANFF
MOUNT ASSINIBOINE PROVINCIAL PARK
ALBERTA
COLOMBIE-BRITANNIQUE
RANGE
SPRAY
Blue Range
Citadel Pass
Fatigue Mountain
Citadel Peak
Fatigue Pass
Nasswald Peak
Golden Mountain
Police Meadows
Simpson Ridge
Golden Valley
Valley of the Rocks
Allenby Pass
Brewster Glacier
Og Mountain
Og Pass
Og Lake
Nestor Peak
Cave Mountain
Mount Allenby
Mount Turbulent
Mount Nestor
Ferro Pass
Indian Peak
Nub Peak
Assiniboine Pass
Mount Mercer
Nublet
Cascade Rock
Gibraltar Rock
Cerulean Lake
Mount Cautley
Octopus Mountain
Sunburst L
Wedgwood Lake
Lake Magog
Gog L
Wonder Pass
Wonder Peak
Mount Watson
Wedgwood Peak
Naiset Point
The Towers
Cone Mountain
Mount Fortune
Terrapin Mountain
The Marshall
Mount Magog
Marvel Lake
Mount Sturdee
Mount Assiniboine
Lunette Peak
Gloria L
Marvel Peak
Owl L
Mount Turner
Mount Engadine
Assiniboine L
Mount Gloria
Watridge L
Aye Mountain
Marvel Pass
Aurora Mountain
Mount Byng
Mount Morrison
Eon Mountain
Mount Shark
Mount Buller
Spray Lakes Reservoir
Mount Smuts
Mount Currie
Mount Alcantara
Red Man Mountain
White Man Pass
Mount Warre
Mount Birdwood
Burstall Lakes
Mount Brussilof
Mount Vavasour
Mount Burstall
Mount Docking
Mount Leval
Leman Lake
White Man Mountain
Spray Pass
Mount Leman
Belgium Lake
Mount King Albert
Mount Queen Elizabeth
Palliser Pass
Mount Williams
Mount Sir Douglas
Haig Glacier
Mount Soderholm
Mount Back
Mount Leroy
Mount Robertson
The Three Sisters
Wind Range
Goat Pond
Cross River
Spray River
Mud L
Companion Ck
Mitchell
Currie Creek
Aurora Creek
Alcantara Ck
Brussilof Ck
Turbulent Creek
Bryant Creek
Mercer Ck
Allenby Ck
Magog Ck
Marvel Ck
Owl Creek
Buller Creek
Smuts Creek
White Man Ck
Warre Ck
Burstall Ck
French Creek
Assiniboine Ck
Magnesite Creek
Surprise
Nestor Ck
Og Ck
2959
2608
2910
2850
2819
2910
3611
3338
2889
2854
2758
3010
2951
2941
2400
2200
2000
1800
1600
2600

Grizzly bears feeding

(also available at the Information Centre in Banff). Observe and respond appropriately to Bear Warning or Trail Closure signs at the trailhead.

~ If you are camping, store your perishables safely. Food smells attract bears (which pose a threat to you and your possessions), rodents (which are capable of removing or spoiling large quantities of edibles and which are very acrobatic at accessing them) and other animals. Use odor-proof storage containers (if attracted by an aroma, a bear is capable of tearing open a car's trunk), store food out of reach of animals, and cook downwind and well away from your tent.

~ For a high risk activity, bring all the safety equipment needed for that sport.

~ There is no substitute for experience. If you don't have it, travel with someone who does.

~ Not long ago, all mountain water was considered safe to drink. One of the unfortunate results of our internationally mobile population is the introduction of pollutants, originating with man and spread by local animals, throughout the mountain environment. The highest incidence of enteric infection in Alberta is Giardia lamblia (a parasite which can cause severe gastrointestinal distress), commonly called *beaver fever* because animals like the beaver, which live in water, are likely to spread the contamination; but any infected warm-blooded animal which happens to defecate near a stream can pollute the water. The risk lessens at higher altitudes, but all backcountry water is suspect. In recent years, Calgary Health Services has dealt with hundreds of cases of Giardia annually, most of them believed to originate from people drinking untreated mountain water. You can no longer count on finding safe drinking water in our mountain parks. (Tunnel Mountain Campground and Johnston Canyon Campground have safe water.)

To protect yourself, you can:

carry water from a known safe source;

boil the water (10 minutes is recommended — just bringing water to a boil won't kill the parasite);

use a proven purifying filter;

treat the water with iodine (you must use tincture of iodine: 4 drops per litre of clear water, or 8 drops per litre for cloudy water; wait 30 minutes for the iodine to do its job before drinking).

Bears

Bear attacks are rare, but it's a good idea to read reliable publications about bear behavior and know how you should respond to potential danger. Watch for Bear Warning or Area Closure signs at the trailhead before you start your hike. The Canadian Parks Service information pamphlet, *You Are in Bear Country*, is readily available from any park Information Centre. *Bear Attacks, Their Causes and Avoidance*, by

Stephen Herrero, a noted authority on bears, has a chapter on avoiding encounters which hikers should read.

Herrero's recommendations for bear encounters (especially grizzly) include the following:

~ Travel with others; the more people in your group, the safer you are.
~ A dog may increase the risk of a bear attack.
~ Be alert. The sooner you spot a bear, the more alternatives you have to avoid a confrontation.
~ If you see a bear at a distance, leave the area as quickly and unobtrusively as possible.
~ Make loud noises. *Bear bells* aren't loud enough.
~ Drop something you are carrying, such as your camera; the bear is likely to pause to investigate, giving you more time to reach safety. If possible, keep your pack on to protect your body if you are caught.
~ Climb a tree — get as high as possible. Remember that bears, even grizzlies, can climb trees. (Wildlife expert Andy Russell advises against climbing trees.)
~ Don't run to escape a charging bear. You are then acting like the animals it hunts for food. Back off slowly and talk in a non-threatening tone of voice.
~ Avoid staring the bear down; it may interpret your stare as a threatening gesture.
~ If attacked by a grizzly, play dead. Curling up with the head protected is recommended. If attacked by a black bear, however, fight back.
~ Leave the campsite if there are signs of bears nearby or if there are food smells from garbage left at the site.
~ Avoid food odors, especially fish. Cook downwind and well away from your tent.
~ Store your food in a safe place (up a storage cable if possible).
~ Sleep inside your tent.

Capsecan sprays are now available, but don't put too much faith in them. You have to be very close (wait till the grizzly is on top of you advises bear authority Brian Horejsi). A canister gives only several short bursts; if you fire too soon, it may be empty before the spray can reach the animal. You have to hit a small target, the bear's face, with a narrow spray which is difficult to aim precisely and is affected by wind. The irritant could damage your eyes and lungs as well as the bear's.

WEATHER

"The seasons vary considerably in a given number of years. There may be a few exceptionally mild winters and a few exceptionally cold winters, a few exceptionally warm summers and a few exceptionally cool summers, a few exceptionally fine spring seasons and a few cool and backward springs, a few exceptionally mild and fine falls and a few exceptionally early and cold falls, as well as a few dry and wet summers and a few exceptional winters of light and heavy falls of snow, and then all the variations possible between these forms. Every year has some peculiarity of its own; every season has some peculiarity of its own; every month has some peculiarity of its own." Norman Sanson, *Canadian Alpine Journal, 1920*

Norman Sanson devoted his long life to the study of Banff's weather. Hikers should apply his experience and be prepared for changing conditions. If you want something more precise, here are some findings of a climate study of the mountain parks by Janz and Storr.

Although frost is rare in the lower Bow Valley in July and August, higher elevations experience frost one night in three throughout the summer. Protection against cold, wind, rain, and sunburn (and snow burn) should be carried on long hikes. A clear dawn is no guarantee that the afternoon will be sunny.

Also, prepare for wet ground: in the mountains, average precipitation is one day in three, increasing to one day in two at higher altitudes.

August is usually the month with the fewest days of precipitation; December to February, followed by May and June, have the most days of precipitation.

In summer, the worst storms are often from the east; take extra precautions if the wind comes that way because it often means bad weather. East—west valleys (such as Lake Minnewanka) have more wind.

As you hike to higher elevations, expect the temperature and air pressure (including oxygen supply) to decrease; also expect precipitation, wind, cloud, radiation, snow cover, and the number of lightning strikes to increase.

Here are a few weather signs that Janz and Storr recommend you watch for:

Continuously falling pressure (12—24 hours), especially if accompanied by increasing cirrus cloud, is probably an indication of the approach of a major bad weather system. On the other hand, rising pressure, while normally meaning the approach of better weather, can also presage unstable showery weather.

Jet trails that dissipate quickly usually indicate good weather for at least 12 hours; if they persist for several hours, the atmosphere is already moist, and a major bad weather system may be near.

A clear dawn with puffy cumulus clouds over the peaks is often a warning of showers or thundershowers approaching.

Lenticular cloud, and in winter, a Chinook arch, warn of strong westerly winds. Banner clouds blowing from the summits also indicate strong winds.

Storm clouds building over Rock Isle Lake

"A succession of storms, very brief but often severe, swept over the mountains and treated us to a grand exhibition of cloud and storm effects.... Sometimes the summit would be clear, and sharply outlined against the blue sky, but suddenly a mass of black clouds would advance from the west and envelope the peak in a dark covering." W. Wilcox, describing the weather at Lake Magog, *Camping in the Canadian Rockies*

Mountain Bluebird. Photo, Cy Hampson.

Weather forecasts are posted daily at the Banff Information Centre. The success of these predictions has improved in recent years; nevertheless, the forecasts are often wrong.

For more detail about the climate of the mountain parks, read the Canadian Parks Service study cited above. You may also wish to check Ben Gadd's *Handbook of the Canadian Rockies*.

ANIMALS

Bugs

"And what shall I say of mosquitoes? I have suffered so much from them, that I cannot leave them unnoticed. In the middle of the day they do not trouble the traveler, if he keep aloof from the shade and walk in the burning sun. But at nightfall they light on him, and hang on him till morning, like leaches sucking his blood. There is no defense against their darts, but to hide under a buffalo skin, or wrap one's self up in some stuff which they cannot pierce, and run the risk of being smothered."

Insect repellents containing DEET offer better protection than Jesuit priest Father De Smet had in 1841 when he made these comments.

If you hike from April to mid-July, you should watch for ticks, nasty parasites which suck blood. They can carry Rocky Mountain Spotted Fever, and if they are not removed, they may cause tick paralysis; both infections are potentially fatal.

Birds

The area attracts numerous song birds. If you come in late spring or early summer, you are likely to hear superb songsters including hermit thrush, Swainson's thrush, Townsend's solitaire, and fox sparrow. More visible are the Clark's nutcracker, gray jay and mountain and boreal chickadee. Near timberline, you are likely to see ptarmigan. Golden eagles are making a return to the mountains, and bald eagles and ospreys seem satisfied with the fishing on many of the lakes in the area. On two separate climbs, I have seen small flocks of bluebirds at the summit of Mt. Norquay.

Mammals

Mountain sheep are common near Lake Minnewanka; elk are abundant near Banff and the meadows in the Bow River Valley. Near the border peaks, mountain goat are most common. Wolves are making a comeback and coyotes are often seen near the back roads. The Bow Valley Parkway and the Banff townsite area are good places to see deer and elk. Porcupines commonly appear in the forests near dusk. Small mammals like the golden-mantled ground squirrel, chipmunk and pika frequent high rock slopes.

Porcupine

"The American porcupine, the *Hystrix dorsata*, is called by modern Zoologists, the *Prickly Beaver*. In fact there is great similarity between the two species in size and form, and both inhabit the same region.... The Flat-heads affirm that the porcupine and beaver are brothers, and relate that anciently they abode together; but that, having frequently been discovered by their enemies, through the indolence, idleness and extreme aversion of the porcupines for the water, the beavers met in council and unanimously agreed upon a separation. The latter availed themselves of a fine day and invited their spiny brethren to accompany them in a long ramble, among the cypress and juniper of the forest. The indolent and heedless porcupines, having copiously regaled themselves with the savory buds of the one, and the tender rind of the other, extended their weary limbs upon the verdant moss, and were soon lost in profound sleep. This was the anticipated moment for the wily beavers to bid a final adieu to their porcupine relatives." Father P. J. De Smet, *Oregon Missions and Travels over the Rocky Mountains*

Floral meadow on Mt. Cautley. Looking to Elly's Dome and Wonder Peak.

"Bourgeau [botanist for the Palliser Expedition] was joyfully anticipating some new forms of plant life, and was delighted over his discoveries when we got there. He could hardly wait to complete his meal before starting out on his search. The captain [Palliser] had assigned a man by the name of Bellcourt as his guide and, I suspect, as caretaker, for the old gentleman [Bourgeau was 45] got so enthused over his work that he never took notice of time or direction.

"The botanist's enthusiasm was almost as great as a gold miner in the discovery of a big nugget. It gave me a lot of amused satisfaction to watch his delight when he found a new species. I watched for new plants in my travels with Dr. Hector, and when I was fortunate enough to bring an addition to his collection, I was treated to a lesson that was most instructive." Peter Erasmus, *Buffalo Days and Nights*

VEGETATION

The lowest elevations of Lake Minnewanka and the Bow River Valley occupy the Montane ecozone where Douglas fir and lodgepole pine are the prominent trees. Most of the Banff—Assiniboine area lies in the subalpine and alpine ecological regions. The subalpine region (to about 2300 m) has Engelmann spruce and alpine fir as the dominant species; lodgepole pine is common, especially in the Bow Valley where many fires occurred during construction of the railway and shortly thereafter when wood-burning locomotives constantly emitted sparks.

Throughout the area, near the upper limit of the subalpine zone, there are many attractive stands of beautifully shaped alpine larch. The light green needles of these trees turn golden in September, enriching the mountain colors. Sunshine Meadows, Healy Pass, Shadow Lake, Egypt Lake and Mt. Assiniboine are good places to see alpine larch. These high locations also have outstanding floral meadows.

GEOLOGY

Geologist Jon Dudley has contributed the following comments on the geology of the area.

Front Ranges: Sawback, Sundance Ranges and East

As you walk among the mountainous ramparts and interceding valleys of this area you are in the midst of the Front Ranges of the Rocky Mountains. You are also in the midst of a never ending geological story. It would take volumes to detail the geological history of this area and new interpretations continue to be offered as geologists gain new understanding. The following brief treatment is therefore akin to a book review of the geological story, to give you some flavor and appreciation of its content and perhaps to entice you to obtain more information or to try reading the story in the rocks yourself as you marvel at the surrounding mountains.

The most obvious feature of the landscape, the occurrence of north-west trending linear ranges of mountains bounded by intervening valleys, is a direct consequence of geology. In general the mountain ramparts consist of older carbonate rocks which are resistant to erosion whereas the valleys are less resistant, younger clastic rocks. Let's consider the older rocks of the mountains first.

In general, the mountains consist of rocks formed from sediments of Upper Devonian to Mississipian age (370—340 million years old). At the time these sediments were being formed, North America and Alberta, as well as other of earth's landmasses, assumed very different positions and configurations than today due to plate tectonics. Then, as now, they rode on moving plates of the earth's crust. Put yourself back in time and picture Alberta as part of a landmass called Laurasia, very close to the equator (moving from 10° to 20° N during this time) dominated by arid to semiarid tropical and subtropical desert climates. Much of the province is inundated by the shallow nearshore waters of the Pacific Ocean's precursor, called Panthalassa Ocean. Reefs and limy muds line the shoreline to the south and east. Today when you look up at the spectacular cliffs of the Front Ranges, Mount Rundle for example, you are looking at rocks, known as carbonates, that were formed from these reefs and limy sediments on the southern Alberta shoreline. As landmasses continued to move, sea levels rose and fell, shorelines shifted, life forms evolved, and changed the type of sediment being deposited at any one place. Evidence for this can be seen in many of the mountains' profiles. The tree-covered lower portion of coral reefs and stromatoporoid (extinct *cousin* of coral) banks known as the Fairholme Group lies beneath a distinctive succession of three units which form the cliffs of the mountains: massive cliff-forming limestones of the Palliser Formation; weaker, eroded shales and shaly limestones of the Banff Formation; and cliff-forming banded limestones of the Rundle Group on top. The Palliser Formation consists of grey carbonate units that were deposited in marine water below and within tidal zones. Laminated units formed by algae, shells of brachiopods and donut-shaped fragments of crinoids are common fossils contained within the Palliser. The Banff Formation is distinctly brown and less precipitous because its sediments were deposited in deeper water and therefore contain more siltstones and shales which are more easily eroded. As the water shallowed again, there was a return to deposition of carbonates in waters below, within and above the tidal zone which eventually became the bedded limestones of the Rundle Group that form the uppermost cliff on mountains such as Mount Rundle. Lime sediments with varying degrees of mud, fossils, and salt flat deposits result in the bedding of subtly different colours seen in the Rundle Group.

In between the linear mountain ranges of carbonate rock are the valleys which consist of less resistant rocks formed from clastic sediments: those derived from the erosion of older rocks into sand and silt-sized grains. These sediments were deposited from the Permian to the early Cretaceous period, after the mountain-forming carbonates, and are therefore younger (285—140 million years old). The change from carbonate to clastic sediments may be due in part, to pre-North America drifting northward as part of Pangea, a landmass comprising most of today's continents. As you stand among the valley-forming rocks, cast yourself back 285 million years; the climate is cooling from tropical to warm to cool temperate, which no longer favors the growth of reefs and warmth-loving carbonate producing fauna. The sediments are being

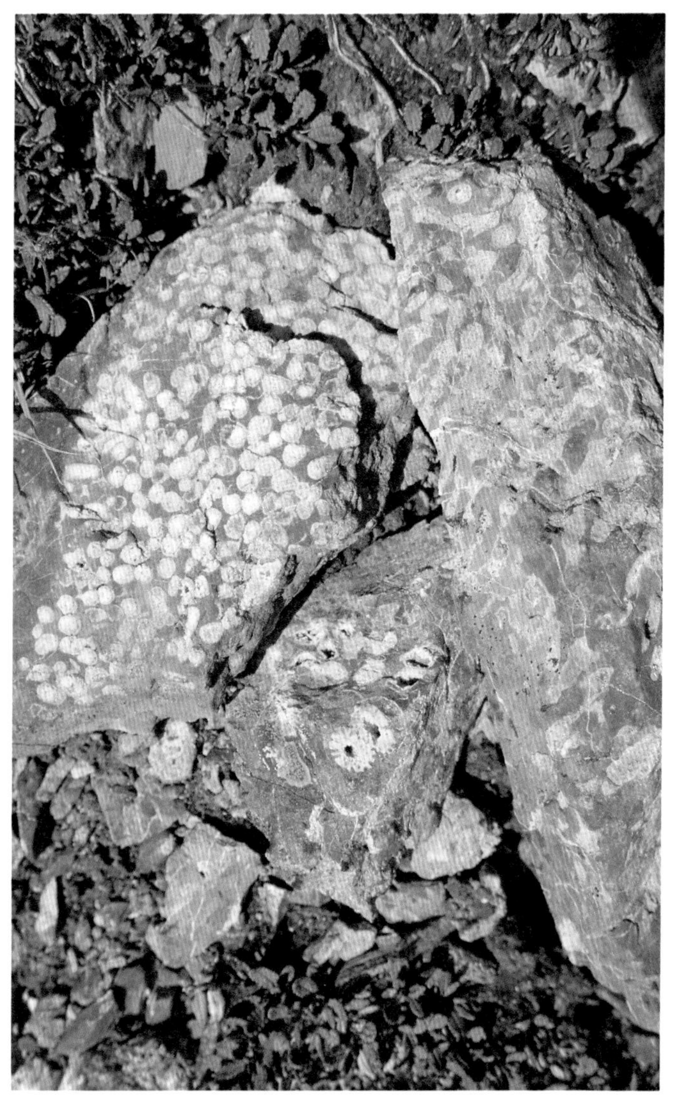

Fossils on Mt. Louis

formed by the erosion of the western edge of the pre-North American landmass which lies to the east and are being deposited in the offshore marine waters in which you are standing (Spray River Group). When the clastics were first deposited, Pangea was beginning to break up with North America, separating as a new landmass. As this rifting occurred, volcanic islands, archipelagos and shoals which were in the Panthalassa Ocean to the west began moving north and east toward the western margin of the new North America. These terranes (land masses foreign to the continent) began docking and colliding with North America causing areas of uplift to the west and southwest that eroded to source these sediments. As more of these terranes were thrust against the edge of North America, their weight caused the earth's crust to be depressed, forming a basin into which the sediments eroded from the thrust slices were deposited.

In places, (e.g. the Fernie Passage Beds on the east side of the Trans-Canada Highway just before the turnoff to Lake Minnewanka) you can find fossilized tree stumps and logs that were deposited in marine waters not far from shore; plants evolved at about the time the transition from carbonates to clastics occurred. Fossilized ammonites (marine mollusks related to the octopus but with a spiral shell) can also be found in these sediments. As time went by, the shoreline shifted partly due to filling of the basin as more terranes collided with North America causing uplift and more sediment supply due to erosion. As a result, the clastic sediments became non-marine sands and muds with lots of plant material which later became coal. These beach and coal deposits (Kootenay Formation) can be seen along the Trans-Canada and are those which were mined in the Banff area. These sediments were eroded from emerging land to the southwest as terranes continued to collide with western North America and mountain-building was beginning. The presence of coal suggests that the climate became moister encouraging lush plant growth.

About 100 million years ago another major terrane collided with the western edge of North America which built much of the mountains you now hike in. The rocks continued to be compressed and thrust up into mountains until about 50 million years ago. Not only were the rocks pushed up vertically, but also laterally. In fact, many of the sediments that you see in the mountains today have been pushed as far as 100 km east of where they were originally deposited.

Main Ranges (on or near the Continental Divide)

As you hike toward Mt. Assiniboine you leave the Front Ranges of the Rockies and enter the Main Ranges. Here are rocks formed from sediments much older than those seen in the Front Ranges. Long before (200—300 million years) the carbonates of the Front Ranges were deposited, a landmass that was to become western North America broke away from a supercontinent. As the continental breakup occurred, large submarine valleys were formed into which sand was deposited (these sediments can be seen in the rocks around Lake Louise). Later, as conditions changed, the western edge of North America had carbonates being deposited which are older than the carbonates in the Front Ranges. These carbonates form most of Mt. Assiniboine and the lower portion of Mount Howard Douglas. The top of Mount Howard Douglas consists of carbonates of the Fairholme Group and the Palliser Formation, the same as found in the Front Ranges.

OUTDOOR ACTIVITIES

Hiking

The extensive trails in the area are fully described in this book. They offer superb hiking for people of all ages and abilities.

Cycling

Biking is permitted on all public roads and highways in Banff Park and on most trails near Banff townsite. Also, Spray River Fireroad, Cascade River Fireroad (to Stony Creek), Redearth Creek Fireroad, Lake Minnewanka, Brewster Creek and Bryant Creek trails are open to bicycles. Of the backcountry trails, the fireroads provide the best cycling.

In Mount Assiniboine Park, bicycles are permitted only on the Assiniboine Pass Trail (to Lake Magog Campground).

The Banff Information Centre can provide a current list of places to rent bicycles.

Horseback Riding

Guide Fred Tabuteau asked one lady if she preferred an English saddle or a western saddle. When asked to explain the difference, he said that the English saddle was flat, whereas the western saddle had a horn. The lady replied that she didn't need a saddle with a horn because she was sure there wouldn't be much traffic on the trail.

Holiday on Horseback, 132 Banff Avenue, offers day rides near Banff. Overnight trips can be planned to their campsites at Stony Creek, Flint's Park and Mystic Camp; or up Brewster Creek to Sundance Lodge and Halfway Lodge. Write Warner Guiding and Outfitting Ltd., Box 2280, Banff, Alberta, T0L 0C0; phone 403-762-4551 (Fax 403-762-8130).

Fishing

"Bryant with unusual imagination had brought along a collapsible canoe.... We camped on the upper [Kananaskis] lake, which is quite large and dotted with wooded islands. Unfortunately this lake has no fish in it. The lower lake is surrounded by burnt timber but is alive with trout. Here it was that Bryant was sitting in his canoe on the first afternoon, casting a fly and smoking a pipe when a band of seventy-five Stoney Indians in full war costume suddenly appeared marching along the shore. One can imagine their surprise at seeing a human being 50 miles from the nearest settlement and a boat where no boat had ever been before. They began to shout:

"'Hey, you no fish here. This Stoney Indian Lake. You fish other lake.'

"In other words we could have the scenery, while they preferred something more substantial." Walter Wilcox, *American Alpine Journal, 1941*

You can get advice on where to fish and on park regulations at the Banff Information Centre. A valid National Park fishing permit is required and is available at Information and Administration buildings, Campgrounds, Warden offices and at Lake Minnewanka Boat Dock. A valid British Columbia fishing license, available at Park Headquarters near Lake Magog, is required to fish in Mount Assiniboine Park.

The Bow River is open to fishing year round. From Victoria Day to Labour Day these lakes are open: Minnewanka, Ghost, Two Jack, Copper, Pilot, Vermilion and Johnson plus the connecting streams and beaver ponds at Vermilion and Johnson lakes. Rock Isle, Larix and Grizzly lakes, and the area near the outlet of Marvel Lake are closed to fishing. All other waters in the area are open from July 1 to October 31.

Cruises, Boating, Kayaking, Canoeing

Minnewanka Tours (1977) Ltd. offers boat cruises on Lake Minnewanka from Mid May to September 30. Write Box 2189, Dept. B, Banff, Alberta, T0L 0C0, phone 403-762-3473 (Fax 403-762-2800). Boat rentals are available at the boat dock at Lake Minnewanka.

In Banff, canoes can be rented at the boat docks at Wolf Street and Bow Avenue daily from 10 am to 8 pm. The Bow River is considered good canoeing upstream from Banff. Don't go beyond the Banff bridge: Bow Falls makes travel downstream impossible.

Mountaineering

"In the immediate vicinity of Banff there are no mountains which put the skill of the practiced Alpine climber to a very severe test, but further west they have opportunities of breaking their necks to their heart's content." Charles E. D. Wood, 1890, quoted in *Alberta History, Summer, 1977*

Glen Boles, co-editor of the climber's guide, *The Rocky Mountains of Canada South*, has provided the following comments on the area.

The wedge-shaped, portion of Banff National Park south of an east—west line through Castle Junction contains some very beautiful mountain terrain, which is quite varied in its interest to the climber. For instance, the portion north of the Trans-Canada Highway is composed of smaller peaks; however, these and some of the spectacular walls and buttresses lower on them, provide some excellent rock; thus they are the domain of the rock climbers. The mountains to the south of The Trans-Canada Highway appeal to the back country mountaineer.

North of the Trans-Canada Highway

Being near Banff and having easy access, the walls and buttresses below Cascade Mountain, Mt. Norquay and Mt. Cory are extremely popular with rock climbers. Cascade Mountain and Mt. Norquay are fairly easy climbs, with great views. They are most often approached from the Mt. Norquay Ski Area parking lot.

Probably the most famous rock peak in the Canadian Rockies, Mt. Louis makes every climber envious. Standing erect between Mt. Edith and Mt. Fifi, Louis, it is a challenge by all of its routes which are reached by the Edith Pass trail. Easy access and routes of all grades also make Mt. Edith a worthy goal. Mt. Finger is another example of a small peak with good rock; access though, is more difficult. The long south ridge of Mt. Ishbel, east of Johnston Canyon, is a good training climb.

At Banff townsite, there are two rock climbing areas great for training. They are Tunnel Mountain and the base of Mt. Rundle, both of which border the golf course. Information on all the above climbs can be found in the climbing guide *Banff Rock Climbs* by Murray Toft.

Looking southwest from the west ridge of Mt. Norquay

South of the Trans-Canada Highway

Of all the mountains shouldering The Continental Divide, stretching between Vermilion Pass and Palliser Pass, a distance of 75 kilometres, only three areas are extremely popular with mountaineers. Predictably they surround the three most lofty peaks: Mt. Ball at 3311 m, Mt. Assiniboine, 3618 m and Mt. Sir Douglas at 3406 m.

Beginning at Vermilion Pass, the mountains of the Ball Group are very accessible; thus the main peaks of this range are climbed quite regularly. Storm Mountain is an easy ascent either in summer or in winter by the west slopes from Highway #93, while the more difficult but not extreme routes of the east side are approached from the trail to Twin Lakes. The more challenging routes on the north and east sides of massive-looking Mt. Ball, the highest of this group, are accessible via the trail to Shadow Lake. The interesting route on the west side may be reached by the trail up Hawk Creek to Ball Pass.

East of the Ball Group, the peaks of the Massive Range receive only a smattering of ascents. Mt. Bourgeau, a mere hike — with a great viewpoint — is climbed most often.

Mt. Howard Douglas, east of Sunshine Village, has a fine 5.8 route on its north face. Proceeding south along The Divide, the mountains between Ball Pass and Assiniboine Pass have had little appeal to mountaineers except for first ascents, Since then, most of them have been virtually left alone. South of Banff, the only peak to receive much attention has been Mt. Nestor at the south end of the Goat Range and gained from Spray Lake. The Mount Assiniboine area is another story.

Mt. Assiniboine is one of the most popular climbs in the Canadian Rockies. It is a fairly easy climb under good (dry) conditions. Yet if conditions are not right, it can be a virtual epic to climb and to get off safely. There have been quite a number of accidents and deaths due to victims who have tackled it when it has been in poor condition. The smaller peaks in this area (Magog, Terrapin, Wedgwood, Sturdee, Sunburst and The Towers) receive only the odd ascent. The adjoining summit, Lunette Peak on Mt. Assiniboine's south shoulder, at 3400 m, is climbed occasionally. The normal north ridge route and the north face routes on Assiniboine are approached from Lake Magog by climbing the headwall southwest of the lake to the R. C. Hind Hut, which is located conveniently right below the climbs. One of the hardest faces to climb in the Rockies is the east face of Mt. Assiniboine.

In recent years, since the Brussilof Mine has been in operation at the forks of the Mitchell River and Aurora Creek, there has been more climbing in that vicinity, southwest of Mt. Assiniboine and west of The Divide. Mt. Eon, Mt. Aye and even Assiniboine and Lunette have received ascents from this side.

Looking southeast from the north peak of Mt. Edith

"We have to go up to build the cairns." C. F. Hogeboom, answering the perennial question, why do you climb? *Canadian Alpine Journal, 1923*

"I am a nature lover more than a mountaineer but of course all alpinists are of necessity admirers of the great world of outdoors as otherwise they would take their exercise in a gymnasium." Walter Wilcox, *letter to J. M. Thorington, Oct. 3, 1945*

"No clan on earth possesses memories that transcend those of the men and women who love the high places.... The mountaineers bring home their priceless mind pictures." Belmore Browne, *American Alpine Journal, 1941*

The mountains along The Divide from Marvel Pass to Palliser Pass are smaller and not of too much interest to climbers; however, east of Palliser Pass a line of peaks east of the Spray River run north; these are the north wing of the British Military Group. They culminate in the summit of lofty Mt. Sir Douglas. Sir Douglas, Birdwood and Smuts are all good climbs by various routes. These peaks are very accessible from the east, via Highway #742, leaving it at Mud Lake. The long extension of the north ridge of Mt. Sir Douglas, called Whistling Ridge, has been very popular with rock climbers in recent years. On the ridge's west side, steep smooth slabs provide challenges of every difficulty.

Bob Hind climbing Mt. Thompson, 1937. Photo, from the collection of Bob Hind.

HOW TO USE THIS GUIDE

This guide is divided into six hiking units: Upper Spray River, Mt. Assiniboine, Sunshine to Vermilion Pass (including Bourgeau Lake, Sunshine, Egypt Lake, Shadow Lake, Altrude Creek, Vermilion Pass), Bow Valley Parkway, Banff and Lake Minnewanka. For some trails I have noted the last place where you can fill your canteen. You should be aware that the rapid spread of dangerous impurities such as Giardia makes it inadvisable to drink this water unless you first treat it.

Height Gains

The height gain shown is the cumulative total and is usually greater than the difference between the maximum and minimum elevations. The maximum height is shown where it is greater than 2400 m, or 8,000'.

Distances

All distances are measured from the stated trailhead. With some satellite trails, in the trip summary after the trail description I also show the total distance to and from the most likely starting point. If there is no common point of departure (a backcountry trail beginning at a trailhead between campgrounds), you will have to add the time and distance from your starting point to the stated trailhead.

Hiking and Biking Times

The intent of giving detailed hiking times is to help you estimate your own times. First, you must make a few comparisons after which, if you hike at a consistent rate, you should know how much to add to or subtract from the times shown for other trips.

Bear in mind that the printed times do not include rest stops and reflect a more leisurely descent than ascent, especially on steep scenic trails.

My biking times tend to be less aggressive than my hiking times.

Trail Descriptions

In ascending order of difficulty, trail grade is described as level, gentle (hardly more than level), easy (you don't quite need traction on your footwear), moderate (you need traction, and you'll probably slow down a little), stiff (a long stretch of moderate to steep), steep (you need very good traction, and you'll slow down a lot), and very steep (this goes straight up the hillside; despite good traction, your feet may slip a little even when the ground is dry).

UPPER SPRAY Introduction

The Upper Spray River Valley is one of the first mountain areas near Banff visited by travellers who left written records. James Sinclair led a band of Red River métis across it in 1841. Although he was of mixed blood, Sinclair traveled widely. Educated at the University of Edinburgh, he would soon make friends with a young American officer named Ulysses S. Grant. His Cree guide, Maskapetoon, had been given an audience with U. S. President Andrew Jackson. Sinclair and his guide repeated the trip in 1850. For some years, fur traders referred to the route as St. Clair's Pass, a corruption of Sinclair's name.

In late July, 1845, lieutenants Warre and Vavasour traversed White Man Pass heading west. Only weeks later, Father P. J. De Smet crossed it heading east. Warre wrote, "The scenery was grand in the extreme; similar in form to the Alps of Switzerland, you felt that you were in the midst of desolation: no habitations, save those of the wild Indians, were within hundreds of miles; but few civilized beings had ever even viewed this."

Little was written about the site by other parties who crossed it until Geologist G. M. Dawson came here in 1883. He translated the Stoney Indian name as *White Man Pass.*

FACILITIES

Campgrounds Campgrounds in the Upper Spray (Us 15 and Us 18) have privies and bearproof storage; fires are not permitted, so bring a portable cookstove. There are no tables.

District Warden Palliser Cabin, on the Palliser Pass Trail, 16 km from Mt. Shark Parking Lot, is occupied some of the summer.

"As regards the scenery of the Rocky Mountains, there is a remarkable absence of peaks." Captain John Palliser, for whom Palliser Pass is named, quoted by Sir Edward Bulwer Lytton.

In 1933, Jack Fuller made this carving in a pine in the Upper Spray Valley. Photo, Bill Vroom.

About 1955, warden Jack Romanson made this axe carving in the trunk of a live pine, visible from the trail near the site of the old Palliser Cabin.

The approach to Palliser Pass. Mount Back and Belgium Lake.

"The summit [Palliser Pass] is nearly level for about two miles, and dotted with several shallow lakes of marvelous colors. The encircling mountains, with their glaciers and waterfalls, made the scenery interesting, but we were disappointed to catch glimpses of a desolate, burned valley ahead which looked very rough." Walter Wilcox, *National Geographic, May, 1902*

Mount Leman and Leman Lake

"We found the walking very rough over a succession of small, wall-like ridges covered with thick woods and charming meadows between crowded with wild flowers. A foamy stream led us to a green pool, the upper end of which was overhung by vertical cliffs of limestone. These cliffs made the end of a small canyon, which led us in half a mile to a blue-green lake three-fourths of a mile long....

"The upper end of this lake is dotted with small islands....

"The remarkable feature of the lake near this pass is that there is no apparent outlet into either valley. The narrow canyon, now partly filled with large masses of rock from its own walls, gives without doubt an underground passage for the water, but it would be hard to explain how the water first cut through a high ridge when the drainage seems more natural in the other direction." Walter Wilcox, The first known visit to Leman Lake, *National Geographic, May, 1902*

PALLISER PASS and UPPER SPRAY VALLEY

~ Lakes, meadows ~

Distance 26.9 km (16.7 mi) from Mt. Shark parking lot
Height Gain 530 m (1,740'); 90 m (200') return
Hiking Time 5 hr 57 min*
5 hr 39 min* return

Trailhead From Canmore, follow the signs to Spray Lakes (the Smith-Dorrien—Spray Trail), going 34.4 km (21.4 mi) past the Nordic Centre. Turn off at the Mt. Engadine Lodge junction; then go an additional 5.3 km (3.3 mi) northwest on the Watridge Logging Road to the Mt. Shark parking lot. Map page 14.

Options You can stay at Us 15 or Us 18 Campgrounds. If you are going to White Man Pass, Us 15 (formerly Us 10) is closer. For Palliser Pass, Burstall Pass or Leman Lake, Us 18 (formerly Us 14) is preferable. You can explore the Palliser Pass area. A rough trail leads down the Palliser River with a side route to North Kananaskis Pass (and Kananaskis Lakes).

≈ Clear lakes in alpine meadows make Palliser Pass a memorable destination. A hogback above the pass gives even better views.

The open meadows and bountiful feed attract abundant wildlife. I saw moose, white-tail deer, elk and black bear, plus the tracks of a grizzly. Bill Vroom said that old timers used to call the warden building (Palliser Cabin) *Grizzly Cabin* because bears broke in so often.

Except for the steep, final hill near Palliser Pass, the grade is mostly easy.

The mountains near the pass have associations with World War I, especially with Belgium: King Albert the Belgian monarch, whose defiance of the invading Germans made him a hero to the Allies, also an accomplished mountaineer, killed in a 1934 climbing accident; Queen Elizabeth his consort; Leval the Belgian lawyer who defended Nurse Edith Cavell at her court martial; Leman the Belgian general who defended the city of Liège; Williams an officer of the Canadian Expeditionary Force taken prisoner in Flanders, Belgium.

Trail From Mt. Shark Parking Lot, you can hike or cycle to the Upper Spray junction. From there you must walk. At this junction, turn left to Palliser Pass. Keep right at the Spray River horse ford. At the north junction to White Man Pass keep ahead and cross bridges over Currie Creek and the Spray River.

Go through a hilly forest, passing the south junction to White Man Pass (right) and Birdwood Campground (Us 15, left).

You enter a long meadow by the Spray River. Cross a footbridge just before the junction (left) to the new warden cabin.

Proceed up valley and ford Birdwood Creek. Three intersections ahead require alertness.

First, watch for the unsigned junction to the Trail Riders' camp, a path that first parallels the main trail, then turns left; keep ahead.

Next, the trail left to Burstall Pass was marked only with a plywood sign, set back 30 m from the main trail in 1992. Keep ahead.

Third, the Leman Lake Trail turns off right and crosses the river. To reach the campground (Us 18, Leman Lake Camp), go 0.1 km via this side trail. The official trail sign (1992) does not show where you turn to get to the campground.

To reach Palliser Pass, continue ahead at this junction, following the Spray River upstream. Cross a minor stream, then ford the Spray River, to its west side. The last ford is at the base of the steep hill before the pass. Climb to open terrain at Belgium Lake.

A scenic meadow leads to the pass.

Trail Section	km from	time out	return time
Trailhead (Mt. Shark)		↓	339 min*
Bryant Creek Jct.	6.2	36 min*	300 min
Horse ford	8.7	72 min	265 min
White Man Pass, north Jct.	9.4	79 min	258 min
Bridge, Spray River	9.8	83 min	254 min
White Man Pass, south Jct.	13.0	129 min	210 min
Us 15	15.5	166 min	175 min
Old Warden Corral site	15.6	170 min	171 min
Warden Cabin	15.8	174 min	167 min
Burstall Pass Jct.	20.1	234 min	110 min
Leman Lake and Us 18 Jct.	20.2	237 min	107 min
Base of large hill	24.8	302 min	38 min
Belgium Lake	26.1	342 min	15 min
Palliser Pass	26.9	357 min	↑

* Cycling time, Mt. Shark Parking Lot to Bryant Creek Jct. Add 40 minutes if you hike this section.

Mt. Soderholm, Leman Lake and Spray Pass from Burstall Pass

LEMAN LAKE and SPRAY PASS

~ Multicolored lake with bays and islands ~

Distance **2.1 km (1.3 mi) Us 18 to Spray Pass**
Height Gain **105 m (350'); 75 m (250') return**
Hiking Time **49 min**
46 min return

Trailhead Campground Us 18. Map page 14.

Options You can also visit Palliser or Burstall passes.

≈ The multicolored lake has many bays and several islands. It provides an interesting foreground for mounts Sir Douglas and Leman.

Trail After a short, moderate climb from the campground, you descend to Leman Lake. The best views are near the far end. After climbing 45 m up a scenic avalanche slope on Mt. Leval, you descend to the west end of the lake.

If you continue to Spray Pass, the grade is gentle. You go through heavy timber, with no views. Beyond the pass, the trail continues through dense timber to a nearby logging road.

Trail Section	km from	time out	return time
US 18		↓	46 min
Leman Lake	1.0	21 min	28 min
End of Lake	2.0	45 min	4 min
Spray Pass	2.1	49 min	↑

Mt. Sir Douglas from Leman Lake

BURSTALL PASS

~ Spectacular panorama ~

Distance **3.9 km (2.4 mi) from Campground Us 18**
Height Gain **485 m (1,590')**
Hiking Time **2 hr**
1 hr 33 min return

Trailhead Campground Us 18, near Leman Lake on the Palliser Pass Trail. Map page 14.

Options You can continue to Mud Lake and the Smith-Dorrien—Spray Trail (road) in Peter Lougheed Provincial Park. Most visitors approach Burstall Pass from Mud Lake, a trip having a much easier grade and which can be done as a day hike.

≈ Mt. Sir Douglas, Mt. Birdwood and Leman Lake are among the scenic splendors viewed from the pass area. The tip of Mt. Assiniboine is also visible. The knoll on the boundary ridge south of the pass, an easy 200 m scree climb, provides even better views (photos pp. 2-3, 30).

This hike is an arduous climb, the grade varying from steep to very steep. Near the pass, the trail is faint.

Trail From Campground Us 18, go east and cross the bridge over the Spray River. Turn left and follow the trail downstream 0.1 km to the junction to Burstall Pass on your right. The plywood sign (1992), is set back 50 m from the junction, where the trail climbs a slight rise.

After going up the low rise, you turn south. The grade is easy until you reach an avalanche slope and commence a grueling ascent. You leave this slope and traverse north to continue the strenuous climb to the ridge where the route becomes faint. A few cairns direct you up the ridge and around a large sinkhole. A short detour leads right to a superb viewpoint overlooking Leman Lake and Spray Pass.

After the sinkhole, the final stretch of trail to the pass is obvious.

Trail Section	km from	time out	return time
Us 18		↓	93 min
Palliser Pass Trail Jct.	0.1	3 min	90 min
Burstall Pass Trail Jct.	0.2	6 min	87 min
Burstall Pass	3.9	120 min	↑

White Man Mountain and Cross of Peace Lake, White Man Pass

"The well-known guide and explorer of early days of Canadian Pacific Railway construction, Tom Wilson of Banff, stated to the writer that he had found at the summit of the pass what seemed to him to be relics of [De Smet's] cross." A. O. Wheeler, *Canadian Alpine Journal 1926-7*

Mount Birdwood, "Pig's Tail," Commonwealth Peak and Mount Chester from Burstall Pass

"Part of our route was through the White Man's Pass, and the white men have burnt up all the woods." [Parties crossing White Man Pass also went over a gap above Canmore which was called *White Man's Pass* by 1900.] Walter Wilcox, *The Rockies of Canada*

WHITE MAN PASS

~ Historic route ~

Distance **17.1 km (10.6 mi) from Mt. Shark parking lot**
Height Gain **455 m (1,500'); 80 m (260') return**
Hiking Time **3 hr 30 min**
3 hr 10 min return

Trailhead From Canmore, follow the signs to Spray Lakes (the Smith-Dorrien—Spray Trail), going 34.4 km (21.4 mi) past the Nordic Centre. Turn off at the Mt. Engadine Lodge junction; then go an additional 5.3 km (3.3 mi) northwest on the Watridge Logging Road to the Mt. Shark parking lot. Map page 14.

Options You can also approach White Man Pass from Campground Us 15 or Us 18.

≈ Until the last hill, the grade is easy. Then comes a stiff ascent to the pass.

White Man Pass is a translation of the Stoney Indian name, probably chosen for the Red River settlers led by James Sinclair who crossed it in 1841; since Sinclair and most of his followers were métis, and their guide a Cree, the translation of the Stoney name may be inaccurate. However, other early parties were white: in 1845 Warre and Vavasour came, then De Smet.

James Sinclair's achievement was remarkable. To support Britain's claim to the Oregon, he led a party of settlers, crossing half the continent, fording rivers, climbing mountain passes and evading hostile Indians (two members of the party had a narrow escape). Three children were born en route. After all their hardships, the migrants experienced unreasonable delays before they were granted land which was inferior to their expectations. In the end, these settlers championed the U. S. claim.

Sinclair, who was educated at the University of Edinburgh, was proud to call himself a half-breed (his maternal grandmother was Cree). Most of his life, he espoused native causes; ironically he was shot dead by insurgent Indians while trying to help a white woman reach safety. He was a friend of Ulysses S. Grant, assisting him in courting his wife.

For some years, fur traders called this St. Clair's Pass, a corruption of Sinclair's name.

Sinclair's guide, a Cree named Maskapetoon, had met U. S. President Andrew Jackson and was accounted a great warrior. However, he had a vicious temper: he scalped his wife for suspected infidelity (she survived). His temperament improved after he was converted by Rev. Robert Rundle in 1840. Unfortunately, dedication to a better life led to his death: while attempting to make peace with the Blackfeet in 1869, he was murdered.

Lt. Henry J. Warre crossed White Man Pass in 1845 on a secret mission. The U. S. was claiming all the western continent from parallel 42, the northern boundary of Spanish territory, to parallel 54° 40', the southern boundary of Russian territory. Britain's claim to the Columbia River and north was countered by American President Polk's jingoistic rallying cry of "Fifty-four forty or fight!"

Warre and Lt. Mervin Vavasour were dispatched from Montreal on May 5 to assess the military situation. They were to pretend to be tourists, hunting, fishing and seeking adventure. On July 27 they reached White Man Pass.

Warre was an amateur artist and made pencil and watercolor sketches of the scenery (and the forts) along the route. A book of lithographs from the trip was published in 1848.

In addition, Warre kept a discreet journal of his activities and observations on the trip.

It proved a hazardous journey. They crossed the mountains on horseback, leaving Edmonton with 60 ponies; when they reached the Columbia River, only 27 remained. "Several of these were so exhausted, they could not have continued many more days.... The steepness of the mountain passes, the want of proper nourishment, the fearful falls that some of these animals sustained, rolling in some instances many hundred feet into the foaming torrent beneath, combined to cause this great loss.

"The scenery was grand in the extreme; similar in form to the Alps of Switzerland. You felt that you were in the midst of desolation: no habitations, save those of the wild Indians, were within hundreds of miles; but few civilized beings had ever even viewed this."

Warre went on to a distinguished career in the Imperial army, including service at Sebastapool in the Crimean War. He was knighted and reached the rank of general.

Warre and Vavasour were led through the Rockies by Peter Skene Ogden, chief factor of the Hudson's Bay Company.

Although convinced of the justice of the British claim, Warre and Vavasour became pessimistic about the chances of holding the Oregon by force. By the time they completed their report in 1846, the issue had been settled by fixing the border at the 49th parallel.

Also in 1845, Father Pierre J. De Smet traversed White Man Pass but in the opposite direction. He met Warre and Vavasour, soon after they crossed the pass. Sensing the real purpose of their journey, he saw through their pretense as sportsmen on holiday.

De Smet weighed more than 200 pounds, but despite his corpulence, he was remarkably strong and undertook many long, fatiguing trips.

He joked about his problems traveling through the mountains. After slipping a third of the way down a steep riverbank, he wrote, "Hung up there 200 feet above the river, I did not find myself very well fixed for meditation or reflection."

He had no better luck on horseback: "In attempting to pass under a tree that inclined across the path, I perceived a small branch in the form of a hook, which threatened me.... It caught me by the collar of my surtout, the horse still continuing his pace. Behold me suspended in the air — struggling like a fish at the end of a hook.... A crushed and torn hat, an eye black and blue, two deep scratches on the cheek would in a civilised country have given me the appearance rather of a bully issuing from the Black Forest than of a missionary."

East of the pass, he erected a giant crucifix. "After much fatigue, labor and admiration, on the 15th [September, 1845] we traversed the high lands.... The Christian's standard, the cross, has been reared at the ... [lake]: may it be a sign of salvation and peace to all the scattered and itinerant tribes east and west of these gigantic and lurid mountains. On the cypress which serves for constructing the cross, the eagle, emblem of the Indian warrior, perches himself. The huntsman aims — the noble bird lies prostrate, and even in his fall, seems to retain his kingly pride.... We breakfasted on the bank of a limpid lake at the base of the *Cross of Peace*."

The Cross River, west of the pass, takes its name from this incident. Like Warre, De Smet was a talented amateur artist. Illustrations in his books were based on his drawings; likely the drawing shown here is his own or of Father Nicholas Pointe who often traveled with him.

There are good views at De Smet's *Cross of Peace Lake* and from several meadows and avalanche slopes en route. The pass is treed, but if you go up the boundary ridge to the south, in three minutes, you reach a gap in the forest with a good view of Mt. Soderholm to the west.

Trail From Mt. Shark Parking Lot, you can hike or cycle to the Bryant Creek Trail Junction at the Spray River. This is as far as you are permitted to take a bike. Turn left onto the Palliser Pass Trail. You reach a narrow meadow shortly before the horse ford (left) at the Spray River. Keep right here and go to the White Man Pass north junction and turn right again.

Head into the forest to the knee-deep ford of Currie Creek. Continue to an easy ford of White Man Creek. Some people have lost the trail here: there are red flags on the wrong side of the creek. You must cross to the west bank.

Travel south to a meadow. At the far end, near White Man Creek, you reach the junction with the south route to White Man Pass. Here, turn southwest in the forest.

You enter open terrain, then ascend a steep, forested hill to the unnamed lakelet where De Smet erected his Cross of Peace. From here, you go through open forest to the nearby pass.

Trail Section	km from	time out	return time
Trailhead (Mt. Shark)		↓	190 min*
Bryant Creek Jct.	6.2	36 min*	151 min
Horse ford	8.7	72 min	117 min
White Man Pass (north) Jct.	9.4	79 min	110 min**
Currie Creek ford	10.7	90 min**	100 min
White Man Creek ford	11.0	94 min	96 min
South trail Jct.	13.3	125 min	70 min
Base of steep hill	15.0	167 min	26 min
Cross of Peace Lake	16.6	198 min	8 min
White Man Pass	17.1	210 min	↑

* Cycling time
** Add 20 min to ford Currie Creek.

The Cross of Peace, probably based on drawing by Father De Smet. Source, Irene Spry, The Beaver, Autumn, 1963.

WHITE MAN PASS, South Route

Distance **8.3 km (5.2 mi) from Us 15**
Height Gain **360 m (1,180')**
Hiking Time **2 hr 19 min**
2 hr 10 min return

Trailhead Us 15 or Us 18 Campground on Palliser Pass Trail. Map page 14.

Trail From Campground Us 15, go 2.5 km down the Upper Spray River trail to the White Man Pass Junction and turn left. Go 100 m to the knee-deep ford and cross the river. (There are plans to bridge these fords in the future.)

You go through forest, at an easy grade, to the ford of White Man Creek, just before the junction with the main trail (north route). Until this is bridged, go a couple of minutes upstream to use a giant spruce log (the branches have been trimmed) straddling the creek.

Cross the creek and angle left to join the main trail which you follow to the pass.

Trail Section	km from	time out	return time
Us 15		↓	130 min
White Man Pass Jct.	2.5	30 min	100 min**
Spray River ford	2.6	31 min**	99 min
North trail Jct.	4.5	54 min	70 min
Base of steep hill	6.2	96 min	26 min
De Smet's Lakelet	7.8	127 min	8 min
White Man Pass	8.3	139 min	↑

** Add 20 min to ford.

The Towers, Naiset Peak, Mts. Terrapin, Eon, Magog, Assiniboine, Sturdee and Wedgwood from the Windy Ridge Trail. Lake Magog shows beneath Mt. Magog.

"The peak is grandest from its northern side. It rises, like a monster tooth, from an entourage of dark cliff and gleaming glacier, 5000 feet above the valley of approach; the magnificent triangular face, barred with horizontal belts of perpendicular cliff and glistening expanses of the purest snow and ice, which constitutes the chief glory of the mountain, soaring more than 3000 feet directly from the glacier that sweeps its base. On the eastern and the southern sides the walls and buttresses are practically sheer precipices 5000 to 6000 feet in vertical height, but the contour and character of the grand northern face more than compensate for the less sheer and lofty precipices." James Outram, *The Alpine Journal, May, 1902*

Legendary guide Ken Jones, Mount Assiniboine Park's first Ranger, at Ferro Pass. Showing Mts. Assiniboine, Sturdee, The Marshall and Wedgwood Lake.

"Barrett … was very efficient in all that concerned camp life and a marvel for taking punishment on the trail. For instance on our trip north to Fortress Lake he would join up with Fred Stephens after seven or eight hours on the trail and explore the new region ahead for half a dozen miles and return to camp with full knowledge of every ford and burnt timber patch in the distance. This of course was a killing proposition for any normal man but it saved us a lot of time the next day.

"While on the Wilcox Pass several days were spent trying to locate some trail or route off the pass and into the Athabasca. Barrett disappeared and did not turn up for three days without so much as saying goodbye and then walked casually into camp one night about eleven pm. So far as I understand it he got lost in burnt timber down the Brazeau." Walter Wilcox, *letter to J. M. Thorington, Dec. 5, 1944*

The first recorded visit to Mt. Assiniboine was in 1893 when Robert L. Barrett came here, guided by Tom Wilson and George Fear. Obviously, Barrett hoped to make the first ascent. Wilson wrote, "We travelled by way of Healy Creek and over the Simpson Pass to the Simpson Valley and then up the Valley to the south branch, finding a good camp with fine feed for the horses. Next day Mr. Barrett and self climbed the ridge, getting a fine view of the lakes and of the mountain itself; Barrett agreeing with me that it was uphill all the way to the top and was not a one boy job."

Barrett must have been overwhelmed by the mountain. In 1924, having since trekked to the world's second highest summit, he fondly remembered his 1893 trip in a letter to Tom Wilson: "I don't think even old K2, the 28,000, looked to me as high and imposing as old Assiniboine when you and I finally won through to where we could have a good look at him."

Ledge, marked "X," where Margaret Stone was trapped. Photo, E. Feuz, CAJ 1921-22.

After eight years of unsuccessful attempts by half a dozen parties, James Outram and two guides made the ascent in September 1901. On their first try they got off route because of mists and climbed Lunette Peak. The second day they were successful, ascending to the Assiniboine—Sturdee col, then to the Assiniboine—Lunette col, and on to the summit via the south ridge. They descended by the north face, completing the traverse in good weather. That night, the mountain was plastered with fresh snow, and rendered unclimbable.

In 1920, A. O. Wheeler organized a series of camps to inaugurate a Walking Tour. The Tour was designed to take participants to Mt. Assiniboine, following the Spray River from Banff to Spray Lakes, and then ascending Bryant Creek to Lake Magog. Half a dozen camps were set up along the route for lunch breaks or overnight accommodation. Cabins were built at two main stops: Trail Centre Camp, at the mouth of Bryant Creek; and Permanent Camp, at Lake Magog. The usual return was via Citadel Pass and Sunshine Meadows. After reaching the Bow River, participants had the option of a boat ride back to Banff. If there were no stopovers, the Walking Tour took five days, but a stay of at least two days at Mt. Assiniboine was recommended in the promotional pamphlet. The destination was flexible; mountaineering parties were encouraged to use the facilities on their way to remote summits.

In 1921, Dr. Winthrop Stone, president of Purdue University, and his wife, Margaret, took the Walking Tour to approach Mt. Eon. What followed is one of the most dramatic episodes in the Rockies.

The Stones bivouacked above Marvel Pass. Late in the day of July 17, they reached a chute below the summit. Dr. Stone had his wife take shelter from falling rocks while he ascended the final chimney. Apparently he removed the rope to explore the summit, stepped on a loose slab and was carried over the ledge. His wife watched the huge rock fall over her head, then saw her husband silently follow, striking a ledge sixty feet below and rolling down the mountainside out of sight. She attempted to descend to him, but was overtaken by darkness.

Next day, Mrs. Stone again endeavored to reach her husband's body. Weakened by shock and lack of sleep and food, she tried to get to a scree slope below, rappelling down a chimney. The rope wasn't quite long enough, so she untied and dropped to a narrow ledge. Still above the scree, and unable now to reach the rope to get back up the chute or to rappel off the small cliff, she was trapped on the high platform. Her food and sweater were in her husband's pack, yet somehow, Margaret survived on the mountain for eight days. In the seven days she spent on the ledge, she managed to get a mere handful of melt water every four hours.

The Stones were expected back at Permanent Camp on July 18, but it was not unusual for mountaineering parties to be a day or so late. Not until July 19 was a man sent with provisions to investigate. He was unable to reach Marvel Pass, so he continued to Trail Centre and reported the pair missing. On July 21, a trail construction crew found the bivouac camp, and searched the slopes of Mt. Eon in vain. The same evening, Swiss guide Rudolph Aemmer was sent from Lake Louise to Banff. Next day, with wardens Bill Peyto and Charlie Phillips plus Constable Pounden of the NWMP, he made the 45 mile trip from Banff to Permanent Camp at Lake Magog. On July 23, the rescue party reached the Stone's vacant bivouac site and ascended to timberline where they spent the night. Next day, they went up the south side of Eon, and scanned the slopes, expecting to find, at best, two bodies. They were about to give up for the day when they heard a faint call.

When they reached Margaret Stone, she was too weak to walk. She murmured, "Oh Rudolph, I knew you would come."

They managed to get her up the chimney. Aemmer wrote, "I carried her for 4 1/2 hours on my back. I cut some rope, made a sling or loop in which Mrs. Stone could sit and also large enough to get my shoulders in, with another rope I tied her to myself; that gave me the arms free to use for holds and the use of the ice-axe."

At timberline, the rescue party set up a bivouac. A doctor gave her what food she could take and after two days she was brought by stretcher to Marvel Pass where she rested two more days before she was taken to Trail Centre. Her son Richard joined her there July 31.

Dr. Stone's body was found August 5. On August 10, Mrs. Stone had recovered sufficiently to leave.

A year before his death, Winthrop Stone published an article on climbing, warning amateurs to learn from a guide before undertaking ascents on their own. Val Fynn, who investigated the tragedy, concluded that the victim (almost 60, with only ten years of mountaineering) shouldn't have made the attempt without a guide. Fynn noted the party was unprepared for a bivouac and chose a dangerous route. Considering how Dr. Stone met his death, Fynn was guilty of an unfortunate choice of words: "It is pure luck that the climbers and some of the search party were not killed by falling *stones*."

After 1926, Wheeler abandoned his Walking Tours and the cabins at Permanent Camp were turned over to the Alpine Club of Canada. The Marquis of Albizzi brought in a party of tourists who used the cabins in 1927.

The CPR applied for a twenty acre lease for a Lodge at Lake Magog which was built in 1928, though the lease was not approved until 1933. Albizzi returned in 1928 with Erling Strom, leasing the new facilities from the CPR plus the ACC cabins. In 1929, while Strom visited his native Norway, the Marquis came back for the last time.

The CPR then leased the Lodge for a few years to Mrs. Bill Brewster. Strom ran the place in the winter. When Mrs. Brewster lost interest, he took over year round.

In 1936, the CPR subleased the property to Strom who enlarged the lodge and added cabins. He gave up winter operations in 1938.

Albizzi had lost interest in wilderness guiding in 1929 after an emergency appendectomy was performed in the Lodge. Perhaps he was prescient. Eleven years later, Strom's daughter Siri developed appendicitis and had to be carried all the way to Banff on a stretcher.

Strom was an entertaining storyteller, who regaled his guests for long hours with anecdotes. He had a ready wit. After carrying a heavy wooden box of painter's supplies from Banff for one guest, Erling learned that the lady had never painted before. "Fine place to start," he said. "I am glad you didn't want to try playing the piano."

Strom had a way with animals. He could pick up a porcupine with his bare hand, reaching underneath, sliding his hand along to grab its tail, then lifting it on his arm to a post. Hans Gmoser saw him do this several times. Nick Morant photographed Strom with a ptarmigan he caught near Allenby Pass. He loved horses: rather than keep one near the Lodge overnight to make it easy to collect the others, he let them all stray together over distant meadows to feed.

Erling's bluntness was legendary. Once, Gmoser overheard him talking to the daughter of a woman he disliked, though he got on fine with the rest of the family. In front of her father, he said with his slight stammer, "Why the h-hell didn't you leave your mother in Banff!"

Strom was precise; there was no ambiguity about how to do things. When Hans washed the horse blankets, he had to add the correct amount of soap, dip and wring them out and rinse them an exact number of times. You had to do things Erling's way.

Yet, Strom ignored the legalism of B. C. Parks. Unable to get permission to build the Pack Shack, he went ahead with construction anyway. When a park official saw the newly finished building and demanded an explanation, Erling replied, "You didn't tell me how to stack my firewood."

In 1954, British Columbia's Parks office began making an inventory of all the Lodge buildings. Their records were inadequate, so officials had to rely on Strom's brochures to identify his building improvements. In 1955, a year after it was up, Strom tried to renew his lease. The best he could do was obtain a Park Use Permit. Since the Lodge had been built on

Rudolph Aemmer. Photo, Nicholas Morant.

From unnamed lake ("Cabin Lake") at Marvel Pass, Unnamed mountain, Mt. Brussilof (in the distance, right center) and Mount Alcantara

"This hard work ended suddenly when we found ourselves in a comparatively level valley, beautified by meandering streams, open meadows, and a few small lakes. On the summit of a pass where the water turned in the opposite direction we ate lunch and took an hour of rest beside a rock-girt pool."
Walter Wilcox, first visit to Marvel Pass, 1895, *The Rockies of Canada*

View from Cautley Meadows: Mt. Assiniboine, rises over Naiset Point. Lunette Peak shows left of Assiniboine. Mt. Strom, Wedgwood and Sunburst Peaks to the right, above Lake Magog.

"In referring to some of the first ascents ... I have, according to mountaineering etiquette — a mighty poor etiquette, to my mind — given the credit to the visitors.... In the large majority of cases the credit really belongs to the professional guides who have been in charge — Feuz, Kaufmann, Häsler, Bohren, Aemmer, Jorriman, Kain — men whose names are linked with our mountain peaks for all time."
A. O. Wheeler, *The Alps of the New World (Canada's Future)*

Erling Strom and ptarmigan at Allenby Pass. Photo, Nicholas Morant.

leased property, it was determined that the Crown, not Strom, owned the Lodge.

Strom retired in 1975, and his daughter Siri ran the concession from 1976-83. Sepp and Barb Renner have operated it since October, 1983. They lead guided hikes, some to their own secret destinations such as Al's Bowl.

Pat Brewster built Sunburst Camp in 1937, and his wife ran it as a fishing camp for a few years. In 1950, Lizzie Rummel, who had worked for Strom from 1938-41, bought it.

Lizzie Rummel was the daughter of a famous aristocratic German actor, Gustav von Rummel, whose stage name was Gustav Waldau. Lizzie kept her noble background quiet; it wasn't until fairly late in her life that people found it out. She wasn't one to try to impress you about herself; she was independent, and could stand on her own feet.

Her generosity and kindness are legendary. Strangers would be invited for tea. Knowing her helper was carrying supplies over Citadel Pass, in winter she would break trail to Og Lake.

Although she was ever the lady, Lizzie knew the packer's vocabulary. Once, she appeared at Strom's at 7:45 am for a trip she had arranged with Erling. Strom and his guests were still at breakfast, and she wouldn't go in uninvited. Standing in the chill morning outside the kitchen door, she muttered to Hans Gmoser, "Jesus Christ, he told me to be here at quarter to eight!"

Lizzie loved a joke. She stored some of her things on a high attic shelf. When she asked Hans to get something down, instead of using a chair, Hans wanted to show off and got up there by chinning himself. Later, if he tried to reach the attic shelf by standing on a chair, she insisted, with a laugh, he repeat the gymnastic effort, "No, no. The way you always do it."

Jack Romanson's fountain, Bryant Creek Cabin

When she retired in 1970, B. C. Parks used the cabin for a youth camp several years. In 1971, B. C. Parks also took over the Naiset Cabins and gave the ACC a lease for the Hind Hut.

The work of warden Jack Romanson can still be seen at the Bryant Creek and Palliser cabins. Axe carvings of Indian heads and a sculpted fountain are typical of his work. At the Bryant Creek Cabin, he had a water wheel operating a moving statue of a man casting with a fish on the line, pointing to the Marvel Lake Trail. Behind the cabin, he built a concrete bath tub supplied by a fresh water stream. Once the tub filled, the inflow was automatically diverted, allowing the water in his bath to warm. You can still see the tub.

Romanson was a born experimenter. He used a parachute to ski in the wind on Spray Lake, long before this kind of thing became popular up north. Jim Deegan told me that Jack was caught in an updraft once. Gliding in the air 15 metres above the frozen lake, he was seen by a surprised Calgary Power motorist who was so startled, he drove off the road.

Romanson always worried about grizzlies. He used to put bells on his pack horses and drive them ahead in case there were bears on the trail. When Chief Warden Herb Ashley visited Bryant Creek, he looked out the window and saw two giant bruins headed toward the cabin. He turned to Romanson and said, "There's a couple of your friends from Canmore coming up the trail." Jack groomed his hair in front of the mirror and rushed to open the cabin door. When he stepped outside, the grizzlies were almost at his porch.

Romanson's successor, Bill Vroom, who was stationed at Bryant Creek from 1958-61, used to see all kinds of people in the back country. One hiker passed by the cabin carrying a suitcase. Another time, Bill watched a group of three big men bearing little packs go by in the company of a tiny slip of a woman who was weighed down under an enormous load.

Ken Jones was appointed Mount Assiniboine Park's first Ranger, serving from 1967-74.

Ken could hike fast. Once when he was packing out of the area for supplies, he got word a guest had a heart attack at Strom's Lodge. The only way to request a rescue helicopter was via the phone line at the Bryant Creek Warden Cabin, a line which was monitored in Banff only twice a day. Ken reached Bill Vroom's cabin in time to put the call through. After the message was sent, Vroom rode to Strom's Lodge to see what he could do until the helicopter arrived. It was getting dark when he returned, so he hurried. "I was on a good horse, and rode at a fast trot most of the way. It took a little longer than Ken, almost 50, who was walking out, and carrying a heavy pack."

Ken is long associated with Assiniboine, making his first visit in 1933 with George Harrison and working for Strom in 1936. In 1992, at age 81, Ken still guides hikers at Mount Assiniboine Lodge.

In 1991, Mount Assiniboine Park was designated a World Heritage Site.

Mount Assiniboine Lodge

FACILITIES

Mount Assiniboine Lodge Built in 1928, the Lodge is located in a spectacular scenic meadow by Lake Magog. Lodge and cabin accommodation are available. No smoking, no pets. In summer, the Lodge is open from late June to early October. Amenities include propane heat and lights in all buildings, a sauna, and in the Lodge, a shower and flush toilet. Gourmet meals are served in a warm family atmosphere. Hosts, Sepp and Barb Renner know the area intimately and lead guided hikes. The facility can be accessed by helicopter.

The lodge is filled with historic photographs and artifacts. It was operated almost 50 years by Erling Strom. Visitors are welcome between 4 pm and 5 pm for afternoon tea, served with a delicious assortment of baked sweets.

Write Mount Assiniboine Lodge, Box 1527, Canmore, Alberta, T0L 0M0, phone 403-678-2883 (Fax 403-678-4877).

Naiset Cabins Located on the south side of Magog Creek, these four cabin shelters, formerly the property of the ACC, accommodate 31 people and are available in summer on a first come, first served basis. Facilities include bunks and wood stoves. Cooking is not permitted inside the cabins. A fee is charged.

Bryant Creek Hiker's Shelter Located just off the Bryant Creek Trail, at Kilometre 12.9, this shelter provides woodstove and axe. A reservation is required and must be picked up at the Banff Information Centre which monitors the bookings to prevent overcrowding.

Campgrounds Mount Assiniboine Park campgrounds in the core area (Lake Magog, Og Lake) have privies and bearproof storage. Bring a portable cookstove: fires are not permitted. Run on a first come first served basis, there is a charge for these campgrounds.

Fires are allowed at other campgrounds in the provincial park which are free. A group camping area is located at O'Brien Meadows; reservations are required and may be obtained from the district office, Box 118, Wasa, B. C. V0B 2K0 (phone 604-422-3212)

Banff Park campgrounds on Bryant Creek (Br 7, Br 13, Br 14, Br 19) and Sunshine Meadows (Su 8) have tables, privies and bearproof storage. Bring a portable campstove: fires are not permitted. Banff Park campgrounds on Lower Spray River (Sp 6, Sp 16, Sp 23 and Sp 35) and on Brewster Creek (Bw 10) have tables, privies, bearproof storage and fire pits. A free permit must be obtained (available at the Banff Information Centre or the Calgary Regional Office).

R. C. Hind Hut The Alpine Club of Canada hut for climbers is located above the headwall west of Lake Magog. The hut is run by B. C. Parks. Free accommodation is on a first come first served basis. Amenities include Coleman stoves, oil heater, foamies, dishes and utensils.

Helicopters At present, two companies are authorized to offer helicopter rides to Mount Assiniboine Park. Flights are restricted to Wednesdays, Fridays, Sundays and statutory holiday Mondays. Contact Canmore Helicopters, Box 2069, Canmore, Alberta, T0L 0M0, phone 403-678-4802 (Fax 403-678-2176) or Canadian Helicopters, Box 2309, Canmore, Alberta, T0L 0M0, phone 403-678-2207 (Fax 403-678-5600).

District Warden and Park Ranger Banff Park warden cabins on Bryant Creek are occupied some of the summer.

Mount Assiniboine Park Rangers are stationed at the Park Headquarters building, located close to the Naiset Cabins near the east shore of Lake Magog.

Sunrise, Mt. Magog and Mt. Assiniboine, 1991. Compare with photo page 216 for glacier recession.

Page 45:	*Top left:*	*Mt. Assiniboine from Lake Terrapin*
	Top right:	*Looking west from Nub Peak. The Marshall shows top left. Mt. Watson, in the centre, rises above a tip of Wedgwood Lake. Mts. Daer and Sam seen in the distance.*
	Bottom left:	*Mt. Eon, rising above Mt. Gloria, Mt. Aye and Lake Gloria from Wonder Lookout. The tip of Lake Terrapin shows bottom left.*
	Bottom right:	*Mt. Magog and Mt. Assiniboine from Sunburst Lake*

ASSINIBOINE PASS from BRYANT CREEK

~ Shortest route to Mt. Assiniboine ~

Distance 25.9 km (16.1 mi) Mt. Shark parking lot to Lake Magog
Height Gain 520 m (1,700')
Hiking Time 6 hr 16 min
5 hr 48 min return

Trailhead From Canmore, follow the signs to Spray Lakes (the Smith-Dorrien—Spray Trail), going 34.4 km (21.4 mi) past the Nordic Centre. Turn off at the Mt. Engadine Lodge junction and go an additional 5.3 km (3.3 mi) to the Mt. Shark parking lot.

Alternately, turn off the Smith-Dorrien—Spray Trail at the Upper Spray Lake dam and follow the west side of Spray Lake to Canyon Dam. From there, hike or cycle to Trail Centre. This trail is 0.2 km longer, is rougher and climbs more than the one from Mt. Shark parking area. Map page 14.

Options The trail may be used by hikers, cyclists, and equestrians. There are separate trails for horses and hikers over the last section to the pass. You can stop at backcountry campgrounds (Br 7, Br 13, Br 14, Br 19 — permit required) or a hiker's shelter (reservation required) from where side trips lead to Owl Lake, Marvel Pass, Marvel Lake, Allenby Pass and Og Pass. Long trips from these campgrounds can also be taken west of Assiniboine Pass, to Wonder Pass, Lake Magog, Sunburst Valley, Nub Peak and Windy Ridge.

Many hikers go to Assiniboine this way, returning by the more scenic (but longer) Wonder Pass route.

If you have two cars, you can return to the Banff area via Citadel Pass or Allenby Pass. You can also leave the area by the Mitchell or Simpson rivers.

≈ The wide trail with long sections of easy grade makes for pleasant cycling as far as Allenby Creek (you save two hours). I prefer to walk from there. The hiker's trail and the horse trail diverge at the Allenby Pass Junction, then rejoin high up the cliff near Assiniboine Pass. The horse trail is 1.5 km shorter (you save 32 minutes going up, 15 minutes down) but is steeper and has brief sections flooded by streams and overgrown with alder.

The two routes separate again at a tiny meadow before the pass where the horse trail diverges into Og Meadows, bypassing the direct way to the Lodge, Naiset Cabins and the campground. The two routes reunite on the Nub Trail, past the Lodge and Naiset Cabins.

When Jack Romanson was warden at Bryant Creek (about 1950) he made some excellent Indian head carvings, one a fountain. He also carved a 50 foot flagpole, removing the bark with a chisel! Unfortunately, this pole no longer stands, but a cement bathtub he made can still be seen back of the cabin.

Jack Romanson. Nicholas Morant photo, courtesy Whyte Museum of the Canadian Rockies.

Trail From the Mt. Shark parking lot, the trail follows an old logging road. Shortly after the Watridge Lake junction, you descend a steep hill. Cross the Upper Spray River, and go by the trail to Palliser Pass (on your left). After the bridge over Bryant Creek, keep ahead to the main path (from Trail Centre) and turn left.

You go through Big Springs Campground (Br 7). The route follows an easy grade, increasing slightly, before the Owl Lake junction. Then the incline steepens to moderate where an ancient rockfall from the Sundance Range encroaches on the forest. You pass a junction (left) to Campground Br 13 and the shortcut to Marvel Lake. In quick succession after this junction, you go by trails to Wonder Pass (and Marvel Lake) and the hiker's shelter, Campground Br 14 and Bryant Creek warden cabin (and another junction to Wonder Pass).

The grade then becomes easy. At Mercer Creek, an unsigned trail leads to the Tall Timbers campsite used by the Skyline Hikers. The easy grade continues past the Trail Riders'

Horse Camp and Br 19. Just before Allenby Creek, the horse trail fords Bryant Creek. After the bridge over Allenby Creek, an easier ford also provides access to the horse trail.

If you stay on the hiking trail, you bend left in the direction of Allenby Creek, leaving the Allenby Pass trail after 0.5 km. A long winding ascent (a vertical climb of 245 m), brings you back to the horse trail near the summit. Then the route ascends almost to the pass before the horse route branches off again, to the right.

Keep ahead. Just after the pass, you descend to O'Brien Meadows. A horse camp now occupies the upper meadow.

You pass junctions to Og Lake (plus Sunshine via Citadel Pass) and Sunburst Valley (plus Nub Peak) before turning left to Mount Assiniboine Lodge, Naiset Cabins (add 0.2 km) and the Ranger station. Keep ahead for the campground at Lake Magog (add 1.3 km).

Trail Section	km from	time out	return time
Mt. Shark Parking Lot		↓	348 min
Palliser Pass Jct.	6.2	76 min	267 min
Trail Centre (Canyon Dam) Jct.	6.9	86 min	257 min
Warden Cabin Jct.	7.1	88 min	255 min
Br 7 (Big Springs)	9.7	120 min	223 min
Owl Lake Jct.	12.1	145 min	195 min
Br 13 (and Marvel L.) Jct.	13.3	166 min	181 min
Wonder Pass (& Shelter) Jct.	13.8	174 min	175 min
Br 14, (McBride Camp) Jct.	14.3	182 min	168 min
Warden (& Wonder Pass Jct.)	14.4	183 min	167 min
Tall Timbers Jct. (Mercer Cr.)	17.1	215 min	135 min
Horse Camp Jct.	17.3	220 min	130 min
Br 19 Jct.	17.8	233 min	117 min
Horse Trail, lower Jct.*	18.0	235 min	115 min
Allenby and Og Pass Jct.	18.5	241 min	107 min
Horse Trail, upper Jct.*	22.9	334 min	41 min
Horse Tr., Og Meadows Jct.	23.2	342 min	35 min
Assiniboine Pass	23.5	346 min	32 min
Sunshine (Citadel Pass) Jct.	24.8	371 min	5 min
Sunburst Lake Jct.	25.8	374 min	2 min
Mount Assiniboine Lodge	25.9	376 min	↑
* Via horse trail		↓	15 min
subtract:	1.5	32 min	↑

Naiset Point, Mts. Magog and Assiniboine from O'Brien Meadows. The meadow (like O'Brien Lake near Lake Louise) is named after an American couple who camped here about 1930. In 1952, pilot Al Gaetz crashed attempting to take off in this sluggish Stinson. Since then, this site has also been called Airplane Meadows. The wreckage was removed not long after this picture was taken in 1965. Another plane crash occurred in Lake Magog (story, Lake Magog Shoreline Trail, Page 64).

Mount Allenby from Allenby Pass

"Far and away the best entertainment were the nights that Erling took the floor. He was a wonderful story teller and a romantic figure with his handsome features, slight stammer and Norwegian accent. The setting helped create the proper atmosphere for his tales of daring do.... Even today a two day 38 mile ski trek over two mountain passes is an accomplishment. In those days it was unheard of, but Erling often did it in one day and alone." Betty Cowie, *letter to Barb Renner, June 25, 1987*

Mount Assiniboine from O'Brien Meadows near Assiniboine Pass

"Assiniboine is one of those mountains you can't sight without feeling excited. Practically twelve thousand feet in altitude and of distinctive shape, it's the most striking thing on the Rocky Mountain horizon for many miles." Brian Meredith, *Escape on Skis*

OWL LAKE and MARVEL PASS Circuit

~ **Floral meadows, luminous lakes, larch stands** (photos pp. 40, 53) ~

Distance **21.5 km (13.4 mi) circuit**
Height Gain **490 m (1,600')**
Hiking Time **6 hr 44 min**

Trailhead Marvel Lake Campground (Br 13). Map page 14.

Options You can explore the lakelets near the pass. You can also make a short detour to the north end of Owl Lake. You can divert to Terrapin and Gloria lakes which have superb views, but this trail has sections which are faint, very steep and boggy; also, since it hasn't been maintained for years, expect deadfall. It takes 15 minutes to reach Lake Terrapin, 20 more to Lake Gloria. (You have to bushwhack a short distance between the two lakes. Keep near the shore of Lake Terrapin and then of Gloria Creek.)

≈ This is a long trip into little-visited country. In two visits, I saw mule deer, white-tail deer and, 0.5 km east of the pass, a grizzly. The bear was perhaps 100 m ahead and 10 m below the trail. There was only a slight cross breeze, but it didn't hear me until my fourth shout. Then it turned in my direction and reared on its hind legs. At the next call, it loped into open timber, making sounds I heard, but not clearly enough to describe. When The Skyline Hikers camped here in 1988 several parties sighted a grizzly. It seemed little concerned by the people and made no attempt to bother them.

Len Black, president of The Skyline Hikers, told me a trapper began constructing a cabin beside the unnamed lake near the pass. When Banff Park authorities found out, he had to abandon construction. His permit allowed him to build in B. C., but the map shows the lake in Alberta. If true, the story is ironic, because the map is wrong. The lake drains to Aurora Creek, B. C. and therefore is not in Banff Park. Wheeler made the mistake on his Boundary Sheet map, probably the source of the error on the current topo map. The remains of the structure prompted The Skyline Hikers to call this *Cabin Lake*.

In 1895, Walter Wilcox, R. L. Barrett and Bill Peyto, while circling Mount Assiniboine, made the first recorded visit to Marvel Pass.

In 1921, Dr. W. Stone and his wife bivouacked near Marvel Pass in their ill-fated attempt to climb Mt. Eon (story, page 38).

"Cabin Lake"

There are problem spots where the trail is faint, especially north of Cabin Lake. Also, watch for cairns at the site of the Skyline Hikers' campsite, where the trail makes a sharp right turn and climbs steeply above the valley.

On both sides of Marvel Lake, the trail is very steep. On the south side, expect overgrown, rough and wet sections.

Near Marvel Lake, the trails are shown inaccurately on the current topo map. There is no water by the path north of Marvel Lake.

Trail If you go clockwise from Marvel Lake Campground (Br 13), hike to the Bryant Creek Trail. Turn right, and go to the Owl Lake Trail Junction. Turn right again and head down to Bryant Creek. Watch for the hiker detour (right) which takes you to the bridge.

After climbing through forest, you attain more open country. A junction left leads to the north shore of Owl Lake, a 5 minute detour.

You follow the west shore of Owl Lake for almost half an hour. Then, after a brief section of forest, you come to a large meadow. Near the south end, where the trail is faint, large cairns direct you up the slope above Owl Creek. From here, you stay high to Marvel Pass. In mid-August these slopes produce lush crops of grouse huckleberry and blueberry — and attract bears.

Just beyond Marvel Pass, you come to an open slope leading down to Cabin Lake and a good view of Mt. Alcantara.

Beyond Cabin Lake, there are diverse trails. The best way to proceed is to take the trail from the outlet (if you keep a little uphill to the north, the path is more obvious). Proceed downhill, staying right of the outlet streambed. The path is faint in places, and like the stream, eventually disappears. After a dozen minutes, you see an open plateau ahead with a stream coming in from the right. Turn right and follow up the stream; a faint trail soon materializes. Continuing north, the path becomes obvious by the time you reach the first of several small lakes. Keep right of the streams.

After passing the first major lakelet on the Alberta drainage, the trail cuts uphill before heading down through open forest and small meadows. At the largest meadow, where the route is faint, watch for hiking signs at both ends. Farther ahead, another trail sign directs you to turn left at a small opening.

Eventually, you reach the steep hillside above Marvel Lake, then follow a very steep, rough trail down to Terrapin Creek.

Left of the horse ford, look for a giant spruce trunk across the creek. Cross this log and go left at the intersecting trail to a set of large weathered logs where you cross the second half of the creek. (There are plans to bridge these fords in the future.)

After this crossing, you reach the old trail (left) to Lake Terrapin. Turn right to Marvel Lake. Then climb to the Wonder Pass Trail and turn right. Follow the hillside to near the east end of Marvel Lake. An unsigned flagged shortcut turns off right to the lake. If you haven't done it previously, you could lose your way following it. To be safe, carry on seven minutes more to the signed intersection and turn right to Marvel Lake.

When the lake is in sight, look for the sign showing the trail to Br 13 and turn left.

Trail Section	km from	time out	return time
Br 13		↓	404 min
Bryant Creek Trail	0.5	7 min	398 min
Owl Lake Jct.	1.7	20 min	384 min
Bryant Creek Bridge	2.0	26 min	376 min
Owl Lake, north shore jct.	5.2	78 min	331 min
Skyline Hikers' Campsite	8.2	132 min	279 min
Marvel Pass	9.9	178 min	251 min
Marvel Lake (west)	14.5	281 min	115 min
Wonder Pass Jct.	15.5	307 min	101 min
Leave Wonder Pass Trail	20.0	376 min	28 min
Marvel Lake (east shore) Jct.	20.5	383 min	18 min
Br 13	21.5	401 min	↑

MARVEL LAKE

~ Scenic shore; fishing ~

Distance **1.8 km (1.1 mi) from Bryant Shelter**
Height Gain **25 m (80'); 55 m (180') return**
Hiking Time **25 min**
26 min return

Trailhead The Bryant Creek Shelter. Map page 14.

Options You can make this a short detour en route to Wonder Pass or Marvel Pass. You can also approach Marvel Lake from campground Br 13. You can explore the lakeshore; from where the trail first meets the lake, you reach the outlet in four minutes.

≈ The lake has always been a good place to fish. Retired warden Bill Vroom told me Marvel Lake is one of the best places to see fish spawning.

Black bears used to be a nuisance at Marvel Lake. One bear learned to grab a fisherman's pack and run into the bush with it. It found if it tried to get at the contents in view of the angler, he would throw rocks at it, so it went first to a safe place before opening the pack. Outfitter Lorne Cripp got so used to chasing bears away, that he'd often dream he heard one rattling nearby, wake up, and rush into the woods swinging a frying pan at an imaginary bear.

About 1960 a grizzly gave Bill Vroom all the work he wanted when it tore down all the trail signs in the area.

The earliest recorded trip to this site was 1895 when Walter Wilcox and James Porter visited Marvel, Terrapin and Gloria lakes while their companion Robert Barrett lingered on Wonder Peak.

In 1910, Tom Longstaff stopped at Marvel Lake after climbing Mt. Assiniboine. His 1907 climb in the Himalayas held the world's altitude record for many years, yet he rated his route on Mt. Assiniboine "the hardest climb I have ever done." When he died in 1964, the route had not been repeated. His guide was Rudolph Aemmer, hero of the 1921 rescue of Mrs. Stone on Mt. Eon.

Longstaff was thrilled by Marvel Lake: "We spent a day visiting the most lovely lake I have ever seen. Surrounded by straight pines to the waters' edge, its outline was broken by narrow projecting points through the columnar stems of whose trees the lake gleamed. It was girt by a circle of rocky peaks culminating in Assiniboine. A blue glacier discharged into a smaller lake beyond it."

Trail From the Shelter, the trail crosses the meadow to a bridge over Bryant Creek and climbs towards Wonder Pass. The first junction to your left leads to Marvel Lake.

Trail Section	km from	time out	return time
Assiniboine Pass Tr., Shelter Jct.		↓	29 min
Shelter	0.2	3 min	26 min
Bryant Creek Bridge	0.7	9 min	20 min
Wonder Pass Jct.	1.5	21 min	9 min
Marvel Lake	2.0	28 min	↑

MARVEL LAKE via SHORTCUT from Br 13

Distance **1.3 km (0.8 mi) from Br 13**
Height Gain **25 m (75')**
Hiking Time **18 min**

Trailhead Marvel Lake Campground (Br 13).

Trail At the end of the campground, cross Bryant Creek. Ascend a hill, then pass a green lakelet (a couple of junctions go left to its shore). You pass the junction, right, to the Wonder Pass Trail 100 m before the shore of Marvel Lake.

Trail Section	km from	time out	return time
Bryant Creek Trail Jct.		↓	25 min
Br 13	0.5	6 min	18 min
Bryant Creek Bridge	0.6	8 min	16 min
Lakelet Jct.	1.3	17 min	8 min
Marvel Lake	1.8	24 min	↑

Mount Eon (above Mount Gloria), Mount Aye, Lunette Peak and Mount Assiniboine from Marvel Lake

"It was only sublime courage that saved the life of Mrs. Stone when marooned for seven days on a narrow mountain ledge without food, making one of the outstanding adventures of all mountain history." Walter Wilcox, *American Alpine Journal, 1941*

Mount Byng and Aurora Mountain from Owl Lake

"The exquisite charm and beauty of the lakes, so numerous in every part of the mountains, is one of the chief delights of the camper. Some are small and solitary, perched in some amphitheater far up among the mountains, surrounded by rocky walls, and hemmed in by great blocks of stone.... Other lakes, at lower altitudes, are concealed among the dark forests, and, with deep waters, richly colored, appear like gems in their seclusion....

"Most of the mountain lakes are small, and hide in secluded valleys, but many are large enough to become rough and angry in a storm, and have beaten out for themselves narrow beaches of gravel and shores lined with sand." Walter Wilcox, *Camping in the Canadian Rockies*

ALLENBY PASS from BRYANT CREEK

~ **Fossils, open views** (photos pp. 48, 137, 157) ~

Distance **5.1 km (3.2 mi) from Br 19**
Height Gain **455 m (1,500')**
Hiking Time **2 hr 6 min**
1 hr 41 min return

Trailhead Campground Br 19, Bryant Creek trail. Map page 14.

Options You may hike or cycle this trail. (It is a stiff climb via a rough trail for a bicycle.)

You can diverge to Og Pass and Windy Ridge. You can cross the pass and follow Brewster Creek to Banff (overnight trip).

≈ You go through a lovely grove of larch to broad grassy meadows and a glacier-scraped ridge above timberline. The peaks flanking the pass are uplifted vertically; seen with binoculars, they are awesome. South, you can see Mt. Sir Douglas, third highest mountain in the area.

The low scenic ridge west of the pass is worth exploring. There are fossils near the pass (especially on this ridge) and an abundance of chert on the glacier-scraped rockshelf on the low ridge west of the pass. Allenby Pass used to be a popular route when Erling Strom's guests arrived from Banff via this trail.

Mount Allenby, southeast of the pass, was named after Field Marshal Viscount Allenby, Commander of the British army in Palestine in World War I. It was called Brewster Pass (head of Brewster Creek) until about 1950.

Beyond the Og Pass junction, the grade is stiff. Loose rocks make sections of the route rough walking.

After climbing the pass in spring on snowshoes, Rex Harrison (Erling Strom's first cook) said he would rather go to the workhouse than over that pass again. Rex had even more problems on skis.

Root-like chert, Allenby Pass

Trail From the Assiniboine Pass Foot Trail Junction, you ascend at a moderate grade to an unsigned junction to the left (marked with red flagging, 1992). This is the junction to Og Pass via the Shortcut Trail.

The grade eases as you proceed to the main (Highline) junction to Og Pass, a much more scenic trail than the Assiniboine Pass route.

A dozen minutes more brings you to an unmarked trail to the right, leading to a campsite which the Skyline Hikers occupied in 1960.

After ascending through a forest of larch, you reach timberline and the grade moderates to the pass. The ridge left of the pass is worth exploring for scenic and geological reasons.

Trail Section	km from	time out	return time
Br 19 Campground		↓	101 min
Bryant Cr., Allenby Pass Jct.	0.2	5 min	96 min
Assiniboine Pass, Hiker's Jct.	0.5	11 min	91 min
Og Pass Shortcut Jct.	1.1	25 min	80 min
Og Pass Highline Jct.	2.3	51 min	60 min
Allenby Pass	5.6	126 min	↑

ALLENBY PASS—OG PASS HIGHLINE

Loose, large rocks make the way unpleasant underfoot, but the path is relatively level, and the open slopes provide views down Bryant Creek valley to Mt. Sir Douglas. After 0.8 km, you intersect with the Shortcut Trail (see page 55) from Assiniboine Pass Trail to Og Pass. You gain 30 m to this unsigned junction.

Trail Section	km from	time out	return time
Og Pass Highline Jct.		↓	16 min
Og Pass, Shortcut Trail Jct.	0.8	18 min	↑

"Mt. Assiniboine's shape is more nearly perfect than the Matterhorn and the foreground... is much prettier." Erling Strom

OG PASS and LAKE MAGOG from BRYANT CREEK (via Og Pass Shortcut Trail)

~ Outstanding views of Mt. Assiniboine ~

Distance 11.6 km (7.2 mi) from Bryant Creek, Allenby Pass Junction
Height Gain 435 m (1,420'); 195 m (640') return
Hiking Time 3 hr 13 min
2 hr 58 min return

Trailhead Campground Br 19, Bryant Creek trail. Map page 14.

Options You can take the Highline Trail or the Shortcut. You can diverge to Windy Ridge. You can circle Cave Mountain, returning via Assiniboine Pass.

≈ In 1928, Erling Strom took his first guests to Mt. Assiniboine via Allenby and Assiniboine passes. By 1931 he changed to this new trail.

Just west of Og Pass, you climb a hogback. If you explore this low ridge a short distance from the trail, you get superb views south to Mt. Assiniboine. To the northwest, you see Mt. Ball with its giant glacier cap.

Much of the trail is rough, with loose rocks on the path. Except for the steep Shortcut Trail section, the grade is easy to moderate.

If you are camped at Bryant Creek, Og Pass is a quicker and more attractive approach to scenic Windy Ridge, than via Assiniboine Pass.

Mts. Magog, Assiniboine, Sturdee and Wedgwood from the Og Pass Trail

Trail Branch right onto the Allenby Pass Trail and follow it to an unsigned junction (flagged with red tape, 1992), the Shortcut Trail. Turn left and follow this steep shortcut up the open forested slopes to join the main Allenby Pass—Og Pass Highline Trail from Allenby Pass. Except for red flagging, this intersection also is unmarked. Turn left.

Not long after this upper junction, Mt. Assiniboine comes in view. You can also see down Bryant Creek to the Spray Mountains (Mt. Birdwood is the striking sharp pyramid; in places, you also see Mt. Sir Douglas with its high, blunt, rounded summit dominating those distant peaks). As you enter the narrow valley to Og Pass, views become restricted. A pond lies near the pass. Just west of the pass, where the trail bends left to climb a low hogback, you pass the Windy Ridge Trail on your right.

You descend the forested hogback to Og Meadows. Near the end of this large opening, the old horse trail from Assiniboine Pass joins from the left. You then intersect with, first the Og Lake trail, then the Sunburst Lake horse trail, both on your right. Keep ahead at both junctions.

After 0.5 km, you reach the new hiking trail from Assiniboine Pass. Turn right for Lake Magog. At the next intersection, turn left for the Lodge (and Naiset Cabins). Keep ahead for the Campground.

Trail Section	km from	time out	return time
Br 19 Campground		↓	178 min
Bryant Cr., Allenby Pass Jct.	0.2	5 min	173 min
Og Pass Shortcut Jct.	0.6	14 min	167 min
Og Pass Highline Jct.	1.6	36 min	153 min
Og Pass	6.2	116 min	83 min
Windy Ridge Jct.	6.5	121 min	77 min
Horse Tr. Jct., Assin. Pass	10.1	172 min	20 min
Og Lake Jct.	10.4	175 min	16 min
Horse Tr. to Sunburst L. Jct.	10.6	178 min	13 min
Assiniboine Pass, Hiker Jct.	11.1	187 min	6 min
Lodge Jct.	11.4	191 min	2 min
Lodge	11.6	193 min	↑

Terrapin Mountain peeping over Naiset Point, Mount Magog, Mount Assiniboine and Mount Sturdee from the Og Pass Trail

"Before turning in we took a last look at the great obelisk above us, brilliant in the moonlight beneath the dark canopy of star-strewn sky; and next morning awoke to a world of snow, which lay thick and soft around, whilst whirling masses of storm clouds drifted across the mountain and wrapped its summit, giving but an occasional glimpse of its steep flanks, covered with freshly fallen snow."

James Outram, describing the change of weather after his ascent of Mt. Assiniboine, *The Alpine Journal, May, 1902*

Mounts Magog, Assiniboine, Sturdee, Wedgwood, Sunburst and The Marshall from the Windy Ridge Trail

"Many larches were mingled with the balsam and spruce trees in the groves, and extensive areas were destitute of trees altogether. These moors were clothed with a variety of bushy plants, mostly dwarfed by the rigor of the climate, while here and there a small balsam tree could be seen, stunted and deformed by its long contest for life, and bearing many dead branches among those still alive. These bleached and lifeless limbs, with their thick, twisted branches resisting the axe, or even the approach of a wood-cutter, resembled those weird and awful illustrations of Doré, where evil spirits in the infernal regions are represented transformed to trees." Walter Wilcox, *Camping in the Canadian Rockies*

WINDY RIDGE

~ Superb views: Mt. Assiniboine, lakes, Brewster Creek Valley ~

Distance 7.2 km (4.5 mi) from Lodge
Height Gain 405 m (1,620'); 60 m (200') return
Maximum Height 2635 m (8,650')
Hiking Time 2 hr 6 min
1 hr 51 min return

Trailhead Lodge. Add 1.3 km if you start from Lake Magog Campground or 0.2 km from Naiset Cabins. Map page 14.

Options You can approach Windy Ridge from Bryant Creek. You can return by the alternate route, circling Cave Mountain. (See Og Pass Trail.) If you don't mind very steep scree, there are easy scrambles to the summits flanking Windy Ridge.

≈ From Windy Ridge, Mt. Assiniboine's summit shows as a sharper pyramid than from any other vantage point I know, except The Nub. En route to Windy Ridge, you pass through a band of larches to a lovely meadow. From here, in addition to Mt. Assiniboine, highest peak in Mount Assiniboine Park and Banff Park, you observe the Goodsirs, highest summits in Yoho Park and the distant Mt. Vaux with its great glacier. As you approach Windy Ridge, you also see Mt. Ball, with its snowy cap, and far away, a few of the Ten Peaks, dominated by the dark wedge of Mt. Deltaform. I prefer the views from the high floral meadows to what you see at the rocky pass, though the higher vantage point looks down a hanging valley with a deep blue tarn and the verdant Brewster Creek valley. Also, as you get higher, you see more of Og and Magog lakes. With binoculars, you can pick out Gog Lake at the base of the Towers.

Mounts Eon and Aye; Marvel, Terrapin and Gloria lakes from Wonder Peak

Trail From the Lodge, turn right and take the trail toward Assiniboine Pass. Turn left at the junction to Citadel Pass. Shortly after the horse path from Sunburst Lake joins on your left, you reach the Og Pass Junction where you turn right. Turn left where the horse trail to Assiniboine Pass separates from the Og Pass Trail.

Hike across Og Meadows and up the hogback 0.3 km west of Og Pass, keeping left where the trail divides near the top of this ridge. (The branch to the right misses the junction to Windy Ridge.) Turn left at the Windy Ridge Junction onto a trail running perpendicular to Og Pass. The route zigzags through a bench of alpine larch, then a floral meadow, and finally through scree to a low saddle of Og Mountain overlooking Brewster Creek.

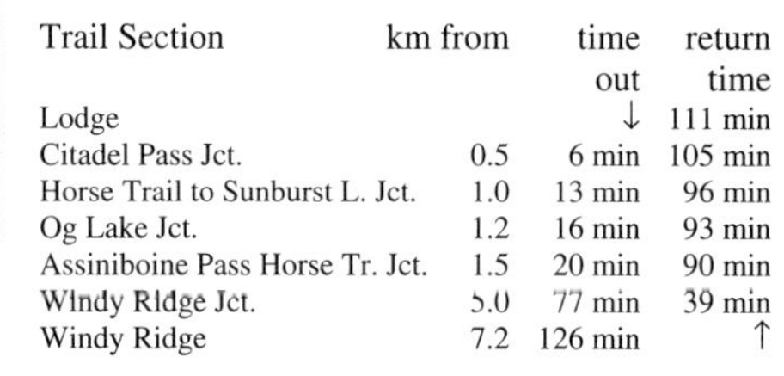

Trail Section	km from	time out	return time
Lodge		↓	111 min
Citadel Pass Jct.	0.5	6 min	105 min
Horse Trail to Sunburst L. Jct.	1.0	13 min	96 min
Og Lake Jct.	1.2	16 min	93 min
Assiniboine Pass Horse Tr. Jct.	1.5	20 min	90 min
Windy Ridge Jct.	5.0	77 min	39 min
Windy Ridge	7.2	126 min	↑

~ Glacial lakes ~

Distance **3.1 km (1.9 mi) from Lodge; plus 9.9 km (6.1 mi) to Bryant Creek (Br 13)**
Height Gain **205 m (670'); 580 m (1,900') loss to Bryant Creek**
Hiking Time **50 min**
41 min return

Trailhead Lodge. (Add 1.3 km from Lake Magog Campground. Subtract 0.2 km from Naiset Cabins.) Alternately, start from Bryant Creek (Campground Br 13 or the Shelter are the closest starting points.) Map page 14.

Options You can diverge to Gog Lake or Wonder Lookout. You can make a circuit of Wonder Peak and Mt. Cautley, returning via Cautley Meadows. This is a gruelling but glorious approach to Lake Magog from Bryant Creek or Marvel Lake.

≈ The grade is stiff, especially from the Bryant Creek side.

There is no water on the trail from Wonder Pass to Bryant Creek.

Wonder Pass is a popular day hike. However, you have to go south of the pass (Wonder Lookout is best) to see the colorful lakes and Mt. Eon, where the tragic death of Dr. Stone, and the heroic survival and dramatic rescue of his wife occurred (story, page 38).

If you are coming from Bryant Creek to Lake Magog, Wonder Pass is almost 300 m higher and 2 km farther than Assiniboine Pass. But the scenery is more rewarding, and many hikers not inclined to pack in this way will take it on their way out, where most of the route is downhill.

The names *Wonder* Pass and *Marvel* and *Gloria* lakes, chosen in 1913 by the Boundary Commission, indicate the thrill of, "the wonderful view that meets the eye ... Marvel Lake, Lake Gloria and a huge amphitheatre of glaciers with a setting of green forest, suddenly appearing". Erling Strom described the scene of the three lakes (Gloria, Terrapin and Marvel) as "one of the most astonishing sights in the Canadian Rockies."

Trail From the Lodge, hike past Naiset Cabins. At 1.4 km, an unmarked trail (250 m, 4 minutes) to the shore of Gog Lake branches right. Keep ahead. Just before timberline, you pass a small waterfall on your left. The meadows near the pass provide expansive views.

If you continue to Bryant Creek, you travel 9.9 km, descending 580 m. You pass the unmarked junction to Wonder Lookout. Just before you enter forest, you get a glimpse of Marvel Lake. The trees restrict your views of the three colorful tarns, though there are open slopes far ahead, near the junction to Marvel Pass which turns off to the right.

You contour above Marvel Lake, passing a junction to the east shore 0.8 km before the bridge over Bryant Creek. From here, an old unmarked path turns left to the Bryant Creek Trail and Warden Cabin which you see across the meadow. The main path angles ahead to the Shelter and the Bryant Creek Trail.

Trail Section	km from	time out	return time
Mt. Assiniboine Lodge		↓	204 min
Naiset Cabins	0.5	7 min	197 min
Gog Lake Jct.	1.4	21 min	186 min
Wonder Pass	3.1	50 min	163 min
Wonder Lookout Jct.	3.8	60 min	151 min
Last View of Marvel Lake	4.7	72 min	135 min
Marvel Pass Jct.	6.4	95 min	106 min
Marvel Lake Jct.	10.9	164 min	29 min
Bryant Creek bridge	11.7	175 min	17 min
Shelter	12.2	181 min	11 min
Shelter Jct.	12.4	184 min	8 min
Bryant Creek, Br 13	13.0	192 min	↑

"We ascended an easy peak on our left and there ... looked upon a magnificent panorama of the entire Assiniboine system." W. D. Wilcox, on the first ascent of Wonder Peak, *CAJ 1909*.

WONDER LOOKOUT (Siri's Lookout)

~ View of Marvel, Terrapin and Gloria Lakes (photo p. 45) ~

Distance **2.0 km (1.2 mi) from Wonder Pass**
Height Gain **30 m (100'); 90 m (300') return**
Hiking Time **31 min**
35 min return

Trailhead Wonder Pass.

Options This trail extends the Wonder Pass trip.

≈ This short walk from Wonder Pass takes you to a hillside with a superb view of Marvel, Terrapin and Gloria lakes, plus mounts Eon, Aye and the southeast face of Assiniboine. The views are like what you see from the south side of the Wonder Pass Trail, but free from dense forest. Ken Jones says it was called *Siri's Lookout* because Erling Strom's daughter, Siri, is said to have discovered it.

If you are coming from Bryant Creek, after you reach timberline, you can see this trail on the slope of Wonder Peak above. There is no trail sign; however, small cairns flank the trailhead to show you where to turn off.

Barb Renner, of Mount Assiniboine Lodge, tells me this is the only place in the area where avalanche lilies grow. Roots of these flowers are sought by grizzlies, sometimes seen here.

Trail From Wonder Pass, hike 0.7 km south to the unsigned junction at the last rise before the larches. Several small cairns show where you angle left. For 0.6 km the route follows an easy grade, then climbs near a small plateau allowing only limited views. Skirting this rise, the trail descends steeply to the Lookout.

Trail Section	km from	time out	return time
Lodge		↓	76 min
Wonder Pass	3.1	50 min	35 min
Lookout Jct.	3.8	60 min	23 min
Wonder Lookout	5.1	81 min	↑

Sunburst Peak, Indian Peak, Nestor Peak and Nub Peak from Wonder Pass

"Whoever goes over the Walking Tour to Assiniboine Camp with a day or two at his disposal, should leave the beaten path and plunge over the edge of Wonder Pass to the Wonderland beyond." L. H. Lindsay, *Canadian Alpine Journal 1921-22*

Mts. Magog, Assiniboine and Sunburst Lake from Elizabeth Lake—Nub Ridge Trail

Mount Assiniboine from Nub Trail

SUNBURST VALLEY LAKES

~ Sunburst, Cerulean and Elizabeth Lakes ~

Distance **4.4 km (2.7 mi) Lodge to Elizabeth L.**
Height Gain **155 m (500'); 45 m (150') return**
Hiking Time **1 hr 1 min**
58 min return

Trailhead Lodge. Add 0.2 km from Naiset Cabins. Subtract 1.3 km from Lake Magog Campground. Map page 14.

Options You can go up Chuck's Ridge or climb The Nub. You can go to Wedgwood Lake or Ferro Pass.

≈ About 1928, Pat Brewster, who was in charge of Brewster's Mountain Pack Trains, constructed a small camp at Sunburst Lake to join with others at Egypt Lake and Banff. His wife, June, ran Sunshine as a fishing camp. One of her parties met a grizzly at Citadel Pass (p. 70). About 1937, Pat had a cabin built at Sunburst Lake. It was made from larch logs cut from the hill near Cerulean Lake and floated across Sunburst Lake. At the end of the season in 1950, he sold the property to Lizzie Rummel who ran Sunburst Lodge for 20 years, selling it to the B. C. Government in 1970. B. C. Parks then operated it for some years as a youth camp. Now, it accommodates the campground attendant.

Lizzie Rummel will always be associated with Sunburst Lake which, with its superb view of Mt. Assiniboine, is the scenic highlight of this hike. The totem pole near her cabin was carved about 1955 during a long spell of bad weather by the B. C. Mountaineers who were camped at Lake Magog. She expressed an interest in the carving, and park ranger Ken Jones moved it to its present location for her.

Trail From the Lodge, follow the trail along the bench above Lake Magog. Turn left towards the Campground at the Nub Peak Junction. Just before you reach the campsite, turn right to Sunburst Lake. At the next junction, again go right.

The trail follows the scenic shore of Sunburst Lake, intersecting with the horse trail from The Nub, before going to Cerulean Lake. Where the trail turns left to follow the southwest shore of the lake, keep straight to go to Elizabeth Lake. At the top of a rise, a trail to the Nub intersects on the right. Keep ahead. You descend to Elizabeth Lake. Keep ahead at the outlet if you want to go up Chuck's Ridge.

Trail Section	km from	time out	return time
Lodge		↓	58 min
Nub Peak Jct.	0.3	4 min	54 min
Campground, northeast Jct.	1.7	20 min	38 min
Campground, northwest Jct.	2.1	26 min	33 min
Sunburst Lake	2.5	33 min	27 min
Horse Trail Jct.	2.9	41 min	20 min
Cerulean Lake (east end)	3.1	44 min	17 min
Ferro Pass Jct.	3.3	46 min	15 min
Nublet Jct.	3.8	55 min	7 min
Elizabeth Lake	4.4	61 min	↑

"It would be impossible to describe our feelings at this sight which at length, after several days of severe marching, now suddenly burst upon our view."
W. D. Wilcox, *Camping in the Canadian Rockies.*

ELIZABETH LAKE and CHUCK'S RIDGE

~ Clear Lake; scenic ridge ~

Distance **3.3 km (2.0 mi) Cerulean Lake to Chuck's Ridge**
Height Gain **120 m (400'); 30 m (100') return**
Hiking Time **1 hr 2 min**
53 min return

Trailhead Start from Cerulean Lake at the Elizabeth Lake Junction. See Sunburst Valley Trail for the most direct route to this trailhead. Map page 14.

Options Nub Peak, Ferro Pass and Wedgwood Lake are alternate extensions of this hike.

≈ Elizabeth Lake has a lush forest of larch on the south. It is named for Baroness Elizabeth von Rummel, who ran Sunburst Lodge from 1951 until 1970. This modest lady preferred to be called Lizzie Rummel; she is remembered affectionately for her warmth, cheerfulness and love of the mountains.

Chuck's Ridge is a narrow arete on the southwest side of Nub Peak named for Chuck Millar, one of Erling Strom's best known packers. He liked to take parties to this viewpoint. Trees inhibit the otherwise spectacular scenery. To the north, you gaze down a sheer cliff to Nestor Creek; to the south, you get a vista to the northwest face of Mt. Assiniboine and a bit of Wedgwood Lake. You have to explore a little to find the best views.

Trail From the junction at Cerulean Lake, you climb 80 m to a low pass where a trail to The Nub turns right. Keep ahead and descend 30 m to Elizabeth Lake. Here a trail branches left to Ferro Pass. Keep ahead for Chuck's Ridge.

Trail Section	km from	time out	return time
Cerulean L.—Elizabeth L. Jct.		↓	53 min
Nub Ridge Jct.	0.5	9 min	45 min
Elizabeth Lake	0.9	15 min	38 min
Ferro Pass Jct.	2.3	34 min	14 min
Chuck's Ridge	3.3	62 min	↑

NUB PEAK

~ **Superb panorama** (photos pp. 61, 185) ~

Distance	**4.6 km (2.9 mi) Lodge to summit**
Height Gain	**550 m (1,800')**
Maximum Height	**2748 m (9,016')**
Hiking Time	**1 hr 49 min**
	1 hr 20 min return

Trailhead Lodge. Map page 14.

Options You can go on to Elizabeth Lake and Chuck's Ridge by a branch trail below the Nublet. You can reach Cerulean Lake and Sunburst Lake from the same trail or via the horse trail.

≈ The trip up the Nub is a delightful panoramic ridge hike. From the summit you see a host of lakes: Sunburst, Magog, Cerulean, Elizabeth, Og, Game, Wedgwood and Gog, plus several ponds. Mt. Assiniboine dominates the scene. Far to the north, Mounts Ball, Temple and Hector are the most prominent. Joffre and Sir Douglas are seen in the distance to the south.

In 1965, three bull elk appeared on the high ridge, the most superb setting for these animals I have seen.

Trail From Mount Assiniboine Lodge, go north. Keep left as you go by, in quick succession, two junctions to Assiniboine Pass. Keep ahead at the next three intersections: to the campground, the horse trail to Assiniboine Pass and the horse trail to the Mitchell River.

The main trail takes you to a superb viewpoint 215 m above the valley. After a brief descent, a trail to Elizabeth (and Cerulean) Lake branches left. A narrower path angles right, up the Nublet (120 m higher). If you wish to continue, a crude trail descends to the sharp ridge then climbs to a broad sloping plateau. Take note of the cairn for your return; there is no trail up this wide plateau. The summit of Nub Peak is 215 m above the Nublet.

Tail Section	km from	time out	return time
Lodge		↓	80 min
Assiniboine Pass Shortcut Jct.	0.1	2 min	78 min
Assiniboine Pass Jct.	0.2	3 min	77 min
Campground Jct.	0.3	5 min	75 min
Horse tr., Assiniboine Pass, Jct.	0.7	10 min	70 min
Horse tr., Mitchell River Jct.	1.3	19 min	62 min
Elizabeth (& Cerulean) L. Jct.	2.8	47 min	44 min
Nublet	3.2	69 min	29 min
Nub Peak	4.6	109 min	↑

ELIZABETH LAKE from NUB RIDGE

≈ This trail allows you to extend the Nub Ridge hike to a low pass from where you can go north to Elizabeth Lake, or south to Cerulean and Sunburst lakes. You descend 75 m to this pass from Nub Ridge. See Chuck's Ridge and Elizabeth Lake Trail for a description of the alternate routes from the pass.

Trail Section	km from	time out	return time
Nub Ridge, Elizabeth L. Jct.		↓	25 min
Elizabeth L., Cerulean L. Jct.	0.7	14 min	7 min
Elizabeth Lake	1.1	20 min	↑

HORSE TRAIL to SUNBURST LAKE

≈ This portion of the horse route through the core area of the park links the Nub Peak trail with Sunburst Lake by an indirect route. The alternate path, to Elizabeth and Cerulean lakes from the Nub, is a shorter, more scenic way to Sunburst Lake if you are also climbing the Nub.

You climb 30 m from the Nub Junction to Sunburst Lake. If you reverse the route, starting at Sunburst Lake, you climb 60 m.

Trail Section	km from	time out	return time
Nub Trail Jct.		↓	23 min
Sunburst Lake	1.7	22 min	↑

Elk on The Nub. Looking to Og Mountain.

LAKE MAGOG SHORELINE

~ Scenic lakeshore ~

Distance 3.4 km (2.1 mi) Lodge to Headwall
Height Gain 30 m (100')
Hiking Time 43 min
43 min return

Trailhead Lodge; alternately, Naiset Cabins or Lake Magog Campground. Map p. 14.

Options Virtually all the trails in the area radiate from Lake Magog.

≈ This is one of the most scenic shorelines in the Rockies. In addition to the lakeshore trail, another path follows the lake from a bench about 30 m above the water.

The grade is easy except for the short rise, on the return, to Naiset Cabins or the Lodge.

Lake Magog has no visible outlet. As winter snow and ice melts, the lake gradually fills, reaching its highest level in late August.

There is an airplane at the bottom of the lake. Pilot Stu Aymes, was caught in a downdraft from the headwall, attempting to fly a Piper off Lake Magog in winter. After breaking a ski in the forced landing, he went to Banff for a replacement. Before he got back, the ice melted and the plane disappeared into the lake.

Trail From the Lodge, take the trail ahead, west, which leads down to Lake Magog. At the northeast corner of the lake, you join a trail left from the back of Naiset Cabins. Keep ahead, and shortly before the Campground, climb a bench. Pass a shortcut to Sunburst Lake (to the right) to enter the campground. A second path to Sunburst turns right at the stream.

At the west end of the campground, a path to some tent facilities branches right. The main trail heads to the end of the meadows under the headwall where a climber's route leads to the R. C. Hind Hut.

Trail Section	km from	time out	return time
Lodge		↓	42 min
Naiset Cabins Jct.	0.4	5 min	36 min
Sunburst Lake, shortcut Jct.	1.4	17 min	24 min
Campground	1.7	21 min	21 min
Sunburst Lake Jct.	1.8	22 min	20 min
End of Campground trails	2.6	32 min	10 min
Southwest end of L. Magog	3.4	42 min	↑

Trail Section	km from	time out	return time
Naiset Cabins		↓	7 min
Lakeshore Trail	0.5	6 min	↑

"The peak is grandest from its northern side. It rises, like a monster tooth, from an entourage of dark cliff and gleaming glacier, 5,000 feet above the valley." James Outram, *In the Heart of the Canadian Rockies*

Mount Assiniboine, after a July storm, from Lake Magog

Mount Assiniboine and Wedgwood Lake from hogback at Ferro Pass. Mount Sturdee is right of Assiniboine; The Marshall, far right.

"As the slope began to fall away in the opposite direction a new world lay before us. It was a desolate valley of burnt timber, beyond which appeared a richly colored lake, girt by green forest and overhung by a barrier of snowy peaks. Above this rough range, the sharp crest of Mt. Assiniboine was faintly seen through the smoky atmosphere, for forest fires were raging somewhere in spite of the rainy season."
Walter Wilcox, View from Ferro Pass, 1895, *The Rockies of Canada*

FERRO PASS

~ Long trip, historic site ~

Distance 10.6 km (6.6 mi)
Height Gain 310 m (1,020'); 280 m (920') return
Hiking Time 2 hr 59 min
2 hr 55 min return

Trailhead Lodge. Add 0.2 km from Naiset Cabins. Subtract 1.3 km from Lake Magog Campground. Map page 14.

Options You get a better view of Wedgwood Lake if you climb the hogback above the pass (0.2 km, 45 m height gain). An alternate section of route (via Elizabeth Lake) allows a variation west of Cerulean Lake. You can backpack down Surprise Creek to the Simpson River; there are backcountry campgrounds at Mitchell Meadows, Rock Lake and Surprise Creek. At the pass, a sign indicates a trail to Mitchell River; guide (and retired park ranger) Ken Jones says this route peters out long before the river.

≈ The scenery of Ferro Pass pales compared with the glories of Magog and Sunburst lakes; but in another location, such a trip, with the rich colors of Wedgwood Lake beneath the sheer cliffs of the Mt. Assiniboine massif, would lure many hikers. This is a long day hike. On the return, a stiff climb from Nestor Creek to Cerulean Lake, almost equals the height gain to the pass.

Historically, the site is pre-eminent. The first recorded visits to Mt. Assiniboine were all made by this pass. In 1893, R. L. Barrett of Chicago was guided here by Tom Wilson. A year later, Samuel Allen, who was the first to describe the area, came in September with Yule Carryer. Allen returned with Dr. Howard Smith in 1895. A few days later, Barrett came back with Walter Wilcox and James Porter, guided by Bill Peyto. Wilcox, Barrett and Peyto circled Mt. Assiniboine, a marathon two day bivouac trip. They met Allen's party on the second day, an awkward visit, because Wilcox was feuding with his former friend who had shared in his discoveries of Moraine Lake and Paradise Valley. Both Wilcox and Allen mention Indian trails in the area, indicating the unknown natives who really came here first.

Wilcox describes his first view from Ferro Pass: "As the slope began to fall away in the opposite direction a new world lay before us. It was a desolate valley of burnt timber, beyond which appeared a richly colored lake, girt by green forest and overhung by a barrier of snowy peaks. Above this rough range, the sharp crest of Mt. Assiniboine was faintly seen through the smoky atmosphere, for forest fires were raging somewhere in spite of the rainy season.... Slightly beyond [Wedgwood Lake], and at a higher elevation, was [Coney Lake], a mere pool of dark blue water, resting against the moraine of a glacier."

Almost fifty years later, Betty Cowie bushwhacked to Rock Lake from Strom's Lodge. She wrote Barb Renner, "It was definitely off the beaten track. Here's a fish story from my 1941 diary: At Rock Lake we caught 54 fish in about 1 1/2 hours. They bit so fast we hardly had time to get them off the hook."

Trail Hike past Sunburst Lake to Cerulean Lake. Follow the north shore of Cerulean Lake almost to the outlet and turn right at the Ferro Pass Junction. You begin a steady descent to Nestor Creek, joining a trail from Elizabeth Lake about half way down, after which the grade steepens. Cross the bridge to the Mitchell Meadows backcountry campsite.

From the campground, you begin the stiff ascent to Ferro Pass. The views improve as you climb. A hogback on the west side of the pass gives the best panorama.

Trail Section	km from	time out	return time
Lodge		↓	175 min
Nub Peak Jct.	0.3	6 min	169 min
Campground east Jct.	1.3	21 min	154 min
Campground west Jct.	1.7	28 min	147 min
Sunburst Lake	2.1	34 min	141 min
Horse Trail Jct.	2.5	41 min	134 min
Cerulean Lake	2.7	44 min	131 min
Elizabeth Lake Jct.	2.9	45 min	129 min
Wedgwood Lake Jct.	3.9	60 min	115 min
Elizabeth Lake west Jct.	5.4	81 min	91 min
Mitchell Meadow Camp	7.0	103 min	62 min
Ferro Pass	10.6	179 min	↑

FERRO PASS, ELIZABETH LAKE Option

~ Alternate route ~

Distance 2.3 km (1.4 mi)
Height Gain 75 m (250'); 120 m (400') on return
Hiking Time 34 min
39 min return

Trailhead Cerulean Lake, (Elizabeth Lake jct.).

Options You can take side trips to Chuck's Ridge or the Nub instead of making the long trip to Ferro Pass.

≈ Elizabeth Lake, named for Elizabeth (Lizzie) Rummel, has a lush forest of larch to the south, contrasting with its bleak north shore.

Trail You ascend a low pass where the route to the Nub branches right. Keep ahead and go down to Elizabeth Lake. After the outlet, the trail ahead goes up Chuck's Ridge. Instead, turn left (downhill) to reach the Ferro Pass trail.

Trail Section	km from	time out	return time
Cerulean L., Elizabeth L. Jct.		↓	39 min
Nub Ridge Jct.	0.5	9 min	31 min
Elizabeth Lake	0.9	15 min	24 min
Ferro Pass Jct.	2.3	34 min	↑

WEDGWOOD LAKE

~ Remote glacial lake ~

Distance 7.3 km (4.5 mi) from Lodge
Height Gain 30 m (100'); 305 m (1,000') return
Hiking Time 2 hr 6 min
2 hr 24 min return

Trailhead Lodge. Add 0.2 km from Naiset Cabins. Subtract 1.3 km from Lake Magog Campground. Map page 14.

Options You can bushwhack to Coney Lake. You can also go to Elizabeth Lake and The Nub.

≈ This attractively colored glacial lake is surrounded by steep cliffs. Yet it cannot match the spectacular views from Magog and Sunburst lakes. Muddy and faint sections of the final stretch plus a demanding climb on the return deter most hikers. Expect overgrown brush. (Take rain pants if the woods are wet). Don't be surprised if you find deadfall; this trail has a low priority for maintenance.

Like the mountain above, Wedgwood Lake is named after A. Felix Wedgwood (1877-1917). A direct descendant of Josiah Wedgwood (creator of Wedgwood china) and a great-grand nephew of Charles Darwin, Felix visited the area on a climbing excursion in 1910. Here, he met Himalayan mountaineer Tom Longstaff, his sister Katherine, and guide Rudolph Aemmer who were just leaving the area. That trio had climbed this summit and named it *Katherine*. The lady met Wedgwood again at the Alpine Club's Consolation Valley camp. After a brief romance, they married. To avoid duplication with Lake Katherine, near Bow Pass, the Geographic Board asked her to suggest another title for the mountain. She graciously chose her husband's name, but it really is her climb the peak commemorates. Felix Wedgwood was killed in action in World War I.

Many of the earliest visitors to Assiniboine stopped here. In 1894 and 1895, Samuel Allen camped by the lake as did Walter Wilcox and Henry Bryant in 1901.

Allen reports that Colonel Robert O'Hara, for whom he named the most famous lake in Yoho Park, tried to reach Mt. Assiniboine from Canmore, but was turned back by forest fires (see Allen's photo). The date of O'Hara's attempt is not given, but it predates Allen's trip of September, 1894. Had he succeeded, it is possible that O'Hara, not Barrett, would have been the first man known to visit Assiniboine.

Trail Shortly after Cerulean Lake, you enter the hunting zone. Also, you glimpse the Moose Bath below. This is not your destination. Wedgwood is much larger and farther away.

You descend a hill to a spring-fed stream where the way is confusing. The horse route crosses the stream (red flag). Hikers, going to an easier ford downstream, have made a *trail* leading away from the route. Note the flag, and head back to the path after you cross the stream.

Three minutes after this ford, you cross the stream from Elizabeth Lake, and after a long descent, you reach the intersection to Wedgwood Lake where you turn left to leave the Mitchell River Trail. In 1991, the sign was on the ground, propped against a large pine.

After 0.2 km you cross a creek. The path to the lake has faint and muddy places.

Trail Section	km from	time out	return time
Assiniboine Lodge		↓	144 min
Sunburst L. via Lakeshore	2.1	38 min	105 min
Horse Trail Jct.	2.5	44 min	99 min
Elizabeth Lake Jct.	2.9	49 min	94 min
Ferro Pass Jct.	3.9	64 min	79 min
Leave Mitchell River Trail	6.5	114 min	13 min
Wedgwood Lake	7.3	126 min	↑

Wedgwood Lake, 1894, showing the results of a recent fire. Photo, S. Allen, The Alpine Journal, 1896.

Mount Assiniboine (left) and The Marshall from Wedgwood Lake. Compare with Samuel Allen's 1894 photo, p. 67.

"When I finally had an opportunity to observe the other side of the valley, the first object I saw was a beautiful lake lying a little below tree-line at the base of a great glacier-crowned wall. Above this lake, encircled by glaciers at the foot of the walls, which rose 3,000 ft. above it, was a smaller lake. The top of the wall was hidden by moving clouds, and I believed it to be Mount Assiniboine at last....

"This beautiful lake, than which I have seen none finer in the Rockies ... is about 1 mile in length and slightly less in width. Its color was a dark green and it was fringed with grass and shrubs and slopes of pine. The great walls rising behind it with their fine blue hanging glaciers and the white snow below made it a scene never to be forgotten."

Samuel Allen, 1894, First description of Wedgwood Lake, *The Alpine Journal, November, 1896*

Mount Aye, Lunette Peak and Mount Assiniboine from Lake Gloria

"A young lady who wanted to see Assiniboine last summer, was horrified when she found that my regular round trip gave two full days at camp. She actually asked me what on earth there could be to do for two whole days, with much emphasis on the word *whole*. There are times in this life when it is a pleasure to be rude, and this was one of them. I told her that there was plenty to do for intelligent people, and I put enough weight on *intelligent* to make her decide that she was not particularly interested in Assiniboine after all.... My difficulty would be to use [two days] to best advantage."
Erling Strom, *The Trail Riders Bulletin, 1937*

CITADEL PASS and OG LAKE

~ Backpacking route, awesome landslide ~

Distance **27.6 km (17.1 mi) Sunshine to Mt. Assiniboine Lodge**
Height Gain **1015 m (3,325'); 975 m (3,200') return**
Hiking Time **7 hr 24 min**
7 hr 5 min return

Trailhead Take the Trans-Canada Highway to the Sunshine Village interchange, 8.6 km (5.3 mi) west of Banff, or 21 km (13 mi) east of Castle Junction. Drive 8 km to the Gondola parking area at the end of the road.

Hike the road to the Interpretive Centre (Ski School) at Sunshine Village starting at the gate before (cast of) the gondola terminal. From July 1 to Labour Day, 9:30 am to 8:00 pm, you might also be able to reach this site by the gondola, but at the time of writing, for economic reasons, the lift has not operated the last two summers. Maps page 12 and 14.

Options You can camp en route at two sites: Howard Douglas Lake (Su 8) and Og Lake. If you detour towards the Simpson River Trail, you can stay at Porcupine Camp.

Many hikers make Citadel Pass (from Sunshine) or Og Lake (from Assiniboine) their destination.

≈ High meadows, flowers, larches, and views of Assiniboine are highlights of this trip. A. O. Wheeler, who ran walking tours to Assiniboine about 1925, considered this "by far the grandest of the three routes to Mt. Assiniboine."

Be prepared for problems. There is no water available after you leave Howard Douglas Lake until Og Lake, and you must go off trail there to reach it. (Giardia warning.) There are steep sections, especially the long hill south of Citadel Pass. Through the Valley of the Rocks, the trail undulates and twists constantly. In September, hunting is permitted north of Og Lake to near Citadel Pass, adding a hazard for hikers.

Although it is possible to reach Mt. Assiniboine in a day, most backpackers will want to stop at one of the campgrounds en route. The Og Lake camper facilities consist of bear pole, privy, and scenery! Porcupine Camp is the only one which permits fires and it is a little off route.

A remarkable animal battle occurred here.

"A death fight between a grizzly and two large wolves, with the bowl of Citadel Pass as the amphitheatre, was the rare drama of the wilds witnessed by Mr. and Mrs. C. Leach of London, England, and East Africa.

"With Mrs. Pat Brewster of Banff, the tourists were on their way to the Mount Assiniboine alpine camp, when, turning a sharp corner of Mount Citadel on the Great Divide, they were horrified to see a grizzly charging madly toward them. But the bear came to a halt about 100 yards away from them, and then they were amazed to notice two large wolves were worrying it, one attacking its head and the other coming in from behind.

"The almost exhausted bear was granted not a moment's respite in the fight that might have been going on for hours, or even days. Another rush and the battle moved to within ten yards of the startled watchers. The grizzly's distress was plain to see. Nimble and with great cunning the wolves darted in, slashed away again, dodging the enraged animal's blows by fractions of inches.

"The next rush carried the fight to a small circular knoll, no higher than the grizzly itself.

"The curtain rang down on this epic of the wilds as the bear fell to its finish behind the knoll." *Crag and Canyon, September 1, 1933*

The Valley of the Rocks was named by A. O. Wheeler. "The valley bed for the greater part of this dry stretch is a wild confusion of piled up masses of rock of quaint form and great size, many of them weighing hundreds of tons. So wild and desolate is the rock-filled valley that it has been named the *Valley of the Rocks*. It would seem that at some bygone age [probably post-glacial] a powerful agency had filled the valley floor with these broken blocks, hurled from the confining limestone masses.... As one travels along the thin twisting trail between the huge fragments one cannot but wonder at the mighty forces ... of primeval desolation, tearing down the mountains and reducing them to fertile areas for the reception of forest growth."

The prehistoric slide has been compared to relatively recent ones at Hope and at Frank but on a much larger scale (over 20 times larger than at Hope). Dr. Stephen Evans, of the Geological Survey of Canada, states the estimated volume of the slide is 1 billion cubic metres, making this by far the largest landslide known in Canada, and probably, North America (one of the top 20 in the world). The rock avalanche displaced the Continental Divide to the east.

Trail From the Interpretive Centre (Ski School, if the winter sign is still up), proceed south, following left of the Strawberry Chair. Pass the Parks Canada Avalanche Control Building and turn left onto the main trail (no sign, 1992).

Ascend the pass east of Standish Ridge. Turn left to Citadel Pass and Quartz Ridge and proceed through the meadow, then up the eastern outlier of Quartz Hill. From here, you descend to diminutive Howard Douglas Lake (misnamed Sundown Lake on the topo map). From the outlet, a path to the left leads to the campground. Keep ahead. Go up a small hill, then down to another large meadow and swing east of The Citadel to reach Citadel Pass, where a route branches left to Fatigue Pass. Stay on the main trail which bends to the right.

Go down a long meadow and enter a steep gully to descend over 300 m to a junction with the trail to Simpson River and Porcupine Camp to the right. Most hikers prefer the higher path ahead, contouring a grassy hillside, which seen in October, gave Golden Valley its name.

You enter a rocky area which becomes more chaotic as you proceed. Just before the Simpson River Junction, you pass an animal trail to the right to a pond which dries up in late summer.

After the junction, you climb steeply, then enter the main portion of the Valley of the Rocks, where there are frequent turns and hills. Finally you reach open country at Og Lake.

At the end of Og Meadows, you join the trail from Og Pass on your left and ascend a narrow valley, passing the horse trail to Sunburst Lake on your right, and climbing Dead Horse Canyon to meet the hiking trail from Assiniboine Pass. Turn right here for Lake Magog. After a short distance, you reach the intersection to the Lodge and Naiset Cabins on your left. If you are going to the campground, keep ahead at this junction and turn left at the Nub junction.

* If you start from the Bourgeau Parking lot at Sunshine, add 6.5 km, plus 465 m height gain (1 hr 30 min; 1 hr 11 min return).

Trail Section	km from	time out	return time
Sunshine (Ski School) *		↓	425 min
Rock Isle Lake Jct.	1.3	25 min	409 min
Satellite crest of Quartz Ridge	5.2	89 min	358 min
Howard Douglas Lake (Su 8)	5.8	101 min	339 min
Citadel Pass (Fatigue Pass Jct.)	9.3	158 min	289 min
Porcupine Campground Jct.	12.5	205 min	220 min
Simpson River Jct.	16.5	267 min	152 min
Og Lake and campground	22.2	360 min	66 min
Mount Assiniboine Lodge	27.6	434 min	↑

Mounts Magog and Assiniboine from Og Lake

The Monarch showing left of Quartz Hill from near Citadel Pass

Page 73:	*Top left:*	*Scarab Lake and Egypt Lake beneath Haiduk Peak seen from Healy Pass*
	Top right:	*Mt. Ball showing above the plateau east of Healy Pass from Wawa Ridge (the Sunshine—Simpson Pass trail)*
	Bottom left:	*"Coronet Towers" and Mt. Ball from the outlet of Shadow Lake*
	Bottom right:	*Castle Mountain from Smith Lake*

SUNSHINE to VERMILION PASS Introduction

This area is bounded on the north and east by the Bow River, on the west by the Ball Range, and on the south by the Sunshine area. There are five trailheads: Bourgeau Lake Parking lot, near Wolverine Creek; Vermilion Pass; Altrude Creek; Redearth Creek; and Healy Creek. Except for the Bourgeau Lake trail, all the paths are interconnected.

Highlights of the area include the vast meadows at Sunshine, spectacular scenery at Shadow Lake and Healy Pass, nine large tarns ringing Egypt Lake, historic Simpson Pass, and many superb stands of giant larches. Prospecting activity was carried on at Copper Mountain and near Redearth Pass until mining was prohibited in the Park.

Since the trails are near the continental divide, they are at high altitude, and you see many richly colored glacier-fed lakes.

Bourgeau Lake and Harvey Pass This scenic pass was first visited by Jim and Bill Brewster with their cousin by marriage, Ralph Harvey. They were traveling on skis from Banff.

Sunshine Sunshine Meadows was used as the last campsite on the Wheeler Walking Tours (1920-26). His campsite is now called Wheeler Meadows. Shortly after Wheeler abandoned this enterprise, a cabin was built in the Meadows by the CPR, registered to the Trail Riders of the Canadian Rockies. Realizing the area's winter potential, Jim Brewster purchased the site for Brewster Transport in 1936. Additional buildings went up, a road was constructed, and in 1942, the first ski tow appeared. Ownership changed several times; in 1981, Ralph Scurfield acquired the property. After a financially unsuccessful attempt to run the gondola in summer, the commercial enterprise confined operations to the ski season.

Pack train departing Sunshine Lodge ca 1944. By permission, Whyte Museum of the Canadian Rockies.

In 1841 Sir George Simpson and his party, the earliest white travelers in the Banff area, crossed the mountains via Simpson Pass. Sir George was delighted to find a plant which closely resembled Scottish heather growing near the pass.

Egypt Lake and Healy Creek Surveyor A. O. Wheeler wrote, "In thirty years of exploration, surveys and mapping of the main ranges of the Canadian Rockies, the writer ... can safely say that outstanding among them for scenic charm and interest may be classed the group of peaks, lakes and alpine meadows of the Egypt Lake area, dominated by the snow-crowned Mt. Ball.... For variety and continuous charm throughout its length, it cannot be surpassed."

Wheeler chose most of the names in the area. "Pharaoh Peaks was a name already in existence when the section was mapped, hence the sequence for the lakes: Egypt, Scarab and Mummy. *Haiduk* is a Polish term for a lively young woman, a hoiden. First seen from a height with sunshine and shadow dancing on the surface of the lake, the name seemed as suitable as any other and has an impressive sound: it was also applied to the peak. Black Rock Lake is due to its location at the base of dark rock precipices of the eastern face of the Pharaoh Peaks. On the western side of the ridge separating Scarab Lake from Haiduk Lake is Whistling Valley, so-named because of the shrill, resounding whistles of a number of hoary marmots ... who greeted me when I first entered the valley." *The Sky Line Trail, July, 1935*

About 1895, Col. Robert O'Hara, for whom Samuel Allen named the most famous lake in Yoho Park, wrote Tom Wilson about the soapy talc he had seen near Redearth Pass. Bill Peyto later prospected the site which he sold to the

National Talc Company, giving Natalco (usually spelled *Natalko*) Lake its name.

Egypt Lake can be reached via Pharaoh Creek, but most visitors use Healy Pass, one of the most scenic heights of land in the Rockies. From Egypt Lake a complex network of trails radiates: to Whistling Pass, Scarab and Mummy lakes, Natalko Lake, Pharaoh Lakes, Shadow Lake and Healy Pass.

Shadow Lake Famed mountaineer artist Belmore Browne visited Shadow Lake in 1921. But Shadow Lake remained remote until a bridge over the Bow River at Massive Siding and a tote road to the Talc mine near Redearth Pass were built in 1928. That year, the CPR erected a guest cabin at a meadow near Shadow Lake. Leonard Leacock had a hiker's camp on the lakeshore in 1935. The horses which supplied the camp were run by Stew Cameron, a talented cartoonist who drew a pencil cartoon on the cabin wall depicting the problems packing around the muddy lakeshore trail. Leacock told me the caption that accompanied it was: "Yes sir, it's a great country for women and children, but it's hell for men and horses."

In 1938, Brewster Transport purchased the cabin, and then sold it to Bud Brewster in 1950. The cabin remained open for hikers until about 1970 when Dorothy Gow leased it for commercial use. In 1991, the building was remodeled as a lodge, and six cabins were added. Brewster's daughter, Allison, now runs it. The wall where Cameron did his cartoon was removed, but the artwork was cut out and framed. It now hangs in the Lodge dining area.

Shadow Lake is one of the most scenic areas in the Rockies. Trails to Gibbon Pass, Twin Lakes, Ball Pass, Egypt Lake and Whistling Pass radiate from the site. The old lakeshore trail, no longer maintained, reveals Shadow Lake at its loveliest and leads to the Ball Glacier Caves.

Altrude Creek Altrude Creek, which drains Vermilion Pass, is the trailhead for three hikes: Twin Lakes, Smith Lake and Copper Lake. Before the road to Radium was begun in 1912, people were transported across the unbridged Bow River by Joe Smith, the legendary prospector of Silver City.

Vermilion Pass Vermilion Pass was first explored in 1858 by James Hector. The name for the pass comes from nearby ochre beds where Indians obtained coloring for ceremonial use, reddish tints being highly prized. In 1968, a catastrophic fire devastated Vermilion Pass, destroying 2500 hectares of forest. The conflagration forced the closure of the Radium Highway. A portion of the Trans-Canada Highway was also closed and used as an airstrip for water bombers fighting the inferno. After four days, a welcome rain helped fire fighters control the disastrous blaze.

Vista Lake Viewpoint, 8.2 km west of Castle Junction, is the trailhead for Arnica Lake (and Twin Lakes).

FACILITIES

Shadow Lake Lodge Located in a scenic meadow near Shadow Lake, the original building was constructed by the CPR in 1928. It is strategically situated, near trails to Gibbon Pass, Ball Pass, Ball Glacier Ice Caves, Shadow Lake and Haiduk Lake.

The Lodge was purchased by Brewster Transport in 1938, and was acquired by Bud Brewster in 1950. His daughter Allison now runs it maintaining a warm friendly atmosphere. In 1991 the Lodge was renovated and six new propane-heated cabins were added. Sumptuous gourmet meals are served in the fully licensed dining room.

In summer, Shadow Lake Lodge is open from mid June to early October. For reservations, write Shadow Lake Lodge, P. O. Box 964, Banff, Alberta, T0L 0C0, phone 403-762-5454 (Fax 403-762-3953).

Storm Mountain Lodge Located near the summit of Vermilion Pass, 5.8 km southwest of Castle Junction on the Radium Highway, Storm Mountain Lodge is open from late May to mid-September. It provides accommodation in log cabins with fireplaces and kitchenettes.

For reservations, write Storm Mountain Lodge, Box 670, Banff, Alberta, T0L 0C0; phone 403-762-4155.

Campgrounds and Hiker Shelter Lost Horse Creek (Re 6), Shadow Lake (Re 14), Ball Pass Junction (Re 21), Twin Lake (Re 24), Pharaoh Creek (Re 16), Healy Creek (E 5) and Egypt Lake (E 13) campgrounds have tables, bear-proof storage and pit toilets. Open fires are permitted only at E 5; bring a portable cookstove if you plan to stay at any of the other campgrounds. A free Park Use Permit is required to stay at any backcountry campground. At Egypt Lake, there is also a hiker's shelter. A reservation is required and must be picked up at the Banff Information Centre which monitors the reservations to prevent overbooking.

BOURGEAU LAKE and HARVEY PASS

~ Steep trail, lakes, high pass ~

Distance	**7.5 km (4.7 mi) to Bourgeau L.**
Height Gain	**670 m (2,200')**
Maximum Height	**2450 m (8,040') at Harvey Pass**
Hiking Time	**2 hr 10 min**
	1 hr 32 min return

Trailhead The Bourgeau Lake parking area is on the west side of the Trans-Canada Highway, 11.8 km (7.3 mi) west of Banff (Mount Norquay overpass) or 17.8 km (11.1 mi) east of Castle Junction. If you are approaching from Banff, be advised that there is no sign on the road showing where to turn and no passing lane to facilitate a safe turn. The parking lot is 1.9 km west of the end of the divided highway. Map page 12.

Options You can go to Harvey Pass and explore the open slopes nearby.

≈ The way to Bourgeau Lake is steep, and you are in forest most of the way. Deep snow often lingers into July in this high shady area.

If you go on to Harvey Pass, you get good views back to Bourgeau Lake. The route takes you through a large verdant amphitheatre dominated by a giant outlier of Mt. Brett. At the pass, across Harvey Lake (often frozen into August) you see the distant wedge of Mt. Assiniboine, highest summit in Banff Park. If you cross the pass, you look over alpine meadows to Sunshine. A knoll to the east, which you can climb in ten minutes, gives even better panoramas.

I associate Bourgeau Lake with the liquid song of the fox sparrow. Golden-mantled ground squirrels, pikas, chipmunks and ptarmigan are also common.

Harvey Pass was named by Jim Brewster for his cousin by marriage, Ralph Harvey, who made the first visit with him. They were looking for a place to put in a ski hill. Soon after, Jim acquired Sunshine Lodge. There was no trail here until the Trans-Canada Highway, built in 1958, facilitated access west of the Bow River.

Mt. Bourgeau (and hence, the lake) was named by James Hector for Eugène Bourgeau (1812-77), botanist with the Palliser Expedition. The 2710 m southeast shoulder of the mountain was later called Mt. Lougheed, the name appearing on the 1926 map of Banff. It was chosen for Sir James Lougheed (1854-1925), pioneer Alberta senator. Some people felt this minor summit was unworthy of the prominent politician, so the name was withdrawn, and a more impressive summit near Exshaw was named for Sir James. Ironically, that peak is one of the few which had been named by Bourgeau: *Wind Mountain.*

Wolverine Creek, which drains Bourgeau Lake, is named for the largest member of the weasel family, often found at high places like this. The wolverine (photo p. 130) has a reputation for ferocity. The largest predators often yield to it. In California, in 1906, Walter Fry observed two bears relinquish to a wolverine the carcass of a cow they were eating. Two years later, he saw a wolverine drive off two cougars from a deer they had killed.

Trail The trail enters forest and then curves uphill high above Wolverine Creek to a major tributary stream. In 1992, the bridge was collapsed, but unless the stream is unusually high, the ford should be no problem.

You continue to a bridge over the cascading main branch of Wolverine Creek, from Bourgeau Lake. Here the grade steepens until you reach the rather wet meadows before Bourgeau Lake.

If you want to go to Harvey Pass, take one of the paths on the north (right) side of Bourgeau Lake and go to either side of the inlet stream. Near both banks there are trails up the steep hillside.

Climb to an unnamed lakelet where both trails unite on the north side. Ascend to a meadowy amphitheatre where the path turns left and climbs to the pass and Harvey Lake. The trail continues across the pass and disappears in alpine meadows.

Trail Section	km from	time out	return time
Trailhead		↓	132 min
Major tributary stream	3.7	60 min	87 min
Wolverine Creek	5.5	84 min	64 min
Bourgeau Lake	7.5	130 min	40 min
Unnamed lakelet	8.8	167 min	12 min
Harvey Pass	9.7	187 min	↑

Bourgeau Lake and Mount Bourgeau

Mt. Assiniboine and Harvey Lake from Harvey Pass

"All us Brewsters are alike … bow-legged and bad-tempered."	Jim Brewster, *Trail Riders Bulletin, May, 1947*

SIMPSON PASS from Bourgeau Parking Lot

~ Historic route ~

Distance 7.2 km (4.5 mi)
Height Gain 150 m (500')
Hiking Time 1 hr 53 min
1 hr 37 min return

Trailhead Take the Trans-Canada Highway to the Sunshine Village interchange, 8.6 km (5.3 mi) west of Banff, or 21 km (13 mi) east of Castle Junction. Drive 8 km to the Gondola parking area at the end of the road. The trail begins at a bridge and kiosk behind (west of) the gondola building. Map page 12.

Options You can also hike to Eohippus Lake, Healy Pass, Rock Isle Lake or Sunshine Village.

≈ Unless you go farther (to Eohippus Lake, Healy Pass or Sunshine), this is not a hike for great scenery, although the floral displays in the small meadow at the pass are attractive.

In 1841 Sir George Simpson and John Rowand carved their initials in a tree at Simpson Pass. In 1904 Lade Brewster found the fallen log with the "Simpson Register" which now resides in the Banff Museum. Photo by permission, Whyte Museum of the Canadian Rockies.

Historically, Simpson Pass is of unusual interest. It was named by explorer James Hector for the earliest recorded visitor to the Banff area. Sir George Simpson (ca 1790-1860) crossed the Rockies in 1841, noting, "We were surrounded by peaks and crags, on whose summits lay perpetual snow; and the only sounds that disturbed the solitude, were the crackling of prostrate branches under the tread of our horses, and the roaring of the stream as it leapt down its rocky course.... About seven hours of hard work brought us to the height of land, the hinge, as it were, between the eastern and the western waters. We breakfasted on the level isthmus, which did not exceed fourteen paces in width, filling our kettles for this our lonely meal at once from the crystal sources of the Columbia and the Saskatchewan."

Simpson noticed the hole (visible from the parking lot) in the mountain now called *The Goat's Eye*. "One peak presented a very peculiar feature in an opening of about eighty feet by fifty, which, at a distance, might have been taken for a spot of snow, but which, as we advanced nearer, assumed the appearance of the gateway of a giant's fortress." Simpson called the peak Hole-in-the-Wall Mountain.

According to Walter Wilcox, in 1896, two prospectors named Smith and Temple lost all their food and gear in a rafting accident on the Vermilion River. While Temple went west, his companion tried to retrace their steps over White Man Pass. Getting hopelessly lost, Smith blundered over Simpson Pass. After eleven days, the starving man had given up hope, when he heard a train whistle. He struggled on and was rescued by a track crew. As he recovered, the great Stoney Indian guide, William Twin, led rescuers in search of Temple whose fate was unknown. To the astonishment of the party, William followed Smith's faint tracks over Simpson Pass to the abandoned raft on the river. Proceeding west, the Stoney traced Temple's footprints to a road near the Columbia River. The rescuers soon learned Temple was safe.

Trail Cross the bridge at the kiosk and proceed west up the rough roadway.

After 0.7 km, you pass a junction left leading to the Sunshine ski area. At 3.0 km, cross to the north side of Healy Creek. You ascend the valley at an easy to moderate rate to the Simpson Pass junction. Turn left. The route becomes steeper after you cross Healy Creek.

At Simpson Pass, you intersect trails to Sunshine Meadows and to Eohippus Lake.

Trail Section	km from	time out	return time
Trailhead		↓	97 min
Sunshine Jct.	0.7	11 min	87 min
Healy Creek Bridge	3.0	46 min	58 min
Campground E 5	5.4	81 min	26 min
Healy Pass Jct.	5.8	86 min	21 min
Simpson Pass	7.2	113 min	↑

SIMPSON PASS and HEALY PASS from SUNSHINE MEADOWS

~ Highline route ~

Distance 5.4 km (3.4 mi) to Simpson Pass
Height Gain 215 m (700'); 245 m (800') return.
Add 290 m (950') to Healy Pass
Hiking Time 1 hr 28 min
1 hr 23 min return

Trailhead From the gondola terminal, go northwest to the trailhead: between the Laryx Staff Accommodation and the Firehall (Sunshine Ski Club). If you are hiking up the Sunshine Road, turn right on the side road just before the gondola terminal. Map page 12.

Options Eohippus Lake, Rock Isle Lake and the Grizzly Lake circuit are short trips nearby.

≈ This is the most scenic approach to Simpson Pass. En route, you see a vast area of open forest, meadows, and lakelets. You get good views of The Monarch and of some impressive larch stands.

Many early visitors referred to the entire Sunshine to Healy Pass area as *Simpson Pass*. One of these, A. O. Wheeler, wrote, "The open grassy alplands of Simpson Pass, thickly strewn with mountain wild flowers, pink heath and white heather, and interspersed with charming little, bright blue tarns and groves of larch are, apart from the historic interest of the pass, most fascinating. Here, when the sun shines is a true mountain paradise."

The area's first known visitor, Sir George Simpson, admired the scenery and was also thrilled by one of the wildflowers he saw near the pass. "In addition to the physical magnificence of the scene, I here met an unexpected reminiscence of my own native hills in the shape of a plant, which appeared to me to be the very heather of the Highlands of Scotland; and I might well regard the reminiscence as unexpected, inasmuch as, in all my wanderings of more than twenty years, I had never found anything of the kind in North America.... I carried away two specimens, which, however, proved on a minute comparison, to differ from the genuine staple of the brown heaths of the 'land o' cakes'."

Trail The Meadow Park Trail climbs steadily following ski trails through scenic meadows to the Rock Isle Lake junction of the Twin Cairns trail. Turn right at this intersection.

After crossing Wawa Ridge, the trail descends steeply in two major steps followed by a long, gentle contour to Simpson Pass.

At this pass, the main trail from Healy Creek joins from the right. Keep ahead for Healy Pass. You climb steeply to a junction (left) to Eohippus Lake. Keep ahead.

The grade becomes easy as you enter more open terrain which you follow to the Healy Pass intersection. Turn left to the pass.

Trail Section	km from	time out	return time
Trailhead: Laryx Staff quarters		↓	139 min
Rock Isle L. (Twin Cairns) Jct.	1.7	32 min	118 min
Simpson Pass	5.4	88 min	56 min
Eohippus Lake Jct.	6.1	101 min	47 min
Healy Pass Jct.	7.9	127 min	23 min
Healy Pass	9.4	159 min	↑

EOHIPPUS LAKE

~ Meadows, larches, small lakes ~

Distance **3.6 km (2.2 mi) from Simpson Pass**
Height Gain **100 m (320'); 60 m (200') return**
Hiking Time **1 hr 1 min**
59 min return

Trailhead Simpson Pass (Add 5.4 km from Sunshine Village or 7.2 km from Sunshine parking lot). Map page 12.

Options You can hike on to Healy Pass or to Sunshine Meadows.

≈ Eohippus is the name of an extinct, fox-sized ancestor of the modern horse. The narrow lake was named by A. O. Wheeler and his Boundary Commission colleagues who left no record why they chose the name. Modern horses are banned from the trail, but on two separate visits I have seen moose at an unnamed lake nearby.

Eohippus Lake is situated beneath the great cliffs of The Monarch, and is surrounded by forests of alpine larch. Fish seem common here and at a nearby nameless lake. You can circle the lake in about 25 minutes.

Trail From Simpson Pass, you climb steeply for 400 m to the junction where you turn left. You then cross a low rise to an unnamed lake. From there, you follow a faint trail up a hillside, and then descend to nearby Eohippus Lake.

Trail Section	km from	time out	return time
Simpson Pass		↓	59 min
Eohippus Lake Jct.	0.4	13 min	50 min
Park boundary	0.7	18 min	45 min
Unnamed Lake	1.7	33 min	30 min
Eohippus Lake	3.6	61 min	↑

"No clan on earth possesses memories that transcend those of the men and women who love the high places." Belmore Browne, *AAJ, 1941*

The Monarch from Simpson Pass

Eohippus Lake and cliffs of The Monarch

"Only once before did I ever make an impromptu speech — it was short, and this will also be short. The first occasion was when a cayuse stamped upon my foot. You can imagine what I said." Tom Wilson, quoted in *The Sky Line Trail, February, 1947*

Rock Isle Lake and Quartz Hill seen from Standish Viewpoint. Mt. Assiniboine shows in the distance, right of Quartz Hill.

"The larches began to appear, and gave a sure sign that open country was near. Presently the slope became gentle. Marching through open meadows and between larch-crowned ridges, we soon entered a delightful upland....

"We made camp by a small lake which was dotted with several rocky islands and enclosed by stern cliffs where a few half-dead larches were standing, or their ancient hulks, bare of bark and bleached by the exposure of centuries, covered the ground.

"The day of our arrival was one of brilliant sunshine." Walter Wilcox, First known visit to Rock Isle Lake, *The Rockies of Canada*

~ Deep blue lake, alpine meadows ~

Distance **8.1 km (5.0 mi) from Bourgeau Parking Lot**
Height Gain **570 m (1,870'); 15 m (50') return**
Hiking Time **2 hr 1 min**
1 hr 35 min return

Trailhead Take the Trans-Canada Highway to the Sunshine Village interchange, 8.6 km (5.3 mi) west of Banff and 21 km (13 mi) east of Castle Junction. Drive 8 km to the Gondola parking area at the end of the road.

Starting at the gate before (east of) the gondola terminal, hike the road to the Interpretive Centre (Ski School) at Sunshine Village. From July 1 to Labour Day, 9:30 am to 8:00 pm, you might also be able to reach this site by the gondola, but at the time of writing, for economic reasons, the lift has not operated the last two summers. Map page 12.

Options Grizzly and Larix lakes are so close to Rock Isle Lake, you will probably want to add them to your destination. Also nearby is a superb viewpoint near the top of the Standish Chair. If you want a longer hike, you can go to Citadel Pass or to Simpson Pass.

≈ There are several attractive destinations after you reach Sunshine Village's Gondola terminus; the lack of trail signs (1992) means that you must know your way about or else bring a detailed description of your route.

The largest of the picturesque islets gives name to Rock Isle Lake. En route to this deep blue tarn, you pass the panoramic Sunshine Meadows with their floral delights. Most of the way is steep. Fishing in the lake is prohibited.

If you hike to Sunshine Village, you should follow the road. You can also start up the Healy Pass Trail, and take the first junction to the left, the winter ski out trail, but this is an unsatisfactory route in summer. (Slippery rocks, greasy and insecure logs make fords of the diminutive creek hazardous. A short distance after the junction, the route comes close to the road, to which you must bushwhack, and better sooner than later. The farther you go, the more you have to climb to reach the road and the worse the ski out route gets: brush becomes a nuisance, and the narrow gorge will eventually force you to scramble up to the road.)

At 4.2 km, you pass Goat's Eye Station which houses the main drive for the lift.

Jim Brewster, whose company owned Sunshine Lodge, made plans for additional accommodation at Rock Isle and Eohippus lakes in 1945. He got approval in 1947, a few days before his sudden death. Lou Crosby, who succeeded him as president of Brewster Transport Company, felt the costs were too high; consequently, the buildings never went up.

Trail From the parking lot, head for the Sunshine Access Road. Follow the steep gravel road to the terminus of the gondola. Proceed south, passing the Ski School building (Interpretive Centre when the gondola runs in summer). Go by the Parks Canada Avalanche Control Building. Just after this log structure, turn left onto the main path (no sign, 1992).

The trail ascends the pass east of Standish Ridge where two junctions branch left to Citadel Pass (Quartz Ridge). Here, the main path swings right and descends to a viewpoint overlooking Rock Isle Lake.

Trail Section	km from	time out	return time
Trailhead (gate)		↓	95 min
Canyon Trail (ski out) Jct.	3.5	48 min	60 min
Goat's Eye Station	4.2	59 min	52 min
Sunshine Meadows (Gondola)	6.5	90 min	24 min
Citadel Pass Jct.	7.7	115 min	8 min
Rock Isle Lake viewpoint	8.1	121 min	↑

"There are few persons so unsusceptible as not to be stirred in their souls by unusual grandeur." Charles Fay, *Appalachia, June 1905*

LARIX and GRIZZLY LAKES

~ Prolific larch stands ~

Distance **4.2 km (2.6 mi)**
Height Gain **45 m (150'); 120 m (400') return**
Hiking Time **1 hr 17 min circuit**

Trailhead Rock Isle Lake. Map page 12.

≈ These lakes are of less interest than Rock Isle Lake, but surrounding slopes abound with stands of countless larch, and provide memorable vistas. Like Rock Isle Lake, they are in Mount Assiniboine Park. You pass two biffies en route.

The circuit actually begins at a junction past the underground outlet from Rock Isle Lake. The sign shows the distances if you go right (counter-clockwise), heading first to Grizzly Lake. Between the two lakes, there is a good view of the Simpson River Valley.

Fishing is prohibited at both bodies of water.

Trail From Rock Isle Lake, walk to the Grizzly Lake intersection and turn left. You climb a low knoll. Then at the end of the lake, go down to a view platform from where you see the small cascade which emanates from an underground channel draining Rock Isle Lake.

You descend to the circuit junction. Keep right if you prefer to go first to Grizzly Lake.

Trail Section	km from	time out	return time
Rock Isle Lake		↓	77 min
Grizzly Lake Jct.	0.2	4 min	73 min
Circuit Junction	1.2	18 min	56 min
Grizzly Lake	1.7	25 min	39 min
Simpson River Viewpoint	2.3	34 min	36 min
Larix Lake	2.5	37 min	26 min
Circuit Junction	3.8	55 min	19 min
Rock Isle Lake Jct.	4.0	71 min	4 min
Rock Isle Lake	4.2	75 min	↑

STANDISH VIEWPOINT

~ Generous panorama ~

Distance **1.2 km (0.7 mi)**
Height Gain **120 m (400') from Rock Isle Lake**
Hiking Time **26 min**
19 min return

Trailhead Rock Isle Lake. Map page 12.

≈ The viewpoint was built in 1984, the first year the gondola operated in summer. It provides a superb overview of the lakes, meadows, and mountains (especially Mt. Assiniboine to the south). The approach passes through the most spectacular of the many exceptional floral displays in the area. The grade is stiff.

Trail From Rock Isle Lake, walk to the Grizzly Lake intersection and turn right on the Twin Cairns Trail. At the first junction, turn right to the viewpoint.

Trail Section	km from	time out	return time
Rock Isle Lake		↓	19 min
Grizzly Lake Jct.	0.2	4 min	15 min
Meadow Park Jct.	0.7	20 min	5 min
View Platform	1.2	26 min	↑

TWIN CAIRNS Trail, ROCK ISLE LAKE to SUNSHINE

Distance **4.0 km (2.5 mi)**
Height Gain **75 m (250'); 200 m (650') return**
Hiking Time **26 min**
19 min return

Trail Section	km from	time out	return time
Rock Isle Lake		↓	76 min
Grizzly Lake Jct.	0.2	4 min	72 min
Standish Chair Jct.	0.7	20 min	62 min
Sunshine (Meadow Park Tr.) Jct.	2.3	50 min	32 min
Sunshine	4.0	71 min	↑

Grizzly Lake

Rock Isle Lake, Larix Lake and Quartz Hill from Standish Viewpoint. Mt. Assiniboine is seen in the distance above Quartz Hill.

"We were told ... that a surveying party was camped near Citadel Pass, that an army truck was going out to them, and we could travel in it. The route was said to be a little rough....

"Time usually palliates unpleasant memories, but mine of that journey are as vivid as though I were enduring it once again, and I get the same squeamish feeling in the pit of my stomach. I have been in some rough seas. I have been flown when a beginner in the RAF., twenty-three years ago, by instructors who believed in stunting and putting the fear of God into their pupils, but never in my life have I known a journey to compare with the one we did from Sunshine Lodge to Citadel Pass, and it stands out in my recollection as two hours of intense internal agony.

"It was said that there was a track. All that there was were some ruts so deep that there was a risk of the vehicle being stuck. Over many sections our driver, a youth of determination and initiative, picked out routes and variations of his own.... We had to cling on for dear life when it seemed we were about to tip over and roll to the bottom of the slope." Frank Smythe, *Climbs in the Canadian Rockies*

The Monarch from Healy Pass

"Even the sounds of the mountains and the forests give constant pleasure. There is every quality and volume of sound, from the loud rumble of thunder, or the terrible crash of avalanches, re-echoed among the mountains, to the sharp, interrupted report of falling rocks, the roar of torrents, or the gentle murmur of some purling stream. The sighing of the wind in the forests, the susurrant pines and spruces, the drowsy hum of insects, the ripple of water on the shores of a lake, and the myriad sounds of nature — half heard, half felt — conspire to make up the sum of the camper's pleasure; though in a manner so vague and indescribable that they must needs be experienced to be understood." Walter Wilcox, *Camping in the Canadian Rockies*

EGYPT LAKE via HEALY PASS

~ Alpine meadows, outstanding panorama ~

Distance 13.3 km (8.3 mi) to Egypt Lake
Height Gain 710 m (2,330')
Hiking Time 3 hr 28 min
3 hr 20 min return

Trailhead From the Trans-Canada Highway, take the Sunshine turnoff, 8.6 km (5.3 mi) west of Banff (west interchange), and drive to the Bourgeau Parking Lot, 8 km (5.6 mi) from the turnoff. The trail begins at a bridge and kiosk behind (west of) the gondola building. Map page 12.

Options You can visit Healy Pass and Egypt Lake starting at Sunshine Meadows, a popular option if the Gondola runs in summer. You can hike to Healy Pass and return via the Monarch Ramparts, cutting down to return via the Eohippus Lake Trail to Simpson Pass.

Most visitors prefer to backpack to Egypt Lake, but strong hikers who get an early start can make the return trip in a day. There is a large campground and a hiker's shelter near Egypt Lake.

≈ Healy Pass has a superb panorama and is a worthy destination on its own. At the summit, you see south to Mt. Assiniboine, The Monarch and a lake-dotted meadow. North, are Mt. Ball and Pharaoh Lake. A few steps across the pass you observe Egypt and Scarab lakes. Walk fifty more paces, and you view Natalko Lake.

The grade to the east Simpson Pass junction is easy to moderate; from there to Healy Pass, it becomes steep.

Healy Pass is named for Joe Healy who located prospect claims on Copper Mountain in 1882. Walter Wilcox asserts that Healy persuaded Edwin Hunter to show him where to find copper ore, so the Stoney became known as Edwin the Gold Seeker. Edwin's friends feared the spirits would punish him, but when nothing happened, they resolved to show the white men other mineral sites so they too would receive tea and blankets. A few weeks later, as Edwin was recounting an exciting buffalo chase, he dropped dead, and his friends decided not to show "where there is money in the rocks". Healy led a colorful life, wandering from Mexico to the Yukon, making his living as hunter, trapper, soldier, prospector, whiskey trader, editor, guide, Indian scout, sheriff and, eventually, business executive.

Trail From the Bourgeau Parking Lot, hike the trail west of the ski lift. (Don't take the Sunshine road.) A kiosk is located at the trailhead, just before a culvert over Healy Creek.

After 0.7 km, you pass a junction left leading to the Sunshine ski area. At 3.0 km, you cross to the north side of Healy Creek. The heavy forest cover is relieved when you go through several openings. As you re-enter the forest at the west end of the second break, you see many recently fallen trees. This was the site of a devastating avalanche in 1990 which killed four skiers who had stopped to rest in what appeared to be the safety of the forest beyond the avalanche slope. At the next opening, 25 m downhill of the trail, are the foundation logs of an old cabin, presumably built by legendary guide Bill Peyto. Campground E 5 and the east junction to Simpson Pass come soon after. Just before the west junction to Simpson Pass you enter lovely floral meadows bounded by alpine larches.

After you cross Healy Pass, you descend steeply to Pharaoh Creek. Shortly before the creek, a sign (1992) points to the old trail down the valley past the warden cabin. The newer trail is on the other side of Pharaoh Creek. Turn left (south) to proceed.

Go to a bridge where the trail to Natalko Lake turns off left. Cross the bridge and ascend a short rise. To your right is the junction to Pharaoh Lake and Redearth Creek.

The hiker's shelter is ahead, in the middle of the spacious campground. Take the trail 0.5 km past the shelter, where a sign directs you to Egypt Lake, 0.3 km to your left.

Trail Section	km from	time out	return time
Trailhead		↓	200 min
Sunshine Ski-out Jct.	0.7	11 min	190 min
Healy Creek Bridge	3.0	46 min	161 min
Campground E 5	5.4	81 min	129 min
Simpson Pass, East Jct.	5.8	86 min	124 min
Simpson Pass, West Jct.	7.7	122 min	100 min
Healy Pass	9.3	154 min	77 min
Warden Cabin Jct.	12.3	191 min	17 min
Natalko Lake Jct.	12.4	193 min	15 min
Campground (shelter)	12.5	196 min	12 min
Egypt Lake Viewpoint Jct.	13.0	202 min	6 min
Egypt Lake	13.3	208 min	↑

Healy Pass. The Monarch is the mountain on the right.

TALC (NATALKO) LAKE

~ Colorful lake, old mine site ~

Distance **4.0 km (2.5 mi) from Egypt Lake Campground**
Height Gain **175 m (570')**
Hiking Time **1 hr 8 min**
1 hr return

Trailhead Egypt Lake Campground. Map page 12.

Options If you are fast and start early, you can hike here via Healy Pass as a day trip. You can do other short hikes from Egypt Lake such as Scarab, Mummy or Pharaoh lakes.

≈ Surrounded by alpine larches, this multi-colored lake beneath a glacier and waterfall is a rewarding sight.

About 1895, Col. Robert O'Hara, for whom Samuel Allen named the most famous lake in Yoho Park, found soapy talc near Redearth Pass. Talc was used for talcum powder and later, for electric insulators and radios.

In 1917 Bill Peyto staked a claim. Ten years later, he sold it to the National Talc Company. (The lake is variously named Talc—or Natalco, an abbreviation for the company, which now is usually misspelled *Natalko*.) The company bridged the Bow River, built a rough road and erected two cabins at the lake, but did little mining before going broke in 1929. Peyto then sold the claim to Western Talc Holdings, but not much work was done during the Depression and the claim lapsed in 1939. In 1943 Wartime Metals Corporation was granted a permit under the War Measures Act to mine the site. Mining ceased after the following winter.

Although the lake is located in Kootenay Park, the main trail starts in Banff Park and takes the old wagon road to the lake at an easy to moderate grade. The trail is well defined and much easier to follow than the alternate route, a longer and steeper trail beginning in Kootenay Park, south of Redearth Pass.

Trail From Egypt Lake Campground, take the Healy Pass Trail. Cross the bridge at 0.1 km and turn south (right) to follow the small creek upstream. The first part is wet and rocky.

At a level spot a little north of Redearth Pass, you reach the intersection for the lake and turn right. The sign for this junction was down in 1992. Until it is replaced, watch for the cairn atop a giant boulder 50 m to your right. Here you reverse directions, ascending a rise to the north. After a few minutes, you turn south and angle toward the lake, arriving at its outlet.

At the lake, the only trail sign directs you back via the Kootenay Park path. Remember to return to the outlet to find your trail.

Trail Section	km from	time out	return time
Egypt Lake Campground		↓	60 min
Talc (Natalko) Lake Jct.	0.1	3 min	57 min
Talc Lake Wagon Jct.	2.3	36 min	27 min
Talc Lake	4.0	68 min	↑

REDEARTH PASS and KOOTENAY PARK ROUTE to TALC LAKE

Trees restrict views at Redearth Pass. The first trips to Assiniboine crossed Simpson Pass and followed the Simpson River to Surprise Creek and then to Ferro Pass. Some early guides (Sid Unwin for one) used Redearth Pass to reach the Simpson River.

If you cross Redearth Pass by mistake, you can take the Kootenay Park route to Talc Lake, but it is steep and hard to follow. For most of the way, you will find that either a path or blazes are visible, but not both. At the trail sign, the way is faint. Follow the meadow in the direction of the arrow on the sign. You soon pick up an old trail, but after a short distance it is blocked by a fallen log. If you continue on this visible path, you won't find the lake. Instead, look for a prominent blaze ahead on the right side of the meadow. You can stay on route here only by following the blazes.

The trail leads across Verdant Creek and ascends near Talc Falls. Sections are steep to very steep.

Trail Section	km from	time out	return time
Egypt Lake Campground		↓	73 min
Talc (Natalko) Lake Jct.	0.1	3 min	70 min
Talc Lake Wagon Jct.	2.3	36 min	40 min
Redearth Pass	2.8	52 min	26 min
Talc Lake Jct.	3.1	60 min	17 min
Talc Lake	5.0	83 min	↑

Cabin at Talc Lake, 1935. Photo, L. Leacock

Haiduk Peak from Haiduk Lake

Page 88: *Top left:* *Scarab Lake and Pharaoh Peak from near Mummy Lake. On the left, Storm Mountain shows above Whistling Pass.*
Top right: *Egypt Lake and unnamed peak which The Skyline Hikers appropriately call "Sugarloaf Mountain". Leonard Leacock called it "Mount Tut," following the Egyptian name sequence. Then with a grin, he said the summit peeping over on the right was "Mount Tut Tut."*
Bottom left: *Natalko Lake and "Sugarloaf Mountain" from abandoned mine entrance*
Bottom right: *Mummy Lake and unnamed peak, Leonard Leacock's "Mount Tut Tut"*

PHARAOH LAKES

~ Rocky cirques, steep cliffs, dark lakes ~

Distance 2.9 km (1.8 mi) Egypt Lake Campground to Black Rock Lake
Height Gain 215 m (700')
Hiking Time 48 min
36 min return

Trailhead Egypt Lake Campground. Map page 12.

Options This short trip can be combined with others near Egypt Lake (Natalko Lake, Scarab and Mummy lakes, Whistling Pass).

You can go on to Sphinx Lake. Although the route is easy, it is vague and difficult to follow. Even experienced route finders have problems following the way.

≈ Pharaoh and Black Rock lakes, lying beneath towering dark cliffs of Pharaoh Peaks, are in bleak but impressive settings, cheered in sunny weather by surrounding larch stands.

Sphinx Lake is a mere pond in an open glade of larch beneath low cliffs of the Pharaoh Peaks ridge. You ascend 60 m, then descend 45 m to Sphinx Lake. From the highest point on the route, you can see Castle Mountain and the Sawback Range in the distance.

The topo map shows a trail to Sphinx Lake, but the way is faint and even if you find it, there is a risk you may lose the way back; unless the route is upgraded, I recommend avoiding this trip.

Trail From the Egypt Lake campground, hike 500 m down the Pharaoh Creek trail to the trailhead. Turn left at the sign.

The trail crosses a short meadow and climbs steeply to Pharaoh Lake.

To go on to Black Rock Lake, cross the outlet of Pharaoh Lake, and shortly after, ascend a larch forest to Black Rock Lake. A faint trail takes you around the tarn.

If you want to go to Sphinx Lake, follow the trail around Black Rock Lake for 174 paces from the outlet. From this point, look to your right a short distance for a big larch with a faded double blaze. Beyond this larch, blazes and cairns mark the start of the route, only parts of which are distinct. By continuing your direction of travel for 100 m, you should be able to pick up the faint route.

If you go on, expect several places where there is nothing to guide you.

Trail Section	km from	time out	return time
Egypt Lake Campground		↓	70 min
Trailhead	0.5	7 min	63 min
Pharaoh Lake	1.8	28 min	50 min
Black Rock Lake	2.9	48 min	34 min
Sphinx Lake	4.5	84 min	↑

Black Rock Lake and North Pharaoh Peak

SCARAB and MUMMY LAKES

~ Alpine lakes, floral meadows ~

Distance 3.5 km (2.2 mi) Mummy Lake from Egypt Lake (E 13)
Height Gain 325 m (1,060'); 95 m (310') return
Hiking Time 86 min
69 min return

Trailhead Egypt Lake Campground (E 13). Map page 12.

Options Plan to spend time exploring the lakes. You can also do other short hikes nearby such as Haiduk Lake, Pharaoh Lakes, or Natalko Lake.

≈ The trail to Scarab Lake is straightforward. Getting to Mummy Lake is another matter. There are alternate routes, each with faint sections; one involves some exposure in a steep gully.

The floral meadows and larch stands near Scarab Lake are outstanding. You might also see ospreys diving for fish in these lakes.

From the outlet of Scarab Lake, a couple of faint trails lead to a nearby spectacular viewpoint cliff (approach with caution) above Egypt Lake.

Of the names he chose for these lakes, surveyor A. O. Wheeler wrote, "Pharaoh Peaks was a name already in existence when the section was mapped, hence the sequence for the lakes: Egypt, Scarab and Mummy."

Trail From Egypt Lake Campground, you pass the junction to Egypt Lake (left), then zigzag steeply up the cliff above Egypt Lake. A brief descent leads to the next junction; turn left for Scarab Lake which you can see ahead, a short way downhill.

To continue to Mummy Lake, cross the outlet of Scarab Lake and follow the steep trail up a ridge. Here the route divides.

The more obvious choice turns left, descends to a pond and climbs a rocky gully to a ridge overlooking Mummy Lake. Small cairns help mark the way which is faint in places. To get better views of the lake, turn right and skirt the tangles of alpine fir to the area near the outlet.

The other route makes a sharp right turn at the ridge, and climbs to a large cairn. From here, you must scramble up a cliff via a gully. This choice is not for everyone, but if you have climbing experience, you will find it easy. You come out atop the cliff near the lake's outlet.

If you explore the lake, watch carefully to find your return route; at present, there are no trail signs to guide you back to either path.

Trail Section	km from	time out	return time
Egypt Lake Campground (E 13)		↓	69 min
Egypt Lake viewpoint	0.4	6 min	63 min
Scarab Lake Jct.	1.8	46 min	32 min
Scarab Lake	2.4	53 min	22 min
Mummy Lake	3.5	86 min	↑

Scarab and Mummy lakes and Haiduk Peak from "Sugarloaf Mountain"

Shadow Lake and Mt. Ball from the ridge west of Gibbon Pass. Haiduk Peak, "Coronet Towers" and Isabelle Peak show left of Mt. Ball.

> "Shadow Lake is one of the most beautiful of the many beautiful lakes in the Rockies. From its western end the precipices of Mt. Ball rise sheer, the avalanches from the snow-capped crown fall continuously into the lake of peacock blue, and the soft green of the embosoming pines completes the harmony."
> Unidentified author, probably Club Director A. O. Wheeler, *Canadian Alpine Journal, 1917*

Sunrise, Shadow Lake. Copper Mountain, the sun peering over The Sawback Range and Pilot Mountain. Photo, Lance Camp.

> "I am sometimes a little uncertain whether the increase in familiarity does not diminish in some degree the power of the mountain to stir the unalloyed sense of sublimity.... I long sometimes for a return of that profound impression by my first view of grand mountain forms near at hand." Charles Fay, *Appalachia, June 1905*

REDEARTH CREEK to SHADOW LAKE

~ Access to famed scenic lake ~

Distance 15.3 km (9.5 mi)
Height Gain 520 m (1,700')
Hiking Time 3 hr 56 min
3 hr 32 min return

Trailhead The Redearth Creek parking area off the Trans-Canada Highway, 19.6 km (12.2 mi) west of the Banff—Mount Norquay traffic exchange or 9.4 km (5.8 mi) east of Castle Junction. Map page 12.

Options You can hike or cycle 11.3 km on the fire road. You can arrange to stay at Shadow Lake Lodge or at Re 14 backcountry campground.

≈ When I first made this trip in 1953 with Leonard Leacock, the 1A Parkway route was the only public road west of Banff. We, left the road where it divided around Jennings' Tree and crossed the Bow River on foot at the bridge at Massive. The bridge and the Redearth Fire Road had been built in 1928 to transport rocks from the Talc Mine near Redearth Pass. In 1953, the last span above the river was a single swaying plank, and as I crossed it, I wondered if my first backpacking trip would also be my last. When we left Shadow Lake ten days later, the plank had fallen into the river, so we returned to Banff by the winding fire road which brought us back past the Cave and Basin. I can't recall being more tired than that night, but happy memories of Shadow Lake tempered my fatigue.

Today, because you can cycle the fire road, it's possible to visit Shadow Lake as a day hike. But the area is so rich in glorious scenery that most visitors, wisely, stay overnight.

Now that Shadow Lake Lodge has been converted to a modern facility, offering overnight accommodation as well as lunch, afternoon tea or spirits, hikers can relax in comfort while exploring the area.

There are remains of an old cabin at Lost Horse Creek, downstream of the fireroad. The letters *RMP* (for Rocky Mountains Park) indicate the structure predates 1930, when the national park was renamed *Banff*. The letters *PYTO* might indicate it was built by famed guide Bill Peyto; if so, it confirms the opinion of Henry Ness that Peyto was "one of the worst men with an axe I ever knew." Probably the shelter was used mainly by Pat Brewster's outfit. The name Lost Horse Creek refers to a Brewster cayuse which disappeared forever up the creek into the forested hanging valley.

Ice Cave, Ball Glacier, 1961

Bud Brewster recalls that two prominent Banff citizens used this cabin to trap small game about 1930. The furs were sold by one of the town's most respected citizens who managed to keep out of the scandal when the poachers were caught.

Trail The trail begins at the east end of the parking area, near the privy. After a short climb, you turn right and cross a meadow to join the old fire road. You climb above the second growth pine as you ascend the forested slopes of Pilot Mountain and then descend to a backcountry campground at Lost Horse Creek. Only 300 m before the road ends at Pharaoh Creek, you reach the Shadow Lake junction. Turn right.

After a steep climb, the trail eases. In quick succession, you pass Re 14 Campground and Shadow Lake Lodge on your left, and the Gibbon Pass Trail on your right.

At the outlet of Shadow Lake there is a superb view of Mt. Ball.

Trail Section	km from	time out	return time
Trailhead (#1 Highway)		↓	122 min*
Lost Horse Creek Campsite	7.8	58 min	84 min
Shadow Lake turnoff	11.3	85 min*	63 min
Shadow L. Lodge (& Re 14)	14.3	130 min	16 min
Gibbon Pass Jct.	14.4	132 min	14 min
Shadow Lake (bridge)	15.3	146 min	↑

* Biking Time. Add 1 hour and 30 min each way for hiking the road 11.3 km.

SHADOW LAKE SHORELINE and BALL GLACIER ICE CAVES

~ Best views of Shadow Lake ~

Distance 5.5 km (3.4 mi) from Lodge to cave
Height Gain 230 m (760'); 75 m (250') return
Hiking Time 1 hr 41 min
1 hr 33 min return

Trailhead Shadow Lake Lodge (or Re 14). Map page 12.

Options The trail is short enough to combine with another hike such as Gibbon Pass or Ball Pass.

≈ The route around the lake has been neglected for decades. In 1935, when Leonard Leacock ran a hiking camp here, his wrangler Stew Cameron drew his memorable cartoon on the wall of Shadow Lake Lodge, depicting problems horses and packers experience on the old lakeshore trail. About 1955, warden Ole Hermanrude supervised construction of a new trail around Shadow Lake. It was routed fairly high to avoid the problems of the original scenic path. Unfortunately, the new trail fell into neglect years ago and at the time of writing, it has a lot of deadfall. Also, there is no trail sign. The path is not even shown on the topo map.

This neglect is deplorable. Although you get a superb view at the outlet, unless you have hiked to the large bay at its west end, you haven't seen Shadow Lake at its most beautiful. Only here, where the water is deep and colored by incoming glacial silt, do you see the rich blues which rival (but don't imitate) Moraine and Peyto lakes. The low shoulder left of Mt. Ball, which Leacock called *The Coronet Towers*, looms picturesquely above. Moose frequent the tarn; several times at dusk I have watched them swim the lake.

I hesitate to recommend the trail beyond the end of the lake. The route is hard to follow and you'll get soaked when the woods are wet. The collapsing caves in the receding glacier are no longer as impressive as I remember from my first visits prior to 1965. You might want to go part way where the view of Shadow Lake benefits from a slight rise, but don't expect too much of the view at the caves.

Trail Hike towards Shadow Lake. One minute before the outlet at the east end, turn right onto an unsigned trail angling uphill. Expect deadfall and several hills before you descend to the lakeshore at the site of Leacock's (and the Skyline Hikers') camp. You can go off trail left to a scenic peninsula, but to see the rich colors of the lake, you must go a little farther where the water is deeper. Expect faint and wet places ahead. After you reach the end of the lake, sections are overgrown; in places, the route is under water when the stream is high.

The route becomes better where you switchback away from the creek. Once you reach the moraine, watch for weathered stakes propped up by rocks (some tipping over) to guide you to the caves.

Trail Section	km from	time out	return time
Shadow Lake Lodge (Re 14)		↓	93 min
Gibbon Pass Jct.	0.1	2 min	91 min
Shadow Lake Jct.	0.9	15 min	78 min
Lakeshore	3.0	37 min	56 min
End of lake	2.8	45 min	48 min
Caves	5.5	101 min	↑

"Yes sir, it's a great country for women and children, but it's hell for men and horses." Stew Cameron's 1935 cartoon of the Shadow Lake trail.

Gibbon Pass

"There's a hell of a lot of space around a goat." Conrad Kain, warning hunting clients that a mountain goat's thick wool coat makes it seem larger than it is. *Reported by Bob Hind*

Shadow Lake and Mt. Ball

Shadow Lake and "The Coronet Towers"

GIBBON PASS and TWIN LAKES

~ Mountain goats, view of Assiniboine ~

Distance **6.9 km (4.3 mi) to Lower Twin Lake**
Height Gain **430 m (1,410'); 245 m (800') return**
Hiking Time **1 hr 52 min**
1 hr 43 min return

Trailhead Shadow Lake Lodge (or Re 14). Map page 12.

Options The short hike to Gibbon Pass can be done as well as Shadow Lake and the Ice Caves. If you scramble up the ridges on either side of the pass (the east side is easier), you get a view of Shadow Lake and Haiduk Creek Valley. You can hike to both Twin Lakes and to Arnica Lake. If you have two cars, you can leave the area via Castle Junction or Vista Lake.

≈ Bring binoculars. The pass is a haunt of mountain goats (photo p. 103) which often feed in the meadow, then climb to the cliffs above to chew the cud. There is a good view of the distant Mt. Assiniboine from the pass.

Jim Brewster named the pass for John Murray Gibbon, the CPR General Publicity Agent who founded The Skyline Hikers and The Trail Riders of the Canadian Rockies. Several times these groups held summer camps in the Shadow Lake area.

From just north of Gibbon Pass, you can glimpse Lower Twin Lake beneath a lesser summit of Storm Mountain.

If you go to Arnica Lake, add 40 minutes each way from Upper Twin Lake.

Trail From the Lodge, take the Shadow Lake trail to the Gibbon Pass junction and turn right. There is a stiff climb through forest to the open meadows just before the pass. The new trail brings you to a giant cairn west of the old trail.

In 1992, there was no marker or other sign of path beyond the cairn. If you want to carry on to Twin Lakes, you must find the old trail, 49 paces towards the low ridge east of the cairn. The path becomes more obvious as you enter heavy forest. You are in dense cover until you reach the stream which drains the lake. Turn left for Lower Twin Lake; cross the outlet stream at the bridge for Upper Twin Lake.

Trail Section	km from	time out	return time
Shadow Lake Lodge (Re 14)		↓	120 min
Gibbon Pass Jct.	0.1	2 min	118 min
Gibbon Pass	4.2	68 min	75 min
Lower Twin Lake	6.9	112 min	17 min
Castle Junction Trail Jct.	7.1	116 min	13 min
Upper Twin Lake	7.9	130 min	↑

BALL PASS

~ South Face of Mt. Ball ~

Distance **8.0 km (5.0 mi) from Lodge**
Height Gain **385 m (1,260')**
Hiking Time **2 hr 15 min**
1 hr 57 min return

Trailhead Shadow L. Lodge (or Re 14). Map page 12.

Options You can hike to Haiduk Lake and Whistling Pass. If you have a second car, you can cross from Redearth Creek Trailhead on Highway 1 to Hawk Creek on Highway 93 in Kootenay Park.

≈ From the outlet of Shadow Lake you see the east face of Mt. Ball; near the pass, you view the south face of Mt. Ball with its great glacier. En route, you pass through stands of larch and floral meadows.

In 1901, famed English mountaineer Edward Whymper made an unsuccessful attempt to climb Mt. Ball. Although his guides wanted to approach via Redearth Creek, he insisted on trying from Vermilion Pass. Three years later, when the peak was first climbed, it was done from Vermilion Pass and Christian Kaufmann, one of Whymper's former guides, led the route.

Mt. Ball from Ball Pass

Trail From the Lodge, hike to Shadow Lake, cross the outlet and head up Haiduk Creek. Keep ahead where the Haiduk Lake Junction turns left at Re 21. Just after this intersection, the grade to the pass becomes stiff. Near the height of land, in the distance you glimpse the east end of Shadow Lake and the Lodge.

Trail Section	km from	time out	return time
Shadow Lake Lodge (Re 14)		↓	117 min
Gibbon Pass Jct.	0.1	2 min	115 min
Shadow Lake Bridge	1.0	16 min	101 min
Haiduk Lake Jct. (Re 21)	5.3	76 min	45 min
Ball Pass	8.0	135 min	↑

SHADOW LAKE—EGYPT LAKE Loop (HAIDUK LAKE, WHISTLING PASS)

~ Lakes, floral meadows, scenic pass ~

Distance **25.9 km (16.1 mi)**
Height Gain **455 m (1,500')**
Hiking Time **6 hr 47 min circuit**

Trailhead Shadow Lake Lodge (or Re 14). Map p. 12.

Options You can make this loop in either direction. There are four campgrounds en route from where you can start this hike. The trip is long enough to satisfy most hikers, but I recommend adding the short (300 m) detour to the Egypt Lake viewpoint. If you get an early start and have energy to burn, you can add a short detour such as Mummy or Black Rock Lake.

≈ The highlight of this trip is Whistling Pass with views of Haiduk, Scarab and Mummy lakes and Mt. Ball. There are lovely floral meadows near Haiduk Lake and Whistling Pass.

A. O. Wheeler chose the name *Whistling* for the rocky valley to Haiduk Lake (it is also used for the pass), "because of the shrill, resounding whistles of a number of hoary marmots who greeted me when I first entered the valley." You are likely to hear their descendents.

Wheeler also chose the name "*Haiduk* ... a Polish term for a lively young woman, a hoiden. First seen from a height with sunshine and shadow dancing on the surface of the lake the name seemed as suitable as any other and has an impressive sound." Nick Topolniski told me Wheeler's idea of the Polish language was defective; that the word means *forester*. Wheeler, who chose most of the names for this area, liked to keep them in some thematic pattern, but he broke with his Egyptian sequence when he crossed Whistling Pass.

I find the trail via Haiduk Lake more interesting than Pharaoh Creek Valley. But if you decide to turn back at Whistling Pass, you should at least go a short way south of the pass to view Scarab Lake.

Trail From the Lodge, hike to Shadow Lake, cross the outlet via the trail near Haiduk Creek. Turn left at the Haiduk Lake junction at campground Re 21. After the campsite, you climb steeply for a dozen minutes, then follow an easy grade to Haiduk Lake. You contour the east shore of the lake, then commence a stiff climb through a rockfall to Whistling Pass.

After crossing the pass, you go down past the Scarab Lake junction, climb a short rise, then descend steeply to the Egypt Lake junction.

A short detour to the right (six minutes each way) leads to a good view of Egypt Lake.

Proceed to the sprawling Egypt Lake Campground. You go by the Healy Pass junction on your right. Keep ahead also at the next junction (Pharaoh Lake). A dozen minutes later, you cross a bridge to join the old trail following the tote road from the mine site at Natalko Lake. Then you make the long descent of Pharaoh Creek Valley. Just after Re 16 Campground, you enter a modest canyon. After crossing seven bridges, you reach the Egypt Lake Trailhead.

Go down the Fire Road 0.3 km, and turn left to reach Shadow Lake Lodge and Re 14.

Trail Section	km from	time out	return time
Shadow Lake Lodge (Re 14)		↓	407 min
Gibbon Pass Jct.	0.1	2 min	405 min
Shadow Lake bridge	1.0	16 min	391 min
Re 21 and Ball Pass Jct.	5.3	76 min	335 min
Haiduk Lake (south end)	8.9	137 min	280 min
Whistling Pass	10.0	184 min	249 min
Scarab Lake Jct.	12.0	209 min	220 min
Egypt Lake Viewpoint Jct.	13.4	240 min	180 min
Egypt Lake Shelter (& E 13)	13.8	246 min	174 min
Healy Creek Jct.	13.9	247 min	173 min
Pharaoh Lake Jct.	14.4	254 min	166 min
Re 16	18.2	314 min	102 min
Pharaoh Cr. (Egypt L. Trailhead)	22.6	364 min	40 min
Shadow Lake Trailhead	22.9	367 min	37 min
Shadow Lake Lodge (Re 14)	25.9	407 min	↑

Haiduk Lake, Mt. Ball and Storm Mountain from Whistling Pass. Photo, Leonard Leacock.

Mt. Ball, peaks of Storm Mountain and Haiduk Lake

"The Canadian Rockies are supreme in the number and beauty of their mountain tarns. In variety of colors and in appearance they resemble rare jewels set in a soft velvet of forest green. At early morn and late eve they are mirrors, reflecting on their placid surfaces the wonderful mountain uplifts that are all about them, and when the breezes blow their tiny wavelets flash and sparkle like myriads of diamonds. They are

Castle Mountain from Copper Lake

of many different shades — emerald green, turquoise blue, sapphire blue, cerulean blue, jade, indigo — and I have even seen a bright chrome yellow. The varied coloring is due to rays of light reflecting through the very finely powdered silt washed into them by glacial torrents and held in suspension in their waters." A. O. Wheeler, *The Alps of the New World (Canada's Future)*

TWIN LAKES from ALTRUDE CREEK

~ Picturesque lakes beneath stark cliffs ~

Distance 8.0 km (5.0 mi) to Lower Twin Lake
Height Gain 560 m (1,830')
Hiking Time 2 hr 32 min
1 hr 58 min return

Trailhead Drive to Castle Junction and turn west onto the Radium Highway. Drive 0.2 km past the Trans-Canada Highway overpass, turn left onto a narrow gravel road and continue 0.4 km to the parking lot. From the kiosk, follow the gravel trail for 0.1 km to the Copper Lake—Smith Lake (and Twin Lakes) Junction and turn right. Map page 12.

Diminutive Joe Smith dwarfed by friends at his cabin. By permission, Whyte Museum of the Canadian Rockies

Options You can hike to both Twin Lakes. You can also go to Smith Lake. Strong hikers could also visit Arnica Lake. You can reach Shadow Lake via Gibbon Pass. There are backcountry campsites at Upper Twin Lake and Shadow Lake. If you have a second vehicle, you can combine this hike with the Arnica Lake Trail.

≈ The Lower Twin Lake, a somber blackish-green tarn, features a lovely waterfall cascading down the steep cliffs of Storm Mountain. Upper Twin Lake lacks the waterfall, but its crystal turquoise colors surpass the sibling tarn.

There is a stiff climb, after which the trail becomes rough and wet. Near the end, the route is faint, with no blazes or flags to guide you through the meadow. You parallel the nearby creek, so the way is obvious on the ascent. On the return, care is needed to find where you leave the stream to enter the forest.

The narrow trail is overgrown in places; bring rain pants if the woods are wet.

Trail Turn right at the Copper Lake junction and keep ahead at the turnoff to Smith Lake. Soon after, you begin a stiff ascent; when it eases (after almost 5 km) the footing becomes rough and wet as you cross numerous streambeds and muddy places.

Near Lower Twin Lake, you emerge in a meadow where the route becomes vague. Keep parallel to the nearby creek.

At the Twin Lakes Junction, turn left for Lower Twin Lake (and Gibbon Pass); turn right for Upper Twin Lake.

Trail Section	km from	time out	return time
Trailhead		↓	118 min
Copper Lake Jct.	0.1	1 min	117 min
Smith Lake Junction	0.2	3 min	116 min
Twin Lakes Junction*	7.9	148 min*	4 min*
Lower Twin Lake	8.0	152 min	↑
* Upper Twin Lake	+0.8	+14 min	+13 min

COPPER LAKE

~ Good view of Castle Mountain ~

Distance 0.7 km (0.4 mi)
Height Gain 10 m (20'); 20 m (30') return
Hiking Time 12 min
12 min return

Trailhead Drive to Castle Junction, 29.6 km west of Banff and turn west onto the Radium Highway. Drive 0.2 km past the Trans-Canada Highway overpass and turn left onto a narrow gravel road, crossing a Texas gate and passing the animal control fence and continue 0.4 km to the parking lot. From the kiosk, follow the gravel trail for 0.1 km to the Copper Lake—Smith Lake (and Twin Lakes) Junction and turn left. Map page 12.

Options You can add this short jaunt to the Smith Lake and Twin Lakes hike.

≈ Only a low hill separates this pond from the Trans-Canada Highway. You see and hear road traffic from Copper Lake.

Although this is not a place to seek tranquility, it provides a lovely foreground for Castle Mountain and is worth the stroll. The rich colors of Castle Mountain show best later in the day.

Trail From the parking lot, hike to the Twin Lakes Junction and turn left. Follow the gravel path to the end. Although you see Copper Lake from the end of the trail, to get a look at Castle Mountain, you must go right and, on a rough trail, follow the shore (0.2 km for the best view).

Trail Section	km from	time out	return time
Trailhead		↓	12 min
Twin Lakes Jct.	0.1	1 min	11 min
End of graveled trail	0.7	8 min	4 min
Viewpoint	0.9	12 min	↑

SMITH LAKE

~ Fishing lake named for famed prospector (photo p. 73) ~

Distance 1.7 km (1.1 mi)
Height Gain 120 m (400'); 25 m (80') return
Hiking Time 31 min
25 min return

Trailhead Drive to Castle Junction and turn west onto the Radium Highway. Drive 0.2 km past the Trans-Canada Highway overpass, turn left onto a narrow gravel road and continue 0.4 km to the parking lot. From the kiosk, follow the gravel trail 0.1 km to the Copper Lake—Smith Lake (and Twin Lakes) Junction and turn right. Map page 12.

Options You can do this short hike in addition to the Twin Lakes hike which shares the same trailhead.

≈ You get a view of Copper Mountain from the lakeshore, and if you circle the lake by a faint, rough path, you see Castle Mountain. But this is not a trail to take for great views.

The lake is named for legendary prospector Joe Smith. Smith arrived at Silver City in 1882 and remained as a squatter more than 50 years after the site became a ghost town.

Joe Smith had an unmistakable Quebec accent. Most people who knew him believe the miner changed his name, taking the most common of English surnames and Christian names, but Dan McCowan thought his father was a Scot and his mother French Canadian.

Although he is remembered as a prospector, he maintained himself by trapping and guiding. At least two pioneer explorers sought his services, though Smith really didn't help them.

W. S. Green tried to hire the French Canadian to guide him to a peak near Vermilion Pass in 1888. Unfortunately, Smith was away prospecting and Green wound up at Lake Louise.

In 1894, Smith gave directions to Samuel Allen to get to Mt. Assiniboine which had only been visited once before, in 1893. However, Allen couldn't find the trail Smith recommended (probably via Gibbon Pass), though he succeeded in getting to the mountain another way.

Marguerite Camp told me Joe Smith was a small man, perhaps five foot three inches tall, who always believed he would find gold. He became a recluse, suspicious of strangers. "He had gun holes in the walls in case robbers came. He hated women, but he allowed me to visit.

"He made his own bread and always had a pan of sourdough batter. The CPR men watched out for him. They knew he must be sick when they noticed one day in 1937 that no smoke came from his cabin. They called the police who took him to the Lacombe Home near Calgary where he could get care. Then they burned his cabin." Although the action was necessary because the aged prospector (about 90 years old) could no longer look after himself, the move probably hastened his death which came only a few weeks later. "You have to have a reason for living, and for Joe Smith it was the cabin at Silver City," Marguerite Camp said.

Trail From the Copper Lake—Smith Lake (and Twin Lakes) Junction, hike 100 m to the next junction and turn left. A blank sign (1992) marks the turn. The grade increases to moderate up the final hill. From here, there are two routes down to the lake. The older one is moderate; the one most used is very steep.

It is almost 1.0 km around the lake. On the far side, the path is faint.

Trail Section	km from	time out	return time
Trailhead		↓	25 min
Copper Lake Jct.	0.1	1 min	24 min
Twin Lakes Jct.	0.2	3 min	23 min
Hill above lake	1.5	29 min	3 min
Lakeshore	1.7	31 min	↑

Mountain Goat, commonly seen on the cliffs of Storm Mountain, especially near Gibbon Pass

Upper Twin Lake and Storm Mountain

"The beauties of Nature retain their glory for the longest period when they are situated in such a place that they are comparatively inaccessible to man, or, at any rate, when they are placed under such conditions and possessed of such a formation that it is practically impossible for man to change their appearance to any great extent.... Surely it is in the mountains that nature achieves the greatest degree of inaccessibility, and

Lower Twin Lake and outliers of Storm Mountain

therefore preserves the greatest quantity of glory, grandeur and splendor....

"No greater contrast is it possible for mortals to enjoy than from the city with its noisy tumult, dusty hot streets, prosy stores, where man and mammon reign, to the Canadian Rockies." A. O. Wheeler, *Our Mountain Heritage*

ARNICA LAKE and TWIN LAKES

~ Clear green lake, steep cliffs ~

Distance **5.1 km to Arnica Lake**
Height Gain **560 m (1,830'); 130 m (430') return**
Hiking Time **1 hr 38 min to Arnica Lake**
1 hr 23 min return

Trailhead The old trail (starting near Storm Mountain Lodge) is no longer maintained. The present trailhead is 3.0 km south of Storm Mountain Lodge (1.3 km south of the Boom Lake Jct.) on the Radium Highway. Because of the passing lane for eastbound traffic, you can reach the parking lot legally only if you are driving east. If you are driving west, go to the Banff Park boundary, turn left into the parking lot and then turn around to drive 2 km east to the trailhead. Map page 12.

Options You can hike farther, to Twin Lakes. If you have a second car, you can return from there to Castle Junction. Backpackers can go on to Shadow Lake via Gibbon Pass. There are backcountry campgrounds at Upper Twin Lake and Shadow Lake.

≈ The trail first descends to Vista Lake, then climbs relentlessly through open slopes of Storm Mountain. On your return, you face a long climb back to the road at the end of the day.

Vista Lake is a fairly large green body of water visible from the parking lot. It lives up to its name, for you look at it through trees from every vantage point save the actual shoreline. Arnica Lake is a smallish green tarn set below sheer cliffs of an outlier of Storm Mountain. Both these lakes are fringed with shallows and so display striking color variations.

En route to Arnica Lake, you travel through the remains of the devastating fire which burned most of the forest on this side of the valley in 1968. Charred skeletons of trees and new growth, dominate the terrain.

Biologist John Macoun, who had visited the Bow Valley before the railway was built, commented on similarly charred forests he saw when he returned later by train. "On looking back now over the country as ... I saw it at that time, it has altogether changed. Everywhere, fine forests were around ... through the Rocky Mountains.... I remember one tree that had been cut and from which thirteen ties, each eight feet and four inches long, had been made. Today, all that fine timber has disappeared and bareness has taken its place. At that time, there was a saw-mill ... in the Rockies ... sawing up fine trees, while fires raged frequently, destroying beautiful standing timber."

As you would expect, arnica grow at the lakeshore of Arnica Lake, but not in profusion.

Child skipping stones, Arnica Lake and Storm Mountain

Trail To begin, you hike steadily downhill to Vista Lake. Then the work begins. The trail is seldom steep, but you never stop climbing until Arnica Lake. You will want to be sure that your canteen is full. Except for a few streams soon after Vista Lake (Giardia warning), the route is dry until you reach Arnica Lake.

The varied greens of Arnica Lake may entice you to explore the shoreline, or you may want to go on to Twin Lake. To reach the Twin Lakes, you first climb 75 m to a narrow pass covered with alpine flowers and an impressive stand of alpine larch. You then descend 160 m to Upper Twin Lake. The first section is steep, but most of the grade is moderate. You descend another 50 m to Lower Twin Lake.

Trail Section	km from	time out	return time
Parking Lot		↓	143 min
Vista Lake	1.4	15 min	118 min
Arnica Lake	5.1	98 min	60 min
Upper Twin Lake	7.3	138 min	20 min
Castle Mountain Jct.	8.2	153 min	4 min
Lower Twin Lake	8.3	157 min	↑

The Bow Valley Parkway follows the route of the original road from Banff to Lake Louise. Since the road is far enough east to provide views of the great boundary peaks like Mt. Ball, it is more scenic than the Trans-Canada Highway, and the lower speed limit gives you many chances to enjoy the sights. The southeast end of the Parkway is 5.4 km west of the Mount Norquay Road at Banff.

FACILITIES

Fireside Picnic Area This turnoff is 0.3 km from the Trans-Canada Highway junction. Drive 0.9 km from the Parkway to the picnic site which is also the trailhead for the Edith Pass and Cory Pass trails. There are picnic tables and a pit toilet.

Backswamp Viewpoint Located 3.9 km from the Trans-Canada Highway junction, this scenic point was formerly called Aften-ro, either an Indian name for *evening peace* or a Nordic word for a place in Scandinavia. The prosaic contemporary name refers to the swampy area where the river backs up when the water is high.

Muleshoe Picnic Area Located 6.3 km from the Trans-Canada Highway junction, this picnic area has views of The Hole-in-the-Wall and of Muleshoe (also spelled *Mule Shoe*) Lake, a backwater channel of the Bow River. Muleshoe Trail commences here. There are picnic tables and a pit toilet.

Sawback Picnic Area Located 11.7 km from the Trans-Canada Highway junction, this interpretive site illustrates the importance of aspen bark as winter feed for elk. There are picnic tables and a pit toilet.

Jennings Tree Site Located 12.2 km from the Trans-Canada Highway junction, this is where the road was diverted around a giant symmetrical spruce. The local name reflects the belief of many Banff residents that this unusual piece of roadwork was carried out at the insistence of park superintendent Major P. J. Jennings. The rotting old tree collapsed in a 1984 storm. Young relatives now grow on the site.

Hillsdale Meadows Located 13.4 km from the Trans-Canada Highway junction, this site gives a tantalizing glimpse of Mt. Ball. The lush pasture used to be a main camp and hay meadow for Pat Brewster's horses. Sir Sandford Fleming, who visited Hillsdale in 1883, when the railway was under construction, said it was named after Mr. Hill, manager of the CPR company store at Aylmer Park, 28 miles east of Kicking Horse Pass. This site is indeed 28 miles from the pass, but Tom Wilson said Aylmer Park was at the site of the Banff Buffalo Paddock, so it may be that Fleming miscalculated the distance, and we've now got the wrong site for Hillsdale. The Hillsdale Trail (to the Ink Pots) commences at the northwest edge of the meadows.

Hillsdale Slide Located 14.1 km from the Trans-Canada Highway junction, this interpretive site is reached on the westbound leg of the divided road. A cataclysmic rockfall occurred here.

Hillsdale Slide and Pilot Pond Located 14.8 km from the Trans-Canada Highway junction, this interpretive site, reached on the eastbound leg of the divided road, is also the start of the path to Pilot Pond.

Johnston Canyon Campground Located 17.0 km from the Trans-Canada Highway junction, this fully serviced facility is one of only two campgrounds with showers in Banff Park.

Johnston Canyon Parking Area Located 17.4 km from the Trans-Canada Highway junction, this is the trailhead for the Johnston Canyon and Ink Pots trails.

Johnston Canyon Resort Located 17.5 km from the Trans-Canada Highway junction, this is the major facility on the Bow Valley Parkway. The resort was developed by Walter Camp.

Camp had been a Calgary taxi driver. In 1921 he came to Banff where his taxi business was so successful that he developed a bus line, *Diamond Tours*. In 1927 he bought the Johnston Canyon facility, consisting of a tea room and a staff house, and began to operate it next season. Until 1939 the site was the only stop between Banff and Lake Louise; it made an ideal stopover for lunch or tea to break the long drive on the twisting gravel road.

Camp's subsequent attempts to improve the facility were determined by politics and rivalry with the Brewsters. Walter was a staunch Conservative who named one of his sons Bennett, after party leader R. B. Bennett whom he got to know when he lived in Calgary. The Brewsters were solid Liberals who had the ear of party leader Mackenzie King.

Camp's applications to improve his resort were denied until 1930 when R. B. Bennett replaced Mackenzie King as prime minister. Then, Walter was given permission to add eight cabins. In 1934, the Prime Minister told him, "If you want to add more cabins, ask now. I'll lose the next election." In 1935 Bennett was defeated, but Camp had already secured permission to build fifteen more units. The facility wasn't enlarged again until John Diefenbaker became the next Conservative prime minister when fifteen more cabins were added.

Walter Camp was a showman who for fifty years gave illustrated lectures each night. The guests loved it; many of them returned annually. "He succeeded because he had no idea of failure," said his second wife, Marguerite.

Walter and Marguerite discovered the upper falls. He had the first trail built and got horses to take guests there. The crew erected a bridge over the creek above the falls, but after a few years it was destroyed in the spring runoff.

Camp hated the spelling *Johnston* and in 1928 put up a sign spelled *Johnson Canyon*. "It took the government 40 years to catch up to him and make him change the sign," said Marguerite. (Precedent is on Walter's side: Dawson's 1882 map uses the spelling *Johnson Creek*.)

One spring when Walter came to open up the facility, he found famed guide Jimmy Simpson swearing mad. Driving his first car, Simpson had taken a side road which followed a short way down Johnston Creek. At a critical moment Simpson put his brand new auto in reverse instead of forward, and backed into the creek.

Walter and Marguerite Camp, 1930. Source, Tim Nokes

The resort survived the Depression and the war years with gas rationing and other restrictions. When plans for the Trans-Canada Highway were being drawn up, an official told Camp the new road would go on the east side of the Bow River. On the strength of this assurance, he built a new tea room. When the highway was routed west of the Bow, business fell off dramatically and the operation struggled for some years until the Parkway was improved.

Facilities include cabins, gift shop, dining room, coffee shop, groceries and gasoline. Write Johnston Canyon Resort, Box 875, Banff, Alberta, T0L 0C0 (phone or Fax 403-762-2971).

Moose Meadows Located 19.0 km from the Trans-Canada Highway junction, this large meadow gives outstanding views of Pilot Mountain and the summits near Vermilion Pass, especially Boom and Whymper mountains. On the southeast corner, a short side road leads to the parking area for the Ink Pots and Johnston Creek trails.

Silver City Located 22.5 km from the Trans-Canada Highway junction, this is the site of an optimistically misnamed mining town. In 1883 it was the largest settlement in the Canadian Rockies. Two years later it was deserted. Legendary prospector Joe Smith stayed on at the site until 1937, still believing he would find gold. A brick kiln is still evident on the east side of the road, the only sign left of the old town.

Castle Mountain Campground Located 23.3 km from the Trans-Canada Highway junction, this campground is open early June to early September. Washrooms have cold water.

Castle Mountain Warden Station Located 23.5 km from the Trans-Canada Highway junction, this warden residence is adjacent to the Rockbound Lake trailhead.

Castle Mountain Village Located 23.7 km from the Trans-Canada Highway junction, this facility is open year round. It has 21 comfortable chalets on 4 acres. The site has an outstanding view of Castle Mountain and is close to hiking trails. Snacks, groceries, gas and propane are available. Write Castle Mountain Village, Box 1655, Banff, Alberta, T0L 0C0 (phone 403-762-3868, Fax 403-762-8629).

Castle Mountain Hostel Located 23.7 km from the Trans-Canada Highway junction, opposite Castle Mountain Village, on the Radium Highway connector, the hostel has accommodation for 36 and provides a kitchen, refrigerator, indoor plumbing, showers, electricity and propane heating. It is closed Wednesdays. For reservations, write to Southern Alberta Hostelling Association, #203, 1414 Kensington road NW, Calgary, Alberta, T2N 3P9 (phone 403-283-5551, Fax 403-283-6503).

Castle Mountain has always been admired for its rich coloring and picturesque cliffs. The landmark is visible from many openings on the Bow Valley Parkway, especially at Castle Junction. The mountain is "the legendary home of the Chinook Wind, that warm dry wind of the western prairies which descends from the mountains in late winter and spring and devours the snow. The story goes that the young and strong West Wind was protecting the beautiful South Wind and her little daughter Chinook when they were attacked by the terrible North Wind, the ruler of the Arctic. The West Wind was victorious, but in the struggle the little Chinook was blinded. Since she could no longer fly with the other winds she was given a home in Castle Mountain, and sometimes, on spring nights, it is said, she glides down to the prairies, seeking her lost mother and leaving spring behind her wherever her feet have trod." Mabel Williams, *Guardians of the Wild*

Johnston Canyon from the Ink Pots trail

Upper Falls, Johnston Canyon

JOHNSTON CANYON to INK POTS

~ Spectacular canyon and falls, Ink Pots ~

Distance **5.9 km (3.7 mi) to Ink Pots**
Height Gain **315 m (1,040'); 105 m (350') return**
Hiking Time **1 hr 30 min**
1 hr 17 min return

Trailhead Take the Bow Valley Parkway (1A) to the Johnston Canyon parking area, on the northeast side of the road, 0.5 km (0.3 mi) east of Johnston Canyon Resort. This is 22.9 km (14.2 mi) west of Banff (Mount Norquay Junction), or 7.3 km (4.5 mi) east of Castle Junction. Map page 12

Options You can go to Forty Mile Creek via Mystic Pass, or to Lake Luellen via Johnston Creek. If you have a second vehicle, you can descend either to Moose Meadows or Hillsdale.

≈ Recently built catwalks and view platforms permit a unique variety of vantage points for enjoying this remarkable canyon and its waterfalls. Tufa, colorful rock deposits from dripping springs, can be seen, especially at the upper falls. Don't miss the new trail to the viewpoint below the upper falls.

The sun reaches the upper falls about noon, the lower falls about 1:00 pm, the other falls later in the afternoon.

Interpretive signs point out local geological features and bird life. Johnston Canyon is one of only three sites in Alberta where black swifts have been found nesting. Evenings are best to see swifts. Dippers also frequent the fast moving water and its spray.

Heed the warning signs about slippery rock and keep to the trail. Some daredevils have fallen into the Canyon. Five people have gone over the upper falls to their death. A mother, who jumped in the creek to rescue her child, somehow survived when she was swept over the upper falls; unhappily, the child, still held in her arms, was drowned. A few people (and one dog) have lived after going over the lower falls.

Be cautious of low overhanging rock above the catwalks; it is easy to bang your head if you peer into the Canyon as you walk.

The trail through the Canyon may be the most popular in Banff Park. Expect your hiking times to be affected when the trail is congested. The Ink Pots, seven quicksand-bottomed ponds, fed by karst springs, can be reached via the Canyon trail. The trail to the Ink Pots climbs above the ancient slide where the Canyon is deepest; you can glimpse a portion of it at the highest point on the trail. In 1992, there was no trail sign to show where to turn to get back to the Johnston Canyon trail.

Backpackers should take the trail from Moose Meadows. Hikers with bulky packs will find the crowded narrow catwalks awkward.

Trail From the parking lot to the lower falls, you climb 30 m. It takes only one minute to take the detour to the cave with its spectacular view of the thundering falls.

The viewpoint just below the upper falls is 95 m higher than the parking lot; to reach the viewpoint at the top, you climb another 30 m.

If you go on to the Ink Pots, you ascend 315 m above the parking lot. You also climb 105 m on the return.

Trail Section	km from	time out	return time
Parking Lot		↓	77 min
Lower Falls, Cave Jct.	1.2	16 min	62 min
Upper Falls, lower viewpoint	2.6	37 min	46 min
Upper Falls, upper viewpoint	2.7	40 min	44 min
Moose Meadows trailhead Jct.	3.2	49 min	37 min
Highest point on trail	4.5	72 min	22 min
Ink Pots	5.9	90 min	↑

"The doctors say I should give up tennis and mountain climbing, so I may eventually turn into a real honest to goodness trail rider and go everywhere on the back of a horse. Fortunately they have not as yet cut me off liquor." Walter Wilcox to Tom Wilson, Jan. 18, 1930

INK POTS from MOOSE MEADOWS

~ Clear ponds, fastest route ~

Distance **5.8 km (3.6 mi)**
Height Gain **315 m (1,040'); 105 m (350') return**
Hiking Time **1 hr 23 min**
1 hr 14 min return

Trailhead Take the Bow Valley Parkway (1A) to the Moose Meadows parking area, on the northeast side of the road, 0.5 km (0.3 mi) west of Johnston Canyon Resort. This is 24.5 km (15.2 mi) west of Banff (Mount Norquay Junction), or 5.7 km (3.5 mi) east of Castle Junction. Map page 12.

≈ This route is less scenic than from Johnston Canyon, but you get to the Ink Pots faster. If you are backpacking, you should go this way instead of via Johnston Canyon where crowds of visitors and narrow catwalks with low overhanging rockfaces will frustrate your progress.

Trail From the trailhead, the route follows a disused roadway. This intersects with several old logging cuts; watch for blocked intersections, flagging and other directional guides, especially on the return. After 2.2 km, you enter a wide road at an unsigned flagged junction. If you miss this diversion on your return, you will end at Johnston Canyon Resort.

Almost 1 km farther, the trail to Johnston Canyon intersects on your right. In 1992, the trail sign showed Moose Meadows and destinations up Johnston Creek, but no indication of the path to Johnston Canyon on the right.

There is a steep hill before the Ink Pots.

Trail Section	km from	time out	return time
Trailhead		↓	74 min
Jct. Old Fire Road	2.2	29 min	48 min
Johnston Canyon Jct.	3.1	42 min	37 min
Summit of Trail	4.5	65 min	22 min
Ink Pots	5.8	83 min	↑

~ Forest trail, small meadow ~

Distance **8.3 km (5.2 mi)**
Height Gain **470 m (1,550'); 235 m (775') return**
Hiking Time **2 hr 3 min**
1 hr 58 min return

Trailhead Take the Bow Valley Parkway (1A) to the Hillsdale parking area, on the northeast side of the road, 4.2 km (2.6 mi) east of Johnston Canyon. This is 18.8 km (11.7 mi) west of Banff (Mount Norquay Junction). Map page 12.

Options You can go to Forty Mile Creek via Mystic Pass, or to Lake Luellen via Johnston Creek. If you have a second vehicle, you can descend to Johnston Canyon or Moose Meadows.

≈ This alternate route to the Ink Pots, is 2.5 km farther and climbs 130 m higher than the usual routes (Johnston Canyon or Moose Meadows), but it is less crowded and easier on the feet. It passes through a richly vegetated forest. Near the pass, you go through a small meadow with a good view of Mt. Ishbel. Bring rain pants if the woods are wet. The Ink Pots are deep ponds, so clear you can see water from underground springs bubbling through the sandy bottom.

The name Hillsdale derives from a railway construction camp. It was "named after Mr. Hill, manager of the company's store." Rev. G. M. Grant held services here in 1883, attracting about 30 people: engineers, doctor, storemen, contractors, prospectors — and one lady.

There is some question if Grant's Hillsdale is this place. He said it was at the west end of Aylmer Park (now the Buffalo Paddock near Banff) but adds it was 28 miles east of the Summit, which is where we now find Hillsdale.

Grant wrote, "The Hillsdale camp ... was the most beautifully situated of any that we had yet seen. It was pitched at the foot of some low aspen and spruce covered hills, looking out to the east on a grassy park of five or six acres.... Every one of these multitudinous peaks is worthy of a separate description, and would be honoured with it over and over again could it only be transported to the plains — say near Winnipeg.... Nothing but the art of the photographer can do justice to their infinite richness."

Grant must have been an effective preacher. Major A. B. Rogers, in charge of constructing the CPR through the mountains, was notorious for his foul language. Yet, after attending one of Grant's services, he resolved to stop swearing, a reformation which astonished his boss, W. C. Van Horne.

Hillsdale Meadow is the site of one of John Brewster's dairy pastures which supplied Banff in 1898. About 1926, Pat Brewster, in charge of outfitting for Brewster Transportation, had a horse camp here. Mary Schäffer calls the place *Hillsdale Hills*, "a wonderful little park ... a succession of low, grass-covered hills surrounded by high peaks".

Hillsdale Meadow is particularly attractive in autumn when the poplars are golden.

Trail From the trailhead, you wind through Hillsdale Meadow; three signs mark the way. At the base of a hill on your left, you can see a cairn erected to commemorate boy scouts (Rangers) who stayed here in 1959 when this area was a group campsite. The nearby Ranger Creek and Ranger Canyon got their names at this time.

You cross Hillsdale Creek three times. The last water before Johnston Creek (Giardia warning) is a spring which dries up in late summer.

The grade doesn't become steep until you are three-quarters of the way to the pass. Shortly after the pass, you reach a small meadow from where you get a good view of Mt. Ishbel.

The trail descends steeply to Johnston Creek; the Ink Pots are directly across the creek, but you must first hike a short distance upstream to the bridge, crossing a short section of bog. Just before the bridge is the junction to Luellen Lake and Mystic Pass.

Trail Section	km from	time out	return time
Hillsdale		↓	118 min
Pass	5.0	85 min	51 min
Johnston Creek Jct.	8.0	119 min	4 min
Ink Pots	8.3	123 min	↑

Black bear (story, page 112)

PILOT POND (Lizard Lake)

~ Small lake set in forest ~

Distance **0.2 km (0.1 mi)**
Height Gain **Nil; 45 m (150') return**
Hiking Time **5 min**
6 min return

Trailhead Take the Bow Valley Parkway (1A) to the Hillsdale Slide display, on the west side of the road, 2.6 km (1.6 mi) east of Johnston Canyon Resort. This is on the divided roadway and can be reached only by eastbound traffic. Map page 12.

≈ Pilot Pond, formerly called Lizard Lake, is larger than many bodies of water called *lakes*. It is a peculiarly twisted body of water filling an old channel of the Bow River.

You get limited views of Massive and Pilot mountains from the hill. If you go a short way around the lake, you see the Sawback Range. The trail is steep (very steep near the lake).

Mount Ishbel and the Ink Pots

About 1920 photographer Walter Wilcox camped here with painter Belmore Browne.

"One day, in early autumn, Browne told me about a pretty lake, tucked away somewhere in the forest a few miles W. of Banff. This lake was very near the road to Lake Louise, but so thoroughly concealed that not one person in a thousand knew of its existence. Browne invited [me] to spend two or three days at the lake, where we could ... devote ourselves to our particular artistic hobbies in a delightful spot. The day of our arrival was one of rare autumnal beauty. Under a sky of cerulean blue, the small round lake resembled an emerald surrounded by thc gold of aspens ... already touched by the frosts of a dying summer. It was not long before we had set up our teepee and arranged our equipment and larder within. While Browne was busily at work on a painting ... I came upon a beaver work-house.... Shortly after, I saw a remarkable rare incident — a beaver swimming at midday and under a bright sun! I was lucky in getting some excellent movie shots....

"Then I went back to the teepee to get more film for my camera. My first glance inside showed that something was radically wrong. A large hole had been torn in the side of the teepee, flour and bacon were spread over the blankets, and an entire ham had disappeared. As I was peering into the semi-darkness I began to imagine in some indescribable but uncanny way that something was right behind me. Turning quickly I was startled to see the largest black bear of all my experience, so close that I could have laid hand on him. This was the robber who had taken our provisions. It must have been his second or third trip. There was no use continuing on into the teepee. The other way was blocked. I realized that the bear must have been annoyed, not to say irritated at my presence and, what is even more important, he must have been one of very bad manners as he had torn a hole in our canvas instead of entering politely by the front door which was open. For a few moments of embarrassing quiet each of us waited for the other to move. Fortunately it was the bear. I shouted to Browne, who came on the run, and with rifle in hand we scoured the neighboring woods, but in vain.

"'It's all over,' said Browne. 'We shall have to go back. It is against the law to shoot game in the Park and if we stay here the bear will be prowling around and annoying us all night.' So we returned to Banff that evening." *AAJ, 1941*

Trail From the parking lot, take the steep trail to the lake. There are two paths. The one to the right leads to a more scenic spot.

Trail Section	km from	time out	return time
Trailhead		↓	6 min
Pilot Pond	0.2	5 min	↑

MULESHOE

~ Douglas firs ~

Distance **0.6 km (0.4 mi) to rest bench**
Height Gain **90 m (300')**
Hiking Time **14 min**
9 min return

Trailhead Take the Bow Valley Parkway (1A) to the Muleshoe parking area, on the southwest side of the road, 6.3 km (3.9 mi) from the southeast end of the Parkway, 11.3 km (7.0 mi) west of Johnston Canyon Resort. This is 11.7 km (7.3 mi) west of Banff (Mount Norquay Junction), or 17.1 km (10.6 mi) east of Castle Junction. Map page 12.

Options You can follow a very steep animal path up a rib of Mt. Cory 800 m above the parking area.

≈ This short nature trail takes you through a stand of aspens, past a group of ancient Douglas firs with their corrugated bark, to a pleasant viewpoint. The grade is easy to moderate as far as the hiking sign and rest bench where the man-made trail ends. From here, an animal path continues upslope, leading very steeply to open slopes 200 m above the trailhead.

A less obvious animal route continues up the crest of a ridge, with many scenic vantage points. As you go higher, however, the tree cover increases and openings with views become infrequent. There is no water on the way; if you are tempted to follow the steep animal path, you will want to carry a supply. If you go before July, expect parasitic ticks to find you.

The picnic site has a good view of two descriptively named features: the giant cave named The Hole-in-the-Wall, and Muleshoe Lake (spelled *Mule Shoe* on the map). The *lake* is man-made; about 1889 Dave White dynamited the riverbank for the CPR, blocking this backwater channel and changing the course of the Bow River.

Trail From the privy site, cross the road to the trail sign. The path swings along the treed slopes of Mt. Cory to the base of an open hillside, marked with a sign pointing the way back. A rest bench (merely a hewn log) is just ahead, but the path to it is faint.

At this point, an obvious animal path continues straight up the hillside. You can follow it to a broad grassy slope where it seems to disappear. If you want to go farther, angle up to your left to pick up the crest of a ridge where the track again becomes obvious.

If you choose to continue, expect very steep sections and vague portions. So long as you stay on the crest, the way should be obvious.

Trail Section	km from	time out	return time
Trailhead		↓	14 min
Sign (end of trail)	0.6	14 min	5 min
Hillside (animal trail peters out)	0.8	25 min	2 min
Brow of hillside	0.9	28 min	↑

Muleshoe Lake, Mounts Bourgeau and Brett from Muleshoe Trail

The history of Banff begins with the railway and the hot springs (see History, page 196.)

In 1886 Dr. R. G. Brett, a medical supervisor for the CPR, built a hotel facility designed to take advantage of the therapeutic value of the nearby hot sulphur springs. A canny promoter, Brett gave the facility a medical name, misspelled *The Sanitarium* and supplied crutches to guests who came for treatment. After they left, the crutches were stacked as mute evidence of cures real and imagined. Wooden boards bore such testimonials as, "A month after I began to take the baths I climbed to the top of Sulphur Mountain. For five years before then I had not been able to walk without a crutch."

Brett's first bathing accommodations were hastily erected: a 4x6' pit dug in the ground surrounded by pine boughs which gave the bather limited privacy.

Water was piped from the Upper Hot Springs. Pat Brewster said that guests were asked to leave their money at the desk for security reasons. He hinted that the cure usually took as long as the money lasted.

Brewster noted that one invalid, a derelict tramp riding the rails, suffering from pneumonia, apparently was forgotten and died. He wasn't discovered until Fred Tabuteau smelled him when raking the gravel outside the tent where he'd been placed. When Fred summoned Brett, the doctor looked inside the tent, then told Tabuteau to rake the far side of the yard while he made discreet attempts to get rid of the corpse without attracting attention.

Brett's hotel, enlarged and renamed *The Bretton Hall Hotel*, burned down in 1933. The Banff Park Administration buildings replaced it in 1936.

W. S. Caine, a British MP advocating temperance, visited Banff in 1887. He admired the scenery, but seemed much more impressed that Banff enforced prohibition.

The CPR named its facility Banff Springs Hotel to emphasize its proximity to the hot sulphur water. The superb site, near the confluence of the Bow and Spray rivers, suggested by Tom Wilson, was chosen by CPR General Manager W. C. Van Horne. When the hotel opened in 1888, it was the largest in the world.

Banff has managed to avoid many prejudices which plague other communities. The stained glass windows installed for the 1990 centennial of the Anglican church, St. George's-in-the-Pines, were designed by a United Church clergyman (Rev. Tom Lonsdale), photographed by an atheist (Nick Morant), assisted by a Roman Catholic elder (Henry Ness). Another ecumenical situation occurred in Banff on November 11, 1918. In an early morning long-distance phone call, a local Orangeman learned of the Armistice, ending World War I. He lit the altar candles (the only light available) and rang the bell of Saint Mary's Roman Catholic Church at 3 am to announce the good news to the town.

SOME TOURIST ATTRACTIONS

Vermilion Lakes Drive In addition to its superb scenery, this is a good place to see coyotes, sheep and deer, especially if you walk or cycle. Osprey and eagles nest near First Lake; beaver and muskrat frequent Second Lake. A century ago, these grassy meadows provided pasture for John Brewster's dairy cows.

Tunnel Mountain Drive and Tunnel Mountain Road The drive on these connected roads is a good place to see elk, deer and coyotes. Views of Cascade and Rundle mountains and of Banff may be seen from several turn-offs. Tunnel Mountain Campground and the trail to The Hoodoos are beside Tunnel Mountain Road. Trails to Tunnel Mountain and the north side of Bow Falls to the Hoodoos commence from Tunnel Mountain Drive.

Hoodoos The path to these famous pillars is near the campground on Tunnel Mountain Road.

Bow Falls One of the most popular sites in Banff, you can reach Bow Falls by road (River Road) or trail (0.7 km; go east of the Bow River Bridge, northeast of Glen Avenue).

Bow River A path follows the north bank of the river 1.3 km from Wolf Street to Beaver Street.

Golf Course Road This scenic road is a popular cycling route. Trails to Mt. Rundle, Spray River, Bow Falls and Canmore commence from the road. Take Spray Avenue and Rundle to Glen Avenue.

Sulphur Mountain Gondola This is the favorite way to reach the top of Sulphur Mountain with its teahouse and superb panoramas. Mountain sheep frequent the summit. Parking is located at the end of Mountain Avenue.

Upper Hot Springs This popular bathing pool utilizes the hottest of the sulphur springs which made Banff famous. Trails to Sulphur Mountain and the Spray River also commence from the parking area, located at the far end of Mountain Avenue.

Mount Norquay Drive The scenic highlight of this switchback drive is The Green Spot. It is near the summit of the road which continues to the Mt. Norquay ski area, located at the end of Mount Norquay Drive where trails to Stoney Squaw, Cascade Amphitheatre, Elk Lake and Forty Mile Creek commence.

Cave & Basin The bathing pool and Cave are synonymous with the history of Banff. An Interpretive Centre features historic displays and an award winning multi-frame slide show. A self-guiding walk leads to a marsh, famous for its unique biological features; another path highlights significant historic and geological aspects of the site. The Cave and Basin are located at the end of Cave Avenue.

Sundance Canyon Now restricted to cyclists and hikers, the road leads to trails through the

Canyon and to Sundance Pass. The trailhead is located at the end of Cave Avenue.

Buffalo Paddock Started in 1897, the site is connected with the preservation of the plains bison. In 1981, they were replaced with Wood bison, which used to be native to Banff Park. Stay in your car. Several visitors have been injured (one fatally) by ignoring this regulation. The site is located north of Banff, on the westbound leg of the Trans-Canada Highway.

Whyte Museum of the Canadian Rockies Located at 111 Bear Street, this facility hosts an outstanding collection of mountain artwork and artifacts plus a treasure of historic information and photographs. It was established in 1968 by Peter and Catharine Whyte.

Banff Park Museum Erected in 1895, this building is designated a National Historic Site. It was run for 30 years by Norman Sanson. Featured are stuffed birds and mammals of western Canada. The Museum is located on Banff Avenue, north of the bridge.

Banff Centre Located on St. Julien Road, The Banff Centre for the Arts provides advanced instruction in all branches of the arts and presents displays and performances by both students and professionals.

Cascade Rock Garden These celebrated displays surround Banff's Administration Buildings, south of the Bow River Bridge.

Central Park This popular picnic area has public washrooms. Open air concerts are held here. It is located on Buffalo Street, opposite Bear Street.

Banff Springs Hotel In addition to its commercial facilities, this CPR hotel has been renowned for its architectural and historic significance. It is located near the east end of Spray Avenue.

Luxton Museum of the Plains Indian Established in 1952 by Norman Luxton, this museum features an outstanding collection of native artifacts and is now run by the Buffalo Nations Cultural Society, a predominantly native group. The Museum is located on Birch Avenue.

FACILITIES

Information Centre Located at 224 Banff Avenue, the Centre gives current information on accommodation and other commercial and recreational facilities and activities. You can also find out about weather, trails, roads, bear sightings and interpretive events. Permits and maps can be obtained here. Phone 762-1550.

Accommodation See Information Centre.

Tunnel Mountain Campground This is the largest campground in Banff Park and offers a wide range of facilities. It is located on Tunnel Mountain Road, northeast of the town.

Police (RCMP) The Banff office is found on the northwest corner of Lynx Street. Phone 762-2226.

Mineral Springs Hospital Located at 301 Lynx Street. Phone 762-2222.

Warden The Banff Warden Office is located on Hawk Avenue, in the industrial compound on the north edge of town. Phone 762-4506.

Bus Station Offices for Greyhound Lines of Canada and Brewster Transportation and Tours are located at 100 Gopher Street. Phone 762-6767. Pacific Western is located at 204 Caribou Street. Phone 762-4337.

Boat Docks Canoes may be rented from the docks at Wolf Street and Bow Avenue.

Log run above Bow Falls, ca 1890. Photo, John Woodruff, by permission Whyte Museum of the Canadian Rockies.

Sunrise, Vermilion Lake. Mount Rundle and Sulphur Mountain.

"Mr. Stewart also proposes, by damming up some portions of the many streams which run through the park to fill up a chain of old marshes, and turn them into lakes. I rather protested against this interference with nature, for I found a special beauty in these marshes such as I had never seen before. But he explained that his chief object was not so much to create lakes as to act as a fire-break from the many conflagrations which rage throughout the Rocky Mountains during the summer and which might at any time sweep through the National Park."
W. S. Caine, *A Trip Round the World*

Mounts Inglismaldie, Girouard and Peechee from beaver pond, Vermilion Lakes

"I cannot find words adequately to describe the unique charms of the primitive and unspoiled scenery. The lake was as smooth as glass; its banks were a wild tangle of brushwood, poplar and maple, a perfect blaze of autumn red and gold, out of which sprang tall and sombre cedars and pine trees. Behind these were the snow-clad mountains, the whole perfectly repeated on the surface of the water."
W. S. Caine, describing Vermilion Lakes, 1887, *A Trip Round the World*

CORY PASS Circuit (GARGOYLE PASS)

~ Sheer cliffs, superb panorama, sheep, ~

Distance **13.4 km (8.3 mi) circuit**
Height Gain **1035 m (3,390')**
Hiking Time **5 hr circuit**

Trailhead Take the Trans-Canada Highway to the 1A Parkway, 5.7 km (3.5 mi) west of Banff (Mount Norquay Road). Go 0.3 km west on the Parkway, turn right and drive 0.9 km to the Fireside picnic area, which is at the end of the access road. Map page 12.

Options You can also go to Edith Pass, but this will seem anticlimactic after this long, spectacular trip.

≈ In 1991, when asked to name her favorite hike near Banff, the town's first mayor, Leslie Taylor, chose this one. Leonard Leacock took me on this circuit, my first big hike, in 1951. It ignited my passion for hiking.

About 1960, the words *Cory Pass* first appeared on a trail sign. The name became official in 1985. Unfortunately, the early local name, Gargoyle Pass (which Leacock remembers it being called in 1920), wasn't known to the park official who made the sign. A gargoyle is a grotesque ornamental rock figure found on Gothic cathedrals such as Notre Dame in Paris. Because the rock towers which give Gargoyle Valley its name are at the pass, *Cory Pass* seems less appropriate than the earlier name.

The spectacular scenery reminds me of the remark A. O. Wheeler read in the field notes of an unidentified surveyor: "Land good for nothing except a fine view from the top of the hill." The steep walls of Louis, and the vertical cliffs of Edith which guard the entrance to Gargoyle Valley are among the wonders of the Rockies.

Mt. Louis is one of the classic climbs in the Rockies. When he made the first ascent in 1916, guide Conrad Kain looked back to the summit and said to his client, "Ye Gods, Mr. MacCarthy, just look at that; they never will believe we climbed it."

Seventeen years later, Kain led H. S. Kingman to the final chimney where they were driven off the mountain "by a terrific sleet and rain storm which encased the entire mountain with slush and verglas. The descent of Louis was quite an experience, and Conrad certainly handled himself beautifully." A week later, they succeeded in climbing Louis, Kain's last difficult climb. He was 50, and six months later would die of encephalitis.

Through Gargoyle Valley, the trail circles Mt. Edith on rough scree. Portions are heartbreakingly steep. For photographic considerations, I like to do the circuit counter-clockwise to get the early sun on Louis from the Edith Pass side, and the afternoon sun from Cory Pass. However, I find the clockwise direction easier to hike since you don't climb so much on loose rock. Whichever way you go, you must turn your back on some glorious scenery, so plan to return and do it in the other direction.

Get in shape before you attempt this hike; it is the steepest in the area. Also, to complete the circuit, you must cross a short exposed cliff-band. Most hikers find it easy, but you could avoid it by taking the eastern (Edith Pass) approach both ways instead of making a circuit.

There are two trails from the Edith Pass Junction to Gargoyle Valley. Lawrence Grassi built the higher one as an approach to Mt. Louis — which he climbed 32 times! It was characteristic of his generous spirit to make a way for others to enjoy, and like his other trails, it is superbly sited and engineered. Present signage shows part of Grassi's path diverging as a climber's route to Mt. Edith. In fact, it also leads to Cory Pass. If you stay on Grassi's trail, you go 15 m higher and get better views; actually you climb less because there isn't so much up and down. Moreover, his route is easier walking (better underfoot, better grade, less overgrown by low shrubs). If you are coming down, be observant at the switchbacks — some people have missed a corner, taking a false *trail* which soon degenerates.

The lower track is a sheep path which has been followed by so many hikers looking for a lower way, that it became more obvious and was chosen for the official trail when it was rebuilt. I think this choice unfortunate, and until deadfall makes the higher way too difficult, I recommend staying on Grassi's trail. Heading to Cory Pass, there is no problem finding his path. Only if you are hiking clockwise, are you apt to have trouble locating the route; where you climb the scree after leaving Gargoyle Valley, you have to go higher than the hiking sign. When you reach this sign, you should see a trail ascending the scree from your right. Turn onto this route which, after a switchback left, leads to a giant boulder. On the other side of the boulder (100 m from where you left the lower trail) Grassi's path is obvious.

Don't be confused by trails branching right as you climb to Gargoyle Valley. They are climbing routes or animal trails leading to Mt. Louis. Snow often lingers at Cory Pass and Gargoyle Valley until mid-July.

On the road near the trailhead, a small enclosure with a ramp was used to capture mountain sheep destined for shipment to zoos. Dan McCowan reports that one workman wanted to pick up a small lamb from a group caught inside. When he cornered it at the fence, a nimble ram escaped the enclosure by leapfrogging first onto the startled man's shoulders, and from there, jumping the high fence.

Trail From the trail sign, cross the creek and turn right to follow an old road 200 m downstream. Go left at the hiker sign and proceed to the Cory Pass Junction where the circuit begins. You can turn left, or keep ahead.

If you continue ahead, you descend a hill and cross Edith Creek to the wide track of the old Edith Pass Trail which you join by turning left.

Head up the narrow valley to a bridge which brings you to the west side of the stream and a steep section of trail.

Turn left onto the Cory Pass—Mt. Louis trail. The forest opens as you ascend, and soon you get glimpses of Mt. Louis ahead. You come to the junction where the lower route separates from Grassi's path. I prefer to keep ahead and follow Grassi's trail (the trail sign shows it as a climber's route to Mt. Edith). Grassi's route brings you to a superb viewpoint from where you descend through loose scree to rejoin the lower trail.

You continue down around a rib of Mt. Edith, then commence the long steep climb to Cory Pass.

From the pass, the trail contours on high slopes of Mt. Edith down to the ridge leading to the Bow Valley. You climb up a short but exposed cliffband onto the ridge, then down the very steep route to the circuit junction.

Turn right to reach the parking area.

Trail Section	km from	time out	return time
Fireside Trailhead		↓	294 min
Cory Pass Jct.	1.1	16 min	278 min
Mt. Louis—Cory Pass Jct.	4.1	78 min	232 min
Grassi Trail Jct.	4.8	94 min	222 min
Trail Sign (Grassi Trail Jct.)	6.2	136 min	191 min
Cory Pass	7.6	192 min	149 min
Top of cliff	9.6	237 min	99 min
Cory Pass Jct.	12.3	283 min	16 min
Fireside	13.4	299 min	↑

Hikers admiring the gargoyles at Cory (Gargoyle) Pass

Mt. Louis from Cory (Gargoyle) Pass

Mt. Louis and Mt. Fifi from the eastern entrance to Gargoyle Valley

Round-leaved orchid

Twinflower, seen close up, resembling ladies in fancy gowns

EDITH PASS

~ Good view of Louis beyond the pass ~

Distance **4.6 km (2.9 mi)**
Height Gain **505 m (1,650')**
Hiking Time **1 hr 30 min**
1 hr 2 min return

Trailhead Take the Trans-Canada Highway and turn off on the Bow Valley Parkway (1A), 5.5 km (3.4 mi) west of Banff (Mount Norquay Road). Go west 0.3 km and turn right onto the Fireside access road. Follow this 0.9 km and park at the picnic site. Cross the creek at the bridge and turn downstream to start the trail. Map page 12.

Options You can take the Cory Pass trail to circle Mount Edith. You can cross the pass to Forty Mile Creek. If you have two vehicles, you can return via Mt. Norquay or backpack to Johnston Canyon via Mystic Pass.

≈ Historian Bill Yeo states the mountains surrounding Edith Pass were named by surveyor Jacob Smith, an employee of park superintendent George Stewart, and probably a friend of his son, Louis. When Lady Macdonald (wife of Prime Minister Sir John A.) visited Banff in 1886, Louis Stewart took her attendant, Mrs. J. F. Orde (née Edith Cox) and her dog Fifi to this pass. So three great summits — Edith, Louis and Fifi — got their names. About the same time, Smith also named the peak east of the pass for John Norquay who is said to have made the first ascent. This giant (300 pound) man of Scottish descent (and it appears he had an Indian grandmother) became Premier of Manitoba (1878-87). He was acknowledged one of the great orators of his day.

The first ascent of Mt. Edith was made in 1900 by famed English climber Norman Collie with outfitter Fred Stephens. Camped on Edith Creek the night before, Collie opened a bottle of champagne, but Stephens would have none of it, saying he'd tasted better cider in Montana. Stephens hated climbing, so Collie "looked forward to experiencing all the pleasures of the initiated, when he should have Fred dangling on the end of an Alpine rope." From Edith pass, they ascended the col between the south and centre peak, descending via the easy west side.

For many years, this trail was little used. In 1921, Brewster Transport manager Lou Crosby wrote, "It must be from ignorance alone that the many tourists who make riding excursions in the vicinity of Banff, do not reach the cool recesses of Edith Pass more frequently. The view from the summit ... well repays one for so easy a climb." *Canadian Alpine Journal, 1921-22*

Mt. Louis from near Edith Pass

The grade is moderate with some short steep sections. In early season, calypsos, Canada violets and clematis are common. I associate the trail with rufous hummingbirds which I have encountered here on four occasions.

You are in trees to the pass where a small meadow permits limited views. The old trail crosses Edith Pass, and just after it enters the forest, there is a view of Mt. Louis. The new path avoids this site, but if you go beyond the pass toward Forty Mile Creek, in 6 minutes, you reach a good vista of Mt. Louis.

Trail From the parking lot, cross the creek via the bridge at the trailhead and turn right to follow an old roadway down 0.2 km. Go left at the trail sign; you parallel the noisy Trans-Canada Highway for 0.9 km, rounding a couple of hills where a few giant Douglas firs grow.

Pass the junction to Cory Pass (on your left) and descend to cross Edith Creek and join the original wide trail.

The route follows the streambed. The grade is moderate until you cross the streambed and ascend a steep hill on the western side of the creek. Soon after the trail returns to the creekbed, you go by the last available water (Giardia warning) on the trip.

Not long after the Cory Pass—Mt. Louis junction, the grade eases and you reach Edith Pass.

Continue beyond the pass for about six minutes if you want to reach a good view (through open trees) of Mts. Edith, Louis and Fifi.

Trail Section	km from	time out	return time
Trailhead		↓	62 min
Cory Pass Jct.	1.1	16 min	46 min
Mt. Louis Highline Jct.	4.0	78 min	8 min
Edith Pass	4.6	90 min	↑

EDITH PASS from FORTY MILE CREEK

~ Mt. Louis, Forty Mile Creek ~

Distance 8.8 km (5.5 mi)
Height Gain 335 m (1,100'); 130 m (425') return
Hiking Time 2 hr 17 min
2 hr 2 min return

Trailhead Follow the Mount Norquay Road north from the west Banff interchange on the Trans-Canada Highway. Drive 5.4 km (3.4 mi) and park at the ski area Parking Lot #2 on your left. (If open, the main lot on your right is closer.) Hike 0.4 km to the hiker's kiosk at the far end of the main winter parking lot (closed in summer). Map page 12.

Options You can cross Edith Pass to combine this with the Fireside trailhead. You can use the Creekside Trail down Forty Mile Creek to return via the Cascade Amphitheatre route. You can go farther up Forty Mile Creek. The trail also connects with the Cory Pass and Stoney Squaw Bridle Path trails.

≈ This route has scenic advantages over the usual Fireside trailhead route: you see more of Mt. Louis (and better views); also, you see Forty Mile Creek. You start higher, and climb less, especially if you avoid the return climb to the Mt. Norquay parking area by taking the Edith Pass Trail to the Fireside trailhead. This route is longer, and the first part, heavily used by horse traffic, is muddier than the Fireside route.

Trail From the hiker's kiosk, cross the paved area between the ski buildings and follow the road past the Cascade Chair. Shortly after, you pass a junction to the Trans-Canada Highway (Stoney Squaw Bridle Path). Continue on the road past the Spirit Chair and turn left, taking the Mystic Lake Trail.

You climb steeply to an old junction with Cascade Amphitheatre. Keep ahead, passing a no bicycling sign, then begin a long descent to Forty Mile Creek. Just before the bridge, another junction (Creekside Trail) branches right.

Cross Forty Mile Creek and follow the wide trail to the Edith Pass junction where you turn left and cross the creek. Begin a stiff ascent to the pass. The best views come about eight minutes before you reach Edith Pass.

Trail Section	km from	time out	return time
Trailhead		↓	122 min
Ski building	0.4	5 min	117 min
Trans-Canada Highway Jct.	1.2	13 min	108 min
Cascade Amphitheatre Jct.	1.4	16 min	105 min
Bridge, Creekside Jct.	4.3	60 min	59 min
Mystic Lake Jct.	6.3	86 min	35 min
Edith Pass	8.8	137 min	↑

CREEKSIDE, FORTY MILE CREEK

~ Quiet trail beside Forty Mile Creek ~

Distance 1.9 km (1.2 mi)
Height Gain 45 m (150')
Hiking Time 29 min
27 min return

Trailhead From the Mt. Norquay Parking area, take the Cascade Amphitheatre Trail to the Creekside Junction (at Forty Mile Creek); alternately, take the Mystic Lake Trail to the Creekside Junction, just before the bridge over Forty Mile Creek. Map p. 12.

Options You can go to Edith Pass or Cascade Amphitheatre. The trail also connects with the Cory Pass, Elk Lake, and Trans-Canada Highway trails. In addition, Stoney Squaw Trail is close to the trailhead.

≈ The path is used mainly as a cross-country ski trail. Although it receives little summer use, soft sections may be muddy.

Though you are never far from Forty Mile Creek, there are few places where the forest permits good views. Often, you can't see the creek. About five minutes from the Cascade Amphitheatre Junction, on the opposite side of Forty Mile Creek you can see streams emptying into the Creek; if you go to the opposite bank (the easiest approach is to cross the bridge on the Cascade Amphitheatre Trail, ford Elk Creek, then follow the Forty Mile creekbed), you will find that these are sulphur springs.

Trail Take the Cascade Amphitheatre Trail to Forty Mile Creek, and where the road doubles back (200 m before the bridge over Forty Mile Creek), watch for the junction. Turn left. The path follows an easy grade to its end, the junction with the Mystic Lake Trail.

Trail Section	km from	time out	return time
Mt. Norquay Parking area		↓	135 min
Forty Mile Cr. (Amphith. Jct.)	3.5	38 min	87 min
Forty Mile Cr. (Mystic L. Jct.)	5.4	67 min	60 min
Mt. Norquay Parking area	9.7	130 min	↑

Mt. Louis from Forty Mile Creek

Mt. Brewster and Elk Pass from Cascade Amphitheatre

"I was hiking along a trail that was new to me — looked like an Indian trail — when I came to a point where it forked. I was about to turn up the right fork when I saw ahead of me a grizzly bear. So not having any other weapon than a hunting knife, I swung to the left and hiked along, pretty fast too — but not so fast as the grizzly, whom I could see over my shoulder following. So I changed from a walk to a run, and so too did the grizzly. Then too late I discovered that I was on a blind alley — ahead of me was a wall of cliff with a ledge about ten feet high. There was nothing to do but make a jump for it, in the hope that I could pull myself up on the ledge. I could feel the grizzly's breath on my neck as I jumped. I caught the ledge with my fingers, but the rock was loose — my fingers slipped —" Tom took out his pipe while the listeners waited for the continuation. "And then what happened?" said one, impatiently. Then Tom said, "I died like a man." Tom Wilson, tall tale, *The Sky Line Trail, February, 1947*

Mts. Inglismaldie, Girouard and Peechee (northern peaks of the Fairholme Range) seen from Stoney Squaw Mountain

"[Banff] is one of the best localities imaginable for the vacation devoted entirely to hiking."	Archie Bell, *Sunset Canada*

CASCADE AMPHITHEATRE

~ High meadow circled by cliffs ~

Distance 8.2 km (5.1 mi)
Height Gain 550 m (1,800') + 155 m (500') return
Hiking Time 2 hr 7 min
1 hr 40 min return

Trailhead Follow the Mount Norquay Road north from the west Banff interchange on the Trans-Canada Highway. Drive 5.4 km (3.4 mi) and park at the ski area Parking Lot #2 on your left. (If open, the main lot on your right is closer.) Hike 0.4 km to the hiker's kiosk at the far end of the main winter parking lot (closed in summer). Map page 12.

Cascade Amphitheatre

Options There are scenic points on the slopes above the easy ridge at the far (south) end of the Amphitheatre. Stoney Squaw is a short trip from the same trailhead.

≈ This demanding route leads through pine forest with few viewpoints before the Amphitheatre. Just after crossing Forty Mile Creek, you see those three striking satellites of the Sawback Range: Edith, Louis and Fifi. The destination is a small high meadow surrounded by steep slopes of Cascade Mountain. You may see mountain goat high up these slopes and bighorn sheep on the Mount Norquay Road.

From Forty Mile Creek, the grade is stiff, the steepest sections coming near the end. On your return, after crossing Forty Mile Creek, you climb at a moderate grade to the parking lot.

The last water source is Forty Mile Creek. (Giardia warning.)

Cascade Mountain has fascinated travelers since man reached Banff. James Hector told Mary Schäffer Warren that he ascended the peak in 1858. There was a proposal to construct an inclined railway up Cascade Mountain. Another scheme suggested placing an airship station to launch Zeppelins from the summit.

The trailhead is at the base of Mt. Norquay, named for a giant (300 pound) man said to have made the first ascent about 1887. The Duchess of Somerset met John Norquay in 1889 in Winnipeg. "The most remarkable person we saw was Mons. Narquet [as she spelled his name], a half-breed, a most able man, who fifteen years had been premier [of Manitoba].... He was by far the most eloquent member of the House, and very proud of his Indian descent. In a former session he was jeered at for this by a Scotchman who should have known better. Narquet's reply, however, was so dignified that it silenced any further remarks, and left the member who had attacked him somewhat humiliated; it was to this effect, that he was proud of the Scotch blood in his veins, but still prouder of his Indian descent, knowing that an attack of the description to which he had been subjected would never have been made by an Indian." The duchess, née Susan McKinnon, was fiercely proud of her Gaelic ancestry and was piqued that it was a Scot who had shown prejudice.

Grant MacEwan gives a slightly different account of the incident. The opposition taunt was, "Now you're showing your Indian." Norquay bared his arm, replying, "I am proud of every drop of blood that flows in my veins."

Shortly after the Duchess met him, at age 48 John Norquay died of appendicitis.

Trail From the hiker's kiosk, cross the paved area between the ski buildings and follow the service road past the Cascade Chair and the Mystic Chair. Take the trail branching to the right, leaving the ski area (no trail sign, 1992).

Descend to Forty Mile Creek. The Creekside Trail — to the Edith Pass and Mystic Lake trails — turns left of the old fire road; stay on the road, making a sharp right turn, and proceeding downstream a short distance to a bridge where you cross Forty Mile Creek and turn left.

You ascend at a steady rate. Soon after you pass the Elk Lake Junction to your left, the grade gets even steeper, easing only as you enter the Amphitheatre.

Trail Section	km from	time out	return time
Gate at Parking Lot		↓	100 min
Ski Building	0.4	5 min	95 min
Trans-Canada Highway Tr. Jct.	1.2	13 min	86 min
Mystic Lake Trail Jct.	1.4	16 min	83 min
Creekside Tr. (Mystic L. Jct.)	3.5	38 min	54 min
Elk Lake Jct.	4.8	68 min	34 min
Cascade Amphitheatre	8.2	127 min	↑

"My brother and I selected Cascade Mountain as our training-ground, and the wearisome and arduous ascent gave us all the exercise we wanted for one day." J. Outram, *In the Heart of the Canadian Rockies*

STONEY SQUAW MOUNTAIN

~ Views of Bow and Cascade Valleys ~

Distance **2.2 km (1.4 mi)**
Height Gain **230 m (750')**
Hiking Time **43 min**
35 min return

Trailhead Follow the Mount Norquay Road north from the west Banff interchange on the Trans-Canada Highway. Drive 5.4 km (3.4 mi) and park at the ski area Parking Lot #2 on your left. (If open, the main lot on your right is closer.) The trail starts near the southeast end (on your right) of the Main parking lot. Map page 12.

Options You can make a loop to the parking lot, returning by a path north of the main trail. (From the summit, head down the rocky rib extending north of the main viewpoint; the trail soon becomes obvious. The way is less scenic, you come out atop a steep disused ski slope above the parking area, and at the end, you have to travel back 0.3 km through the parking lot, making the loop slightly longer.)

From the Mt. Norquay parking area, you also can hike to Cascade Amphitheatre, Edith Pass, Forty Mile Creek or the Stoney Squaw Bridle Path.

≈ This short hike is in trees most of the way. Many hikers stop at the false summit at the end of the obvious trail from where you get good views of the valley, the Fairholme Range, Cascade Mountain and Mt. Rundle. The true summit of Stoney Squaw is hidden in trees 50 m to your left (if you are looking at Cascade Mountain). Twenty metres beyond this point, an old cairn marks an opening with views to the west.

The grade is easy to moderate. There is no water on the trail.

The name Stoney Squaw predates 1884, and its origin is uncertain. There is a story that the name ties in with *Stoney Chief* which some people think is an old Indian name for Cascade Mountain. (James Hector named Cascade Mountain in 1858, a translation of the name he learned from his Indian guides, *Mountain Where the Water Falls.*) According to another story the mountain name honours an unidentified Stoney woman who hunted on these slopes to provide for her sick husband.

Mountain sheep frequent the Mount Norquay Road leading to the parking area, especially the scenic Green Spot, a place with royal associations: in 1939 Jim Brewster drove King George VI and his queen here.

Trail From the trail sign, you ascend the forested western slope of the mountain. Except for a brief dip over a rock rib, you go uphill all the way, reaching a scenic opening 0.2 km before the summit of Stoney Squaw.

Trail Section	km from	time out	return time
Trailhead		↓	35 min
Summit	2.2	43 min	↑

Bighorn sheep chewing the cud

STONEY SQUAW BRIDLE PATH (TRANS-CANADA HIGHWAY)

~ Horse route ~

Distance **4.5 km (2.8 mi)**
Height Gain **30 m (100'); 335 m (1,100') return**
Hiking Time **1 hr 1 min**
1 hr 18 min return

Trailhead As for Stoney Squaw.

Alternately, start near the Buffalo Paddock or Forty Mile Creek bridge on the westbound side of the Trans-Canada Highway. Finding a nearby place to park is a problem. Map page 12.

≈ The path follows dense forest with little to see except for the vegetation (pine forest, calypsos in June, moss-covered trail higher up). It is used mainly by horses as a route from the corrals near the Buffalo Paddock to the network of trails at Forty Mile Creek.

Trail From the kiosk, cross the paved area between the buildings and follow the road past the Cascade Chair. After 0.6 km, turn right onto the bridle path (in 1992, the trail sign reads: *Trans-Canada Highway*).

Cross a bridge and ascend at an easy-to-moderate grade, then undulate until you reach a steady descent (stiff uphill on the return). The pine forest gives way to spruce and Douglas fir.

A short detour to the left, 0.4 km before the highway, leads to a viewpoint. After this, you pass two horse trails branching left to a ford. The hiking path bends right to end at a trail sign by the animal control fence. If you go left 50 m, you come to a highway access gate.

Trail Section	km from	time out	return time
Parking lot		↓	78 min
Trailhead	0.6	8 min	68 min
End of trail	4.4	60 min	1 min
Gate	4.5	61 min	↑

ELK LAKE

~ Quiet lake, larches, Mt. Brewster ~

Distance **14.3 km (8.9 mi)**
Height Gain **675 m (2,210'); 285 m (940') return**
Hiking Time **3 hr 41 min**
3 hr 19 min return

Trailhead Follow the Mount Norquay Road north from the west Banff interchange on the Trans-Canada Highway. Drive 5.4 km (3.4 mi) and park at the ski area Parking Lot #2 on your left. (If open, the main lot on your right is closer.) Hike 0.4 km to the hiker's kiosk at the far end of the main parking lot. Map p. 12.

Options You can return via Stony Creek and Cascade Fire Road. There is a backcountry campground at Elk Pass, near Elk Lake.

≈ This is a long trip and the trail is steep. Forest cover permits few views before the long snaking meadow at Elk Pass, not far from your destination. The lake is small, but it is so tight to Mt. Brewster that the cliffs are awesome, especially above the south end of the lake.

The mountain is named for John Brewster, a pioneer Banff dairyman whose four sons (Jim was the most famous) became noted guides, outfitters and tourist operators.

Elk Lake seems to be well named. On a September trip, I heard elk bugling on the slope of Cascade Mountain near Elk Pass. At the lake, I saw many end products of elk digestion.

About 1950, elk in Banff Park were culled to prevent overpopulation. After each elk was shot, a warden took a blood sample to determine the animal's health. The warden would straddle the carcass to get a knife in the neck.

Wardens Neil Wooledge and Ernie Young got a surprise when they worked together on this job. Young approached one fallen stag which seemed dead. When he straddled it, the elk leapt to its feet and commenced to run. The helpless warden, still on the animal's back, hollered to his startled companion, "Shoot, Neil, shoot!" Naturally, Wooledge couldn't shoot an elk with a man riding it. Fortunately, the dying beast collapsed after a dozen bounds.

Trail Follow the service road beyond the ski lodge. Shortly (100 m) after the Mystic Chair, turn right onto the trail marked only with a no cycling sign (1992) and take this to Forty Mile Creek. Your trail makes a sharp right down stream to a bridge after which there is a stiff climb to the Cascade Amphitheatre Junction where you turn left.

Head through a mature second growth forest on a trail high above the valley floor. The forest begins to open shortly before you enter the long, snaking meadow at Elk Pass.

Just before the pass, there is a turnoff to Elk Lake Summit Campground. The campsite is tucked in trees to your left near a tiny stream which disappears just before it reaches the main trail.

At the pass you turn left to Elk Lake. (The main trail continues across the summit to Stony Creek and the Cascade Fire Road.)

The path to the lake angles up a ridge to its crest, then descends to Elk Lake.

Mt. Brewster and Elk Lake

Trail Section	km from	time out	return time
Parking Lot		↓	199 min
Ski buildings	0.4	5 min	194 min
Trans-Canada Highway Tr. Jct.	1.2	13 min	185 min
Mystic Lake Jct.	1.4	16 min	182 min
Creekside Tr. (Mystic L. Jct.)	3.3	40 min	154 min
Forty Mile Creek Bridge	3.5	43 min	151 min
Cascade Amphitheatre Jct.	4.8	69 min	134 min
Bridge	7.9	110 min	95 min
Elk Pass and Ek 13	11.7	179 min	38 min
Elk Lake	14.3	221 min	↑

ELK LAKE from STONY CREEK

Distance **12.6 km (7.8 mi) from Cascade Fire Road***
Height Gain **380 m (2,900')**
Hiking Time **3 hr 28 min**
2 hr 57 min return

Trailhead From the east Banff interchange on the Trans-Canada Highway turn north onto the Lake Minnewanka Road. Drive 3.6 km (2.2 mi) and turn left to the Upper Bankhead parking area. Hike or cycle 15.3 km to Stony Creek via the Cascade Fire Road. The trailhead is on your left, shortly before the Stony Creek Bridge. Map page 13.

Options From Elk Pass, you can hike via the Mount Norquay trailhead back to Banff. You can stay overnight at backcountry campgrounds at Stony Creek and at Elk Pass (permit required) or at Stony Creek Camp (reserve through Holiday on Horseback, Banff).

≈ Most of the grade to Elk Lake is easy. You are more likely to meet equestrians than hikers on this remote route.

The Cascade Valley is prime grizzly country. In 1989, park naturalist Mike Potter was confronted by an aggressive bear near the campground at Stony Creek.

Potter dropped his pack and climbed a tree. First, the grizzly bolted. But after rearing on its hind feet, it approached and circled the tree. Discovering the pack, it ripped it open and devoured the gorp inside. Mike detailed the encounter in Banff's *Crag and Canyon.*

The grizzly the pursued Mike up the tree, "slowly but methodically, including grabbing at branches with his teeth to haul up on....

"I scrambled to get higher: soon finding myself in the very crown of the tree. I knelt up on two branches about an inch in diameter, so as not to leave a leg dangling that it could grab.... The bear kept coming up until it was two metres or less below me, then stopped — apparently because the branches would not support its weight (I had broken one myself)." The bear went part way down the tree. Several times it came back up, always stopping where the branches were too narrow for its weight. Finally, it went to the bottom, where it began shaking the tree before finally leaving. Potter estimates the bear climbed 13 m up the tree.

Trail At the trail sign, there is a confusing diversity of trails (old roads, horse routes from a rider's camp, foot trails). Take the main path heading left of the road (west). It shows a lot of horse use and leads to a ford. After 0.5 km, take a trail angling right to the first bridge. If you miss it and find yourself at the ford, go upstream and you should find the bridge in a couple of minutes.

Cross Stony Creek and Cascade River on successive footbridges, then enter a narrow valley which you ascend for 2.3 km to an open plateau. Here you turn south and cross a bridge.

Continue south, climbing steadily, and passing in and out of timber until you reach the long curving meadow leading to Elk Pass.

At the pass, turn right for Elk Lake.

Note: If you come from Upper Bankhead, at 6.7 km you cross the Cascade River by a footbridge. A little before the bridge, horses take a prominent detour left to a ford. Don't take this detour.

Trail Section	km from	time out	return time
Stony Creek Trailhead *		↓	177 min
Stony Creek Bridge	0.6	9 min	167 min
Cascade River Bridge	0.9	14 min	163 min
Bridge	3.2	54 min	130 min
Elk Pass	10.0	166 min	38 min
Elk Lake	12.6	208 min	↑

* From Upper Bankhead via Cascade R. Fire Road, add:
Distance 15.3 km (9.2 mi)
Cycling Time 1 hr 40 min; 1 hr 10 min return
Height Gain 285 m (930'); 110 m (360') return.

People used to say grizzlies can't climb trees. This one is on its way down a larch. It tried to reach two campers, but turned back when the tree began swaying. Photo, Kelly Smith.

MYSTIC LAKE

~ Quiet green lake, rocky cirque ~

Distance 12.3 km (7.6 mi) from Fm 10
Height Gain 185 m (610')
Hiking Time 3 hr 3 min
2 hr 53 min return

Trailhead Fm 10 Campground. Alternately, Fm 19 or Ml 22 campgrounds, or Mount Norquay Parking Lot. Map page 12.

Options You can go on to Mystic Pass and Johnston Creek. Although it is possible to make a long day hike from Banff to Mystic Lake, most visitors use one of the nearby campgrounds, permitting a less frenzied visit. You can also stay at Mystic Camp (reserve through Holiday on Horseback, Banff — for details, see page 23).

≈ I associate this placid tarn with wildlife. On my first visit to Mystic Lake in 1970, I saw a distant wolverine loping east along the lake-shore. As I watched through binoculars, a mature grizzly emerged from the woods, 100 m to my right. While I was assessing my situation, a second bear appeared. The bruins headed west toward the wolverine. I didn't wait to see if the converging predators ever met.

Wolverine on a patch of snow

The earliest record of a visit to Mystic Lake was 1891, when the great Stony Indian guide, William Twin, brought Bill and Jim Brewster here. William told the young boys, who were 11 and 9 years old respectively, "Mystic Lake was the lake where fish were like fallen leaves." It is still popular with anglers.

In 1923, Leonard Leacock, his brother Ernie, and three chums: Jack Brown, Eric Stewart and Earle Birney (who became one of Canada's greatest poets) spent four days at Mystic Lake. They went via Edith Pass and Forty Mile Creek. When they reached Mystic Lake, Leacock was enchanted. He wrote, "We hurried forward and in a few minutes one of the most beautiful little lakes in the Rockies lay sleeping at our feet.

"Across it the great rock wall towered to the sky and a little star peeped out.... The lake lay in a cup-like basin, three sides being formed by the mountain, the other by the hill on which we were standing. On two sides were huge rock slides, while opposite was a forest that sloped up to a cliff.... The only sound came from a little waterfall on the other side. And the indescribable colour of the water — a deep green that merged into a deeper green where the shadows darkened the surface! For a while we stood there overawed by the solemn and splendid grandeur of the scene."

Years later, memories of Mystic Lake and a nearby CPR cabin (no longer standing) would provide Earle Birney with the setting for his poem *Bushed.*

The boys had rather poor luck angling, catching only a few trout at what is usually a good fishing lake. Birney blamed this on Leonard who had disturbed the others when he wakened at 4 am with his feet sticking out of the tent in the cold. "Earle said the fish must have seen my feet during the night and had been so frightened they had sought the deepest parts of the lake in safety. I told him fish couldn't see in the dark. 'Then,' he said, 'they must have smelt them.'"

When they returned, the boys had difficulty with the horse's pack. Ernie and Jack thought they knew how to tie the diamond hitch, and had been given a review by Jack Cooley, who loaned them a packhorse for the trip. Leacock recalls, "Every mile the pack fell off. We took turns trying and found twenty ways of tying the diamond hitch. None of them worked."

Trail See Forty Mile Summit: *Trail*, p. 131. At Mystic Lake Junction turn left. Cross the bridge at Forty Mile Creek and loop to the right around the warden cabin to a junction (right) from Fm 19 Campground. Keep ahead.

There are steep sections to Ml 22 Campground (left). One kilometre after the campground, you reach the Mystic Lake Junction. Turn left to the lake, 500 m ahead.

Trail Section	km from	time out	return time
Fm 10 Campground		↓	173 min
Horse Camp Jct.	5.9	94 min	82 min
Mystic Lake Jct.	8.1	122 min	55 min
Warden Cabin	8.2	124 min	53 min
Fm 19 Jct.	8.3	126 min	51 min
Ml 22 Campground	10.8	162 min	18 min
Mystic Lake Jct.	11.8	176 min	6 min
Mystic Lake	12.3	183 min	↑

MYSTIC LAKE SHORTCUT from Fm 19

If you are staying at Mystic Junction Campground (Fm 19), you can reach Mystic Lake via this shortcut to the Warden Cabin which follows west of Forty Mile Creek instead of the east side.

Trail Section	km from	time out	return time
Fm 19		↓	9 min
Warden Cabin Jct.	0.8	8 min	↑

FORTY MILE SUMMIT

MYSTIC PASS

~ Rugged alpine pass ~

Distance 10.9 km (6.8 mi) Ml 22 to Jo 9
Height Gain 340 m (1,110') from Ml 22; 550 m (1,800') return
Hiking Time 2 hr 45 min
3 hr 1 min return

Trailhead Campground Ml 22. Alternately, Larry's Camp (Jo 9) or Mystic Camp (see page 23). Map p. 12.

Options This trail connects destinations in Forty Mile Creek Valley with Johnston Creek's trails. You can make a detour to Mystic Lake.

≈ During my four trips over the pass, I have met only one pair of hikers. It's hardly surprising that it's not more popular because on the Johnston Creek side, the trail is not up to the usual park standard: it is very steep near the top; sections are overgrown, faint or covered with loose gravel; part of the route is flooded by seasonal streams; passing the big rockslide the way is obscure (watch for cairns on either side of the route).

On the Mystic Lake side, the trail is better, but expect a stiff climb.

If you are undaunted by the trail condition, the rewards are dramatic views of the stark terrain near Mystic Pass.

Trail From Campground Ml 22, climb to the Mystic Lake Junction. Keep ahead. Switchback up the forest to an alpine hillside above the mound of an ancient moraine.

Cross the pass to begin the very steep descent. When you reach the Johnston Creek Trail, turn left to Jo 9 and Johnston Canyon.

Trail Section	km from	time out	return time
Mystic Lake Campground		↓	181 min
Mystic Lake Jct.	1.0	14 min	170 min
Mystic Pass	4.4	74 min	125 min
Johnston Creek Jct.	10.8	163 min	2 min
Campground Jo 9	10.9	165 min	↑

~ Backpacker route ~

Distance 23.9 km (14.8 mi)
Height Gain 725 m (2,375'); 235 m (765') return
Hiking Time 5 hr 43 min
5 hr 22 min return

Trailhead Follow the Mount Norquay Road north from the west Banff interchange on the Trans-Canada Highway. Drive 5.4 km (3.4 mi) and park at the ski area Parking Lot #2 on your left. (If open, the main lot is closer.) Hike 0.4 km to the hiker's kiosk at the far end of the main winter parking lot (closed in summer). Map page 12.

Options You can stay at Fm 10 or Fm 19 Campgrounds on the way. Most hikers use this route to reach Flint's Park en route to Badger Pass and Pulsatilla Pass. You can make side trips to Sawback Lake and Rainbow Lake.

≈ Walter Wilcox traveled down Forty Mile Creek in 1895, and called the route "absolutely the worst traveling I have anywhere met with in the Rockies. The horses were compelled to make long detours among the dead timber, and the axe was frequently required to cut out a passage-way.... We had only found a small insignificant axe-mark on some dead tree, about once in every quarter mile, or often none at all during hours of progress."

Today, a good trail with an easy-to-moderate grade follows the valley, but since it is a circuit used by trail riders, portions may be muddy. The country is remote and seldom visited except by equestrians. If you go on to Flint's Park, be aware that you are in prime grizzly country.

Much of the time you are in forest, but there are frequent openings. You get views of Mt. Louis and the Sawback Range from the meadow at the pass.

Upstream from the Mystic Lake junction, the main trail is muddy and there are four fords. A recently constructed hiker bypass provides a drier route to the pass.

At Mystic Camp (run by Holiday on Horseback) a marten was observed sliding down sloping tent roofs on rainy days. Martens can be playful, but the one at the Castle Junction Youth Hostel went too far when, in the outhouse, it nipped a young man in the privates.

Forty Mile Creek is a railway name: the railway bridge over the creek is forty miles from the old siding at Morley.

Trail From the hiker's kiosk, cross the paved area between the ski buildings and follow the road past the Cascade Chair and the Spirit Chair to the junction with the Cascade Amphitheatre Trail and turn left, taking the Mystic Lake Trail.

You climb steeply to an old junction with Cascade Amphitheatre. Keep ahead, pass a *no bicycling* sign, then begin a long descent to Forty Mile Creek. Just before the bridge, another junction (Creekside Trail) branches right to Cascade Amphitheatre.

Cross Forty Mile Creek and follow the wide trail past the Edith Pass junction (left) and backcountry Campground Fm 10 (right). There is a short separation between the hiking and horse trail at the Holiday on Horseback outfitter's camp junction.

Keep ahead at the Mystic Lake junction (left). Just before Campground Fm 19, the hiker bypass trail turns off right. It rejoins the main trail near the Summit.

Trail Section	km from	time out	return time
Gate at Parking Lot		↓	322 min
Ski Building	0.4	5 min	317 min
Trans-Canada Highway Jct.	1.2	13 min	308 min
Mystic L., Forty Mile Creek Jct.	1.4	16 min	305 min
Creekside Trail Jct.	4.3	55 min	261 min
Edith Pass Jct.	6.2	81 min	237 min
Fm 10 Campground	8.4	114 min	210 min
Horse Camp Jct.	14.3	208 min	119 min
Mystic Lake Jct.	16.5	236 min	92 min
Hiker Bypass and Fm 19 Jct.	17.0	244 min	86 min
Horse Trail Jct.	22.6	322 min	17 min
Forty Mile Summit	23.9	343 min	↑

Mystic Lake

"The trail across to Johnston Creek is not very good and there are a couple of very steep hills. Before reaching the divide we came across a glacier-fed lake about one-half mile in diameter, which is full of trout averaging about one pound in weight. On the evening of 30th August we pitched our camp on the summit of the Sawback Range above timber line. Next morning we made the ascent of a mountain to the right of the pass.... On the morning of 1st September ... it was snowing.... We made a trip to the lake and caught two dozen trout."

J. J. McArthur, describing Mystic Lake and Mystic Pass, *Survey Report 23rd January, 1891*

Mystic Pass and Sawback Range

"The trail down to Johnston Creek is very steep in places and has not been much travelled of late. The slope of the mountains to the north of where we struck the creek is strewn with crinoid fossils." J. J. McArthur, *Survey Report 23rd January, 1891*

TUNNEL MOUNTAIN

~ Panoramic views ~

Distance **2.3 km (1.4 mi)**
Height Gain **305 m (1,000')**
Hiking Time **43 min**
29 min return

Trailhead Follow St. Julien Road (turn east off Banff Avenue via Moose or Wolf Street); shortly after you pass the angled junction to Grizzly Street, turn left (uphill) to the parking lot with the trail sign, just north of the Banff Centre. Map page 12.

Options You can shorten the hike by driving to the upper trailhead (the trail sign on Tunnel Mountain Drive, south of the junction with Tunnel Mountain Road); this way, you miss the steepest section of trail and reduce the height gain by 45 m. Of the many other trails at Banff you can take, the closest is the Hoodoos Trail, starting on Tunnel Mountain Drive.

Anne Ness. Photo, courtesy Henry Ness.

≈ In 1858, James Hector named this diminutive peak *The Hill*. In 1882, Major Rogers planned to construct a tunnel through this mountain for the railway line, not realizing he could easily avoid the problem of the cliffs above the Bow River by following the Cascade River and going north of *The Hill*. When CPR General Manager William Van Horne saw Rogers' plans he was furious. "Are we going to hold up this railway for a year and a half while they build their damned tunnel? Take it out!" So the tunnel was never built, but the mountain name commemorates Rogers' intended folly.

There used to be a fire lookout on the peak, called King's Lookout because King George VI and Queen Elizabeth hiked there in 1939.

Connoisseurs of mountain beauty have a deep affection for this trip. James Outram recommended hiking up Tunnel, commenting, "the view will never be forgotten." He went up it in 1900, his first climb in the Rockies. A year later, he made the first ascent of Mt. Assiniboine. Thus in one year, Outram became the first man to climb both the highest and perhaps the lowest summits in Banff Park.

Others have praised the trip. The late Jon Whyte chose Tunnel as his favorite hike near Banff. The ashes of famed wildlife artist Carl Rungius are scattered on Tunnel Mountain, a site his closest friends considered appropriate for a man who loved the view of Banff and the Bow Valley. Stoney Indian Noah Cecil said his grandfather helped carry a dying tribesman atop Tunnel Mountain, and erect a teepee for his departing spirit, commenting, "A man's a long time dead. On mountain he see more." (Harriet Hartley Thomas, *From Barnacle to Banff*)

No one loved this hike more than Anne Ness who went up Tunnel more than 8,000 times! For forty years she climbed it every day, missing only a few times in bitterest winter. Some days, she climbed it twice: first during slack time at work; then again in the evening. Norman Sanson is renowned for his 1,000 ascents of Sulphur Mountain; Anne Ness' record deserves similar recognition.

Not everyone shares this passion for hiking or love of superb scenery. One friend asked Anne, "Don't you find it boring?" But as A. O. Wheeler pointed out, "Although only 5500 feet in altitude above sea level, the summit is a magnificent viewpoint, covering the Bow River valley both east and west. The chief advantage is that, set at a position … midway between the valley bottom and the crests of the encircling mountain ranges, it does full value in perspective to the depths and to the heights."

When Jim Brewster was a small boy, he was given a horse to round up his father's dairy cows. Many mornings, he found the steed at the top of Tunnel Mountain. He was convinced it went there to watch the sunrise.

Leonard Leacock used to hike here to listen to the massed pipe band when Banff hosted the Highland Gatherings (before 1930). Although Leacock hated the sound of the bagpipes, he found them thrilling from a distance. Marching bands can still be heard from the site on ceremonial occasions such as Canada Day, July 1, but I find this distance too great to thrill to the small bands I have heard in recent years.

Most of the grade is easy to moderate; there are a few short steep sections, especially near the trailhead.

After you reach the summit ridge, views open east to Lake Minnewanka, Mount Aylmer and the Fairholme Range.

This is a hike for all seasons. The west-facing slope at the start loses snow early, so except for a few weeks when the path is icy this trail makes a great spring training climb to get in shape for longer trips. In summer, cool shady sections combine with scenic openings to provide delights. So many people now do this trip from the Banff Centre in winter, that the trail is usually packed.

Douglas firs can be seen all the way to the summit. Beside the trail, Crocuses bloom in May. Mule deer frequent the slopes. Photographer Halle Flygare got a superb picture of a cougar on the mountainside.

Be wary of the sheer cliffs near the summit ridge, especially if the trail is icy. Among the mountain's victims is a twelve year old boy killed in 1952 when trying to take a shortcut from the summit to the campground.

Bikes are not permitted on the trail.

Trail From the parking lot, you climb steeply, zig-zagging to a viewpoint where you cross Tunnel Mountain Drive.

You continue to switchback upwards and the rewards increase as you gain height. You are almost in line with the Banff Springs Hotel when you reach the summit ridge. The trail moves to the east side of the mountain where there are breathtaking viewpoints atop the sheer cliff en route to the summit.

Trail Section	km from	time out	return time
Trailhead		↓	29 min
Tunnel Mountain Drive	0.3	9 min	23 min
Summit Ridge	1.9	34 min	7 min
Summit	2.3	43 min	↑

Mount Rundle from Tunnel Mountain

Mt. Aylmer above Mt. Astley and Lake Minnewanka (frozen) from Tunnel Mountain. Douglas firs frame the view.

Goat Range and Sulphur Mountain from Tunnel Mountain

"One of [Stewart's] greatest works is the partial ascent of Tunnel Mountain by a carriage road. The different glimpses of the valley from this road are perfectly superb. The mountain is 1,000 feet above the valley. The carriage road ascends about half way, and the rest of the distance there is a bridle path. The top of this mountain is long and narrow, and from its crest, there is a grand view both ways. I went to the top of this mountain, Mr. Stewart kindly acting as guide,

Banff Hoodoos above Bow River Valley

Brewster Creek Hoodoos *(see page 158)*

and one of the ladies of the party pluckily accompanying us all the way. It does not look much, but I shall remember it as one of the hardest pulls I ever had. From the top of this mountain the view is very fine."

Charles E. D. Wood, 1890, *Macleod Gazette, quoted in Alberta History, Summer, 1977*

HOODOOS Trail

~ Douglas firs, views of Mt. Rundle ~

Distance 5.0 km (3.1 mi)
Height Gain 105 m (350'); 50 m (170') return
Hiking Time 1 hr 8 min from Bow Falls
1 hr 4 min return

Trailhead The Bow Falls Viewpoint on Tunnel Mountain Drive, near the Banff Fine Arts Centre. You can reach this site from Banff Avenue by turning east (left if you are coming from downtown Banff) on Buffalo Street, then keeping right at the Cemetery.

Alternately, start at the Hoodoos Parking Lot on Tunnel Mountain Road, east of Tunnel Mountain Campground. Map page 12.

Options I like to start in Banff at the boat landing at Echo Creek, and follow the scenic Bow River shore, adding 2.1 km (25 min each way) to the hike. Also, you can go beyond the Hoodoos to the Cascade River.

There are alternate trails leading from Tunnel Mountain Campground and Douglas Fir Resorts which intersect this trail.

Tunnel Mountain from trail to Cascade River

≈ The view of the Hoodoos has long been famous. In 1914, it was even featured in the advertisement of the Park Liquor Store in Banff.

Although you can drive to the Hoodoos, there are bonus rewards if you take the trail: views of giant Douglas firs, the Fairholme Range and Mt. Rundle. Except for a few short sections, the trail is free of snow in late April.

The grade varies from gentle to moderate. There is no water on the way.

You might see and hear rock climbers on nearby cliffs of Rundle and Tunnel mountains.

The path follows the Bow River where CPR surveyor Major Rogers intended to build the railway, planning to blast a hole through Tunnel Mountain. At the last moment, surveyor Charles A. Shaw changed the route of the track, commenting, "I cannot understand why they failed to investigate the valley to the west [of Tunnel Mountain]. Rogers' location here was the most extraordinary blunder I have ever known in the way of engineering."

Trail At the Bow Falls parking area, stairs lead down to the path. A branch right takes you to a view of the falls; go left. You descend to the level of the river, and after a short distance, the trail divides. The path to the right gives a better view of Tunnel Mountain. After four minutes of hiking, the alternate routes rejoin.

A little ahead, at a hill, the trail divides again. The obvious way is up a set of stairs, but when the river is low, there is an alternate detour by the riverbank. Both choices have some attractive viewpoints.

Where the routes rejoin, you go through a broad meadow, then gradually uphill to a small parking area beside Tunnel Mountain Road.

Cut across or loop around the parking area to continue the trail to the Hoodoos Parking Lot where an asphalt track leads to three viewpoints with interpretive displays.

Trail Section	km from	time out	return time
Bow Falls		↓	64 min
Campground Jct.	2.5	33 min	31 min
Hoodoos Parking Lot	4.0	62 min	5 min
Upper Display Viewpoint	5.0	68 min	↑

CASCADE RIVER

≈ This extension of the Hoodoos Trail is of more interest to cyclists than hikers. It is a good trail, although the route is not maintained and two hills are very steep. You climb 40 m, then descend 120 m to the riverbank.

Beside the trail, there are some large middens (mounds of debris from evergreen cones left by generations of squirrels). In early season, calypsos are common near the trail.

Trail After the Hoodoos, at the base of the long steep hill, the trail divides at a T-junction. Keep ahead for the Cascade River. If you go right, you reach the Bow River (about 8 minutes; after the power line cut, it's easier to walk). If you go left, you get to a steep hill above the Cascade River (about 6 minutes). There is more deadfall on these options than on the main trail.

Although the main path, ahead of the T-junction, has fallen trees, you can hop your bike over most of them (1992). It is 0.8 km from the T-junction to the fence atop the hill above the Cascade River. From here to the riverbank, 0.1 km below, the trail is very steep, narrow and rough. Leave your bike at the top of the hill.

Be warned that the Cascade River can rise quickly and unexpectedly when water is released from the power dam upstream.

Trail Section	km from	time out	return time
Hoodoos Parking Lot		↓	35 min*
Cascade River	3.7	30 min*	↑

* Cycling time

FENLAND

~ Interpretive trail, varied wetland habitat ~

Distance 1.5 km (0.9 mi) loop
Height Gain Negligible
Hiking Time 25 min circuit

Trailhead The Fenland picnic area, 0.4 km north of the CPR crossing on the Mount Norquay—Trans-Canada Highway connector road on the west side of Banff. If you are walking from Banff, you can pick up the trail at an unsigned trailhead north of the rail crossing. Map page 12.

Options You can hike or cycle this short trail. You can continue on the scenic Vermilion Lakes road by a connecting path.

≈ This is a self-guiding nature walk. You pass through a rich breeding ground for birds and mammals. There are opportunities to see beaver, bald eagle and osprey in a variety of habitats near the banks of Forty Mile Creek which loops beside First Vermilion Lake on its way to Echo Creek and the Bow River. (Forty Mile Creek becomes Echo Creek where it meets the outlet stream from Vermilion Lakes.) Interpretive pamphlets for the self-guiding trail are available at the trailhead.

In early June the trail is often closed because an elk uses the area to raise her calf. In calving season, cow elk become aggressive (several people getting too close to these animals have been seriously injured, especially at this time of year); it is dangerous as well as illegal to use the trail when it is closed.

In 1887, visitor W. S. Caine was enchanted by the beauty of the nearby Vermilion Lakes. He wrote, "I cannot find words adequately to describe the unique charms of the primitive and unspoiled scenery."

Trail If you start at the picnic site, cross the bridge after #1 interpretive site. At the far end of the bridge, the trail divides three ways at a T-junction. The path to the left leads away from the Fenland, following the other side of the creek back to the road. Go ahead. At all other junctions, turn clockwise if you wish to visit the interpretive sites in sequence. If you go clockwise, note that the paths to the left lead away from the Fenland Trail to the Banff and Vermilion Lakes roads.

Trail Section	km from	time out	return time
Trailhead		↓	25 min
Return	1.5	25 min	↑

Henry Ness atop a giant midden (see p. 138)

Cascade Mountain and Cascade River from extension of Hoodoo trail

Spray River, Mt. Norquay and Mt. Brewster from the Spray River Circuit. The Quarry bridge shows below the Banff Springs Hotel.

Mt. Nestor and Spray River

Coyote

"All these [game animals and bears] Mr. Stewart proposes strictly to preserve and encourage, while at the same time he will endeavour to exterminate all those animals which prey upon others, such as wolves, coyotes, foxes, lynxes, skunks, wild cats, catamounts, panthers, and porcupines, together with such birds of prey as feed upon fish."

W. S. Caine, reporting National Park Policy, 1887, *A Trip Round the World*

SPRAY RIVER

~ Good cycling road ~

Distance 46.7 km (29.0 mi)
Height Gain 875 m (2,870'); 510 m (1,680') return
Cycling Time 4 hr 3 min
3 hr 30 min return

Trailhead From Banff, go to the parking area at the end of Spray Avenue, just past the Banff Springs Hotel. Maps page 12 and 14.

Options You can return to the Golf Course via the east side of the Spray River for the last 5.9 km; the distance is 1 km farther, but there is less climbing.

If you have a second car, you can make a through trip from parking areas in Kananaskis Country: at Spray Lakes (Mt. Shark or Canyon Dam), or Goat Creek (White Man's Pass). You climb more if you start at Banff. There are three campgrounds beside the fireroad (Sp 16, Sp 23, Sp 35).

Tree near Fortune Cabin, clawed by a grizzly

≈ This is a good cycling road. There are some steep hills, especially between campgrounds Sp 23 and Sp 35. Be alert for washouts from spring runoff streams. Park policy is not to repair such obstacles so long as the road is passable.

At 8.7 km, a side road on the east leads to the mouth of Goat Creek. The Spray River was dammed above the confluence, but in the last few years, the dam was destroyed. It takes 5 minutes to hike the 0.5 km to the site.

The largest of the Spray Lakes was originally named Trout Lake, and fishing was good. In 1899, Walter Wilcox caught four fish within an hour, two of them nine and ten pounds.

In 1900 a scandalous example of irresponsibility and incompetence occurred in this valley. Two brothers named Walling had hired three Swiss guides to attempt Mt. Assiniboine. The brothers failed to make the climb, and on the return, the outfitters went to Canmore with most of the horses. Failing to keep up with the Swiss going down the Spray to the Banff Springs Hotel, the Wallings got lost. The disgruntled guides waited a day to report the missing dudes. The brothers were found within fifty yards of the road, making no attempt to go farther, having killed a saddle horse for meat.

Outfitter Pat Brewster got an early start in the guiding business, leading a trip up the Spray River to the Spray Lakes in 1904 when he was 8 years old. He was called the youngest guide in Canada. "I had been there before, you see; I knew how to get there.... Of course there was a packer with me, a trail man, but I showed them the way."

Pat remembered guide Fred Tabuteau taking a pair of dudes camping up the Spray. When supper was ready, Fred called his guests and the other wranglers to eat while the food was hot. The man haughtily replied that his wife wasn't accustomed to eating with the staff. Fred replied, "I quite understand, Sir. Go back and tell her that we'll be finished soon."

Several place names go back to the 1925 Wheeler Walking Tours which approached Mt. Assiniboine by this valley. Wheeler's main camp at Spray Lake, *Trail Centre*, now is only the name of a trailhead. *Rink's Camp* recalls Wheeler's packer, Ralph Rink. Another of Wheeler's camps, *Eau Claire Camp* (his packers pronounced it *You Claire*), originated with the Eau Claire logging company which had timber rights in the Spray River Valley.

Near the corral at Fortune Warden Cabin, I found a couple of pines which a grizzly has clawed. Bear authority Brian Horejsi says no one knows why a grizzly does this; perhaps only to show it has been there. If he's trying to show how high he can reach, this bruin has me beat by a couple of metres.

Trail The route, following an old fireroad, is obvious. Don't cycle too fast: in 1992, there were three washouts, one near Sp 16, the others upstream of Sp 23 where the road is on the east side of the Spray River. Also, every time I have traveled this road, I have seen bear tracks on the road; a speeding cyclist might surprise a bear.

Trail Section	km from	time out	return time
Trailhead (Banff Springs Hotel)		↓	210 min
Spray River East Jct.	5.9	27 min	184 min
Goat Creek Trail Jct.	10.2	53 min	167 min
Sundance Trail Jct.	12.5	67 min	159 min
Sp 16	15.9	80 min	148 min
Sp 23 & Spray R. Cabin	24.0	115 min	113 min
Bridge (Spray R.)	24.5	119 min	109 min
Sp 35	35.7	193 min	48 min
Fortune Warden Cabin	37.2	208 min	39 min
Park boundary	39.4	219 min	30 min
Canyon Dam Jct.	41.0	229 min	20 min
Bryant Creek, Mt. Shark Jct.	46.7	243 min	↑

SPRAY RIVER Circuit

Distance 12.5 km (7.8 mi)
Height Gain 75 m (250')
Hiking Time 2 hr 31 min circuit

Options There are many variations of the circuit possible. You can complete the trip by hiking from the Hotel to the Golf Course, though it is easier to use the Quarry Bridge to get back to your trailhead. (The Quarry Bridge is near the site where stone was cut for the Banff Springs Hotel.) There are two routes from the west road to the east road via the Quarry bridge: the distance is 1.0 km if you take the lower route directly to the Golf Course, or 1.1 km if you come out up the valley near the Mt. Rundle Trail.

Another option from the Quarry Bridge is to go upstream on a horse trail on the east bank to a ford. The distance from the Bridge is 1.6 km. The rough trail is easier to hike than cycle and offers some of the best views in the vicinity of the Circuit Trail.

Campground Sp 6 permits overnight stays.

≈ This circuit is popular with cyclists, hikers and joggers.

The fulcrum of the route is the footbridge over the Spray River which rests on the concrete foundation of a structure built during World War I. The men who made the original bridge were immigrants, most of them Ukrainians. Many had fled the Austrian Empire to avoid conscription. In 1915, they were interned because some people feared they might return to Europe and join the army of Austria.

You pass the site of the Youth Hostel. In 1984 a new Hostel was built on Tunnel Mountain and the old structures here were removed from here.

Trail The route follows the Spray River Fireroad 5.9 km to a picnic site where you turn left and cross the Spray River to return down the fireroad on the east side.

Trail Section	km from	time out	return time
Trailhead (Banff Springs Hotel)		↓	151 min
Quarry Bridge Jct.	0.7	7 min	144 min
Youth Hostel site	3.7	42 min	109 min
Sulphur Mtn. Highline Jct.	4.1	55 min	96 min
Spray River East, bridge	5.9	70 min	81 min
Campground Sp 6	6.6	78 min	73 min
Quarry Jct.	10.4	125 min	26 min
Mt. Rundle Jct.	11.0	133 min	18 min
Elk fence site	11.4	138 min	13 min
Quarry Bridge Jct.	11.6	141 min	10 min
Golf Course Road	11.8	144 min	7 min
Bridge	12.4	149 min	2 min
Bow Falls Parking Lot	12.5	151 min	↑

GOAT CREEK

~ Cycling route ~

Distance 7.6 km (4.7 mi) Smith-Dorrien—Spray Trail to Spray River Fireroad
Height Gain 70 m (225'); 250 m (825') return
Cycling Time 35 min (2 hr 2 min hiking)
40 min return (2 hr 20 min hiking)

Trailhead From Canmore, take the rough gravel road toward Spray Lakes. Cross the narrow pass, and turn right to the parking area, 8.8 km from downtown Canmore (8 Ave. and 8 St.) or 5.3 km from the Nordic Centre. Map page 12.

Alternately, from Banff go to the parking area at the end of Spray Avenue, just past the Banff Springs Hotel. Follow the Spray River Fireroad 9.5 km to the Goat Creek Junction.

Options You can start from Banff or from a trailhead near White Man's Pass, 0.8 km outside Banff Park. Most people prefer the latter choice because the trip is mostly downhill.

You can follow the Spray River Fireroad — on foot or bicycle — up river (to Spray Lakes and Bryant Creek) or down river (to Banff). If you go to Banff, you can take either the east or the west side of the Spray River Circuit for the last 5.9 km.

≈ You are in trees most of the way. Except for the Goat Range, you get mere glimpses of the mountains. There is an interesting view of Mt. Rundle from the bridge over the Spray River. It gets better if you go off trail a short way down the riverbank. On the return, you get a look at the steep cliff of Chinaman's Peak.

Although this is hardly a scenic route, the roadbed is good for cycling. Except for a steep hill down to the Goat Creek bridge, the grade is easy to moderate.

Trail From the parking area, follow the old road to the park boundary. Shortly after, you reach the gravel fireroad which you follow to the Spray River Fireroad.

Trail Section	km from	time out	return time
Trailhead		↓	93 min
Spray River Fireroad	7.6	35 min	53 min
Sp 6, North Spray Rd. Jct.	11.9	60 min	27 min
Trailhead, Banff Springs Hotel	17.8	81 min	↑

A. O. Wheeler. By permission, Whyte Museum of the Canadian Rockies.

UPPER HOT SPRINGS from BANFF SPRINGS HOTEL

~ Quiet, short hike to the popular hot springs ~

Distance **2.0 km (1.2 mi)**
Height Gain **170 m (550')**
Hiking Time **28 min**
20 min return

Trailhead From Banff, go to the parking lot at the end of Spray Avenue, just past the Banff Springs Hotel. From the parking area, walk back toward the hotel parking lot. A trail sign with only a hiker symbol marks the trailhead on your left. Map p. 12.

Options You can carry on from the Hot Springs up Sulphur Mountain or via the Sulphur Mountain Highline trail to the Spray River Fireroad.

≈ This is a short path to the Upper Hot Springs. It follows the pipeline which used to carry warm sulphur water from the Kidney Springs to the Banff Springs Hotel swimming pool.

The grade varies from easy to moderate. You are in forest most of the way.

Trail From the trailhead, hike uphill for a minute to a trail sign to the Upper Hot Springs where you turn left. At 0.9 km, you cross the old roadway. At 1.4 km, you reach the new road shortly before the Rimrock Hotel. Here, the trail runs out and you must walk beside the road to where an unsigned wide track on the west side of the road provides a shortcut to the pool, just a minute away.

Trail Section	km from	time out	return time
Trailhead		↓	20 min
Upper Hot Springs (pool)	2.0	28 min	↑

SULPHUR MOUNTAIN HIGHLINE

~ Horse trail ~

Distance **3.9 km (2.4 mi) to Spray R. Fireroad**
Height Gain **30 m (100'); 185 m (600') return**
Hiking Time **46 min**
54 min return

Trailhead From downtown Banff, take Banff Avenue south across the Bow River Bridge and turn left onto Spray Avenue. After 0.1 km, branch right onto Sulphur Mountain Drive and follow it 3.3 km to the Upper Hot Springs. Go to the upper parking lot (to the right). The trailhead is near the southwest corner, above the Gondola terminal. Map page 12.

Options You can also hike the Spray River Circuit, returning to the Banff Springs Hotel. The trail up Sulphur Mountain also starts at the Hot Springs parking area.

≈ This is a forest route, with little to see except from a couple of avalanche slopes you pass. It is used mainly by horses. The way is rough, but a few cyclists try it.

The grade is easy to moderate.

Trail The route goes under the Gondola and crosses a streambed. At the far side, a satellite track to the site of a derelict dam above (85 m vertical), turns off right. Keep ahead. Follow the forested hillside of Sulphur Mountain, then descend to the Spray River Fireroad 4.1 km from the Banff Springs Hotel (see page 143). The pony trail proceeds to a ford of the Spray River, so use the road if you want to go farther.

Trail Section	km from	time out	return time
Upper Hot Springs		↓	68 min
Spray River Fire Road	3.9	46 min	14 min
Spray River East Bridge & Jct.	5.7	60 min	↑

Striped Coralroot orchids grow in moist shady locations in the Bow Valley.

Grizzly bears digging for roots

"When the snow begins to fall, the bears, plump and fat, resume the road back to their dens in the thick of the forests and hollows of rocks, there to pass the four sad wintry months in complete indolence, with no other pastime or occupation than that of sucking their four paws. If we may credit the Indians, each paw occupies the bear for one moon, (a month) and the task accomplished, he turns on the other side and begins to suck the second, and so on with the rest.... Where they go — what becomes of them during the period they carry their young — is a problem yet to be solved by our mountain hunters." Father P. J. De Smet, *Oregon Missions and Travels over the Rocky Mountains in 1845-46*

MOUNT RUNDLE

~ Strenuous hike to near timberline ~

Distance 4.6 km (2.9 mi)
Height Gain 565 m (1,850')
Hiking Time 1 hr 48 min
1 hr 8 min return

Trailhead From downtown Banff, cross the Bow River bridge. Turn left onto Spray Avenue and follow it 0.8 km (0.5 mi). Turn left onto Rundle Avenue, and follow it downhill, keeping right, 0.6 km (0.4 mi) to the Bow Falls parking area. Walk across the Spray River bridge and follow the golf course road 0.6 km to the trailhead on the right (south) side of the road. You will find the trail sign where a horse trail crosses the road. (You have just passed the fifteenth tee on your right.) Map page 12.

Options You can detour to the Spray River Circuit.

≈ Former warden Sid Marty says the many fatal accidents on Mt. Rundle cause staff to call it the 9,000' tombstone. Although First Peak is technically a simple climb, it is easy to get off route on the return; if you miss the best way through the cliffbands, you can find yourself in trouble. Mt. Rundle has taken a melancholy toll of victims, mostly novices who got off route. Inexperienced climbers should hire a guide.

Evening shower, Bow Valley, from Mt. Rundle trail. Photo, Leonard Leacock.

The route is intended for climbers. It can be enjoyed by hikers, but the views from this trail are inferior to those from Tunnel or Sulphur.

There is no other water en route.

Explorer John Palliser named this mountain for Methodist Missionary Rev. Robert Rundle, who climbed part way up a mountain nearby. Some people say this is what he climbed, but that seems unlikely. (See page 193)

Trail From the trailhead, the path loops to the right beside the fifteenth tee to another trail sign where you turn left. In about 5 minutes, you reach a junction at the former site of an animal fence (which never did keep elk off the golf course). Follow the wide trail ahead for five more minutes to where the Mt. Rundle trail turns off left. Watch carefully for the sign.

Here you begin to ascend the slopes of Mt. Rundle. You climb steadily through fairly open forest, but there is little to see until the trail crosses a wide gully, almost two thirds of the way. Soon after crossing a second gully, you come to the first of the switchbacks that bring you to open slopes where there are views of the Spray and Bow river valleys. The trail ends where the climbing routes begin. A sign points to the main routes up the first and second peaks of the mountain. This can be followed a short distance, but the way is very steep, and becomes faint. Also, from the end of the trail, you can follow 0.7 km to the start of a climbing route to the higher third peak. There is little to see on this section.

Trail Section	km from	time out	return time
Bow Falls Parking Lot		↓	68 min
Bridge	0.1	2 min	66 min
Trailhead (horse crossing)	0.7	7 min	61 min
Spray River Jct.	1.0	10 min	58 min
Mt. Rundle Jct.	1.7	19 min	50 min
First switchback	3.6	77 min	18 min
End of trail (sign to peaks)	4.6	108 min	↑

GRASSI'S LOOKOUT

~ Good view of Banff townsite ~

Distance 1.0 km (0.6 mi)
Height Gain 185 m (600')
Hiking Time 22 min
19 min return

Trailhead Park at the site of the old Clubhouse of the Alpine Club, a pull-off to your right as you drive to the Upper Hot Springs, 1.9 km from the traffic lights at the south end of the Bow River bridge. Map p. 12.

Options This trip makes a pleasant evening walk after a nearby hike such as Sulphur Mountain.

≈ This trail leads you from the site of the clubhouse of the Alpine Club of Canada to a scenic bluff on Sulphur Mountain. The path was built about 1925 by Lawrence Grassi who did volunteer work here. Guests called this Grassi's Lookout, honoring one of the most generous spirits who ever lived in these mountains.

A Canmore coal miner, Grassi was the finest trail builder, and one of the greatest mountain guides in the Rockies. He never accepted pay for his trail work or his guiding. Remains of benches he fashioned can be seen en route. Despite encroaching trees, you still get good views of Banff townsite and the surrounding mountains. Not maintained by the park, the trail is cleared periodically by Grassi's admirers.

Trail From the parking area, walk to the clearing where the clubhouse stood. Proceed uphill towards Sulphur Mountain to where a tiny stream enters the opening from the right. The trail commences here, running north and climbing several switchbacks to the viewpoint.

Trail Section	km from	time out	return time
Parking area		↓	19 min
Viewpoint	1.0	22 min	↑

GOLF COURSE to CANMORE NORDIC CENTRE (CANMORE—BANFF TRAIL)

~ Riverbank views ~

Distance 19.6 km (12.2 mi) Bow Falls to Nordic Centre
Height Gain 180 m (600')
Cycling Time 2 hr
1 hr 35 min return

Trailhead From downtown Banff, cross the Bow River bridge. Turn left onto Spray Avenue and follow it 0.8 km (0.5 mi). Turn left onto Rundle Avenue, and follow it downhill, keeping right, 0.6 km (0.4 mi) to the Bow Falls parking area. You can shorten the hike if you drive across the Spray River bridge 4.5 km east to the parking lot (and trail sign) at the farthest end of the golf course. Map page 12

Options The Spray River and Mount Rundle trails also start at the Golf Course. This trail is open to hikers and cyclists.

≈ The trail follows near the Bow River almost to the park boundary. After you pass the Cascade River, there are a few scenic places before you again enter forest. Near the Canmore Nordic Centre, you cross a scenic meadow, a grassed-over open pit mine from the final days of the Georgetown coal development.

Much of the route is rough: sections of loose rock near Banff, and bumpy ski trails and loose gravel near Canmore. The grade to the park boundary is easy. At this border, there is one steep hill.

This path has been incorporated into the National Trail, a modestly advertised project by the National Trail Association (organized in 1977) to construct a course from the Atlantic to the Pacific. In 1991, the local section of the undertaking extended from Barrier Lake to the Cave & Basin.

A tiny lake in a dark cirque by the golf course has been known, locally, as The Cauldron (or The Devil's Cauldron). About 1900, outfitter Bob Campbell said he went skating here each August. The pond froze after two cold nights.

Trail Follow the golf course road 4.5 km east to the trailhead, a small parking area on the south side of the sharp bend. (The road divides at the loop junction; the branch to the right is shorter.) The path leads to the river and follows near its bank until a hill near the park boundary.

If you go farther, you ascend to a ski road. The main route brings you to the Canmore Nordic Centre.

Trail Section	km from	time out	return time
Spray River Bridge		↓	115 min*
Trailhead	4.5	15 min	100 min
Cascade River confluence	7.3	36 min	79 min
Park boundary	13.1	85 min	33 min
Nordic ski trail	13.6	90 min	30 min
Meadow	16.5	106 min	17 min
Nordic Centre (Day Lodge)	19.6	120 min*	↑

* Slow cycling time.

Lawrence Grassi. By permission, Whyte Museum of the Canadian Rockies.

Above Mt. Rundle trail, looking west. Pilot Mountain, on the left, and Mount Cory, right of center, dominate the skyline.

"Douglas Dick was an interesting figure of those days. His favorite resort was Field, for the Mollisons [the Mollison sisters managed the CPR hotels at Field and Lake Louise] were the only women in the world of whom he had no fear. Neither tiger nor grizzly could strike more terror into the heart of the average man than a pretty girl could inspire in this old bachelor, who was reputed to have been a wealthy Ceylon tea planter and the victim of an unfortunate love affair. Many a time have I seen him make a dash out of the dining room at Banff, sometimes by way of a window, upon the arrival of some group of femininity, and thence by first train to Field. Yet, withal he was a most delightful companion

View from Sanson Peak, Sulphur Mountain. Mt. Aylmer and the Fairholme Range (Mts. Inglismaldie, Girouard and Peechee) show on the skyline. Lake Minnewanka is seen above Tunnel Mountain in the gap between Aylmer and Inglismaldie.

on the trail or in the woods. When, on rare occasions, he deigned to visit Banff, he indulged in the extraordinary custom of taking a midnight swim in the icy waters of the Bow below the hotel. One morning the hospitable and popular manager of the hotel, Mr. Mathews, said to me, rather excitedly, 'Have ye seen Douglas Dick? He said he was going for a swim last night, but no one has seen him since.' Telegrams were sent to Field. He was not there. The alarm was spread as Tom Wilson and the Mounted Police started a search. Three days later his body was found several miles down the river." Walter Wilcox, *American Alpine Journal, 1941*

SULPHUR MOUNTAIN (from Upper Hot Springs)

~ Superb panorama ~

Distance 5.3 km (3.3 mi) to top of gondola
Height Gain 645 m (2,110')
Hiking Time 1 hr 51 min
1 hr 6 min return

Trailhead From downtown Banff, take Banff Avenue south across the Bow River Bridge and turn left onto Spray Avenue. After 0.1 km, branch right onto Sulphur Mountain Drive and follow it 3.3 km to the Upper Hot Springs. Go to the upper parking lot (to the right). The trailhead is near the northwest corner, by the access road to the swimming pool. Map page 12.

Options From the end of the trail, you can continue north to Sanson Peak, or go south to a viewpoint on the west side of the summit ridge. You can descend by a disused road on the west side of Sanson Peak to a distant trailhead on the Sundance Canyon Road.

≈ The trail approximates the route of the Gondola. Though you are in trees all the way, views improve as you ascend. At the summit, you get a generous panorama, especially if you go to Sanson Peak.

Sanson Peak is named for Norman Sanson (1862-1949), meteorologist and director of the Banff Museum from 1896 to 1931. Starting from Banff, thus adding 3.5 km to the length of the trip, he ascended this peak more than a thousand times on foot or snowshoe.

In summer, he often had to make a hasty retreat to avoid electric storms. Once, when caught in the observatory, he noted, "With a deafening roar, the first flash struck the building, entered and leapt demoniacally along the wires from machine to machine, destroying everything in its path. Then it shot along the cable down the mountain slope and started a fire in the Upper Hot Springs bath house."

Frequently he climbed in vicious weather. One stormy day, it took him seven and a quarter hours to reach the summit. His long-haired collie contracted pneumonia on one trip. At times Sanson left sub-zero temperatures in the valley and climbed to Chinook-warmed upper currents. One wintry day it was -30° F as he left Banff; before he got to the Hot Springs, he froze a toe; when he reached the observatory, the wind had shifted from northeast to southwest and the temperature had risen to +4° F. Sometimes he was marooned overnight inside the observatory because of sudden blizzards.

Sanson had bachelor's habits. Once, warden Henry Ness returned from patrol to his Stoney Creek cabin to find a young helper and Sanson, who was collecting specimens for the Banff Museum, just finishing supper. The boy asked Sanson if they should wash the dishes. The older man replied, "No, just turn them over. We'll have them for breakfast."

Late hours were not unusual for this unmarried man. His friend Harry Leacock purchased a record of the national anthem, *God Save the King*, which he played when the meteorologist stayed too late. His guest always took the hint.

Sanson chose the site for the observatory, built, like this trail, in 1903; he made weekly, later biweekly, trips to record data. On July 1, 1931, a procession of townspeople accompanied him on his thousandth official ascent.

Always fit, when he was 70, Sanson still made the trip to the summit in less than two hours. At age 80, after hiking 13.7 km earlier in the day, he led a group up Sulphur Mountain to await the sunrise. In 1945, now 83, he climbed to the observatory, possibly for the last time, to observe a solar eclipse.

The meteorologist is credited with 32,000 km of hiking. He joined the Alpine Club of Canada in 1913 and in 1933 was a founding member and first president of the Skyline Hikers.

When he was 86, Sanson Peak was named in his honour. He died the following spring. A devout Anglican, he asked that his tombstone be inscribed, "Gone higher".

Not everyone shares Sanson's enthusiasm for climbing Sulphur Mountain. Calgary Eye-Opener editor Bob Edwards said, "There are two kinds of fools in the world; those who have not been up Sulphur Mountain, and those who have been up more than once." In the 1950's, a tractor pulled tourists in a trailer to a resthouse half way up the mountain. The gondola was built in 1959. In the Zeppelin era, there was a proposal to build an airship station on the summit.

There is no water en route. You can detour to a waterfall on the way (Giardia warning).

Mountain sheep frequent the high slopes.

Trail The trail sign is found by a service road to the Hot Springs at the north end of the upper parking lot.

Head straight up the mountainside on a roadway which turns right, then, after 100 m, makes an abrupt switchback left (don't continue ahead on the service road) and the grade moderates.

At 2.2 km, a trail branches left to a small waterfall. At the next switchback, you reach the old resthouse. Soon after this, the grade steepens, and is stiff to the summit ridge.

You must cross the Gondola platform to reach Sanson Peak (0.4 km), an additional climb of 30 m to a much better view.

Trail Section	km from	time out	return time
Trailhead		↓	76 min
Waterfall jct.	2.2	45 min	49 min
Resthouse	2.5	50 min	45 min
Summit (Gondola)	5.3	111 min	10 min
Sanson Peak	5.7	124 min	↑

SOUTH SUMMIT RIDGE Trail

A trail follows the skyline south 0.8 km (18 minutes). You descend 30 m, then climb 60 m. Although more restricted than Sanson Peak, the viewpoint brings you closer to the peaks of Rundle and the Sundance Range. You pass some beautifully-shaped whitebark pine and a few larches on the way.

SULPHUR MOUNTAIN, WEST (Comic Ray Station Road)

~ Steep scenic route to superb viewpoint ~

Distance 8.4 km (5.2 mi) from Cave and Basin
Height Gain 840 m (2,760')
Hiking Time 2 hr 24 min*
1 hr 21 min return*

Trailhead From the Cave and Basin, take the Sundance Canyon Trail to the trailhead, directly opposite the road to Brewster Creek. Map page 12.

Options You can hike or cycle, but the steep road will discourage most cyclists beyond Sundance Canyon Road. You can descend to the Upper Hot Springs (bicycles prohibited), via trail or Gondola. You can also go to Sundance Canyon or Sundance Pass.

≈ The grade is stiff all the way. The rocky road is hard on the feet.

The route is more open and scenic than the main trail from the Upper Hot Springs. Snow clears early from the southwest-facing slopes. Mountain sheep frequent the high terrain. Check for ticks if you hike before July. I associate the way with the Townsend's solitaire, whose burbling song rings from timberline in early summer. Marmots inhabit rockslides near the top.

Norman Sanson chose Sulphur Mountain as the site for a weather observatory which was erected in 1903.

In 1956 the National Research Council built this road up the west side of the mountain and erected a building adjacent to Sanson's observatory atop Sulphur Mountain. This was one of eight Canadian (and 98 world) cosmic ray stations, an international research program for 1957, the International Geophysical Year. Cosmic rays are produced by explosions on the sun. They also cause the Northern Lights. Without the Earth's atmosphere and magnetic field to protect us, they would be fatal.

The Sulphur Mountain site was Canada's highest and most important cosmic ray research station. In 1960 the University of Calgary took it over and continued research until 1978. The road was often icy, and the four-wheel drive vehicles occasionally had to be winched around the hairpin turns. One machine rolled off the road and plunged 300 m down the mountainside. Fortunately, the two occupants escaped serious injury. Today, only Sanson's building remains at the mountain top.

Nick Morant remembers an employee of the Banff Springs who requested that she be cremated and her ashes scattered around the hotel and on Sulphur Mountain.

After her death, her sister arrived with three young children. Fearing that there might be difficulties obtaining the necessary permits, she decided to carry out the request discreetly.

Using a paper bag hidden under her coat, she went to the conservatory of the hotel, and scattered some ashes around the palms. The children looked the other way, pretending they were admiring the plants.

Then they ascended Sulphur Mountain in the gondola, casting ashes out the window as they went. At the top, they waited for the omnipresent throngs to leave the platform. Finally, when the crowd eased momentarily, she rushed to the edge of the platform, reached under her coat for the last remains, and hoisted the bag over the railing. In her haste, the bag slipped from her grasp and fell to the ground below.

Two mountain sheep saw the sack descend, and, accustomed to handouts, rushed forward to investigate. Dumbfounded, the sister watched as the animals consumed bag and contents. The children, who had thus far concealed their purpose so well, wailed in astonishment: "Look what they're doing to auntie!"

Trail From the trailhead, the route follows a steep road to the summit. Most of the way you parallel the skyline ridge.

Trail Section	km from	time out	return time
Cave and Basin Parking		↓	81 min*
Trailhead	2.8	11 min*	71 min
Join Gondola Trail	8.2	138 min	5 min
Sanson Peak	8.4	144 min	↑

* Biking time from parking lot to Trailhead.

Norman Sanson (bottom left) and Banff townsfolk on Sulphur Mountain celebrating Sanson's thousandth ascent. By permission, Whyte Museum of the Canadian Rockies.

Hiker petting dog, Cosmic Ray Station Road on the west side of Sulphur Mountain. Seen above the Bow River Valley are Mt. Cory and, above the hiker, Mt. Edith (with the tip of Mt. Louis peeping over the ridge on its right).

> "Magnificent views, overlooking, southwest, the Sundance Creek valley and pass, and, northeast, the Spray River and Spray Lakes valley and the enclosing ranges on both sides, are to be had for all of the distance along the ridge."
>
> A. O. Wheeler, Sulphur Mountain, *Climbs Near Banff*

Bow River, Mts. Bourgeau and Brett from the Sundance Canyon Road

"Near [Banff] are the Hot Springs, which are already becoming noted for their curative powers. There is the wild, rugged scenery surrounding them, the beautiful Bow meandering through the mountains, and whose waters afford recreation for boating and canoeing, the cave and basin and a multitude of favorable circumstances to attract both invalid and tourist." Otto J. Klotz, *Survey Report, Jan. 7, 1887*

CAVE AND BASIN

~ Interpretive site, swimming, short walks ~

≈ The Cave and Basin, a famed recreation site, is also important for its history, geology and unique plants and animals.

David McDougall says that Stoney Indians brought their sick to the Springs and called it their peace grounds. Various people claim to be the first Whites to find the Cave.

Mabel Williams, who wrote interpretive booklets for the national parks, credits the discovery to a rheumatic grizzly bear. "A year or so before the construction of the railway, a trapper had come across a well-beaten grizzly trail. He followed the tracks down the Bow Valley and came to a natural pool on the slopes of Sulphur Mountain, fed by a spring of unusually high temperature. There were unmistakable signs that the old bear had used the pool as a bathtub. Later it was even said that the trapper had actually seen him limping down the trail and lowering himself into the warm waters, so grateful to aching bones." If the story is true, the bear's pool could hardly have been the inaccessible Cave.

Mts. Inglismaldie, Girouard and Tunnel from the Marsh Trail

Most accounts credit the discovery to railway construction workers Frank McCabe and the McCardell brothers, Bill and Tom, who crossed the Bow River in 1883 and found the site. They staked a claim, but since it wasn't surveyed, they obtained no lease. D. B. Woodworth, an Ottawa MP from Nova Scotia, heard about the springs and came west to investigate. While the McCardells were off working on the railway, he persuaded McCabe to sign away the rights to the springs for $1,500. When the McCardells learned that McCabe had not only signed this paper but had also forged Bill's name, they hired Calgary lawyer James Lougheed. The upshot was the formation of Canada's first national park, *Banff Hot Spring's Reserve*, and cash payments to the claimants.

McCabe never saw the money Woodworth had promised. Perhaps this experience made him mistrustful. Years later, near Fort Steele, writes Bob Campbell, he set up a burglar trap at his cabin. He rigged a seven foot cross-cut saw over the entry so it would fall down when the door was opened. In the middle of the night McCabe got up to answer a call of nature and opened the door. He spent the next two months in hospital.

Geologist R. G. McConnell described the Cave in 1887. "The cave is about thirty feet deep, and is reached by an opening in the roof. The water rises through quicksands, and its ascending force is just about sufficient to prevent a man from sinking through the yielding floor." Many distinguished people, including Sir John A Macdonald, his wife, and the Prince of Wales, used a hazardous tree ladder to descend to the Cave from the opening in the roof.

The government built a bath house beside the Basin Spring in 1887. A Montana man claimed he was cured of eczema by bathing in the springs for three weeks. Soon it was promoted as a cure for everything from syphilis to rheumatism. Crutches were hung from a nearby tree with the testimonial, "The owner of these has left the springs — cured!" Doubtless the warm waters did relieve some ailments, but for years wild claims were made about the curative powers of the hot springs.

Also in 1887, George Fear was hired to build the tunnel now used to enter the Cave. Construction in the porous rock formation disturbed the pool and its underground streams. In consequence, the pool had to be dammed.

Cold air from the new passageway was blamed for cooling the water which used to be so hot in the cave that one man boiled an egg in the water. About 1970, after an earthquake centered in the United States, the water temperature dropped again.

In 1972, the deteriorating pool was closed. It was repaired and reopened in 1985 as part of Banff Park's centennial. The same summer, the Cave & Basin Centennial Centre opened. Here, you can see a free, award winning multi-frame slide show, taking 15 minutes. The complex also features a licensed tea room and gift shop, picnic tables and public washrooms. Free interpretive pamphlets are available.

From the Centre, you can take two short self-guiding boardwalk paths: The Marsh Trail and The Discovery Trail, both completed for 1985. Each takes about 10 minutes to walk if it is uncrowded, but you'll want more time to browse and read the displays.

MARSH TRAIL

≈ This walk details unusual vegetation, fish, reptiles, and birds near the warm sulphur spring.

DISCOVERY TRAIL

≈ This path reveals some of the history and geology of the site and its role in forming Canada's first national park.

SUNDANCE PASS

~ Long, easy forest hike ~

Distance 15.4 km (9.6 mi) Spray River Fireroad from Cave & Basin
Height Gain 395 m (1,300'); 90 m (300') return
Hiking Time 3 hr 8 min*
2 hr 55 min return*

Trailhead Park near the Cave and Basin (at the west end of Cave Avenue, south of the Bow River Bridge in Banff) and walk or cycle the Sundance Canyon road to the trailhead, 3.4 km (2.1 mi). This is 0.6 km (0.4 mi) before Sundance Canyon. Map page 12.

Options You can return via the Spray River Fireroad. This brings you back to a trailhead near the Banff Springs Hotel. You can also go on to Sundance Canyon and hike the Canyon trail.

≈ The trail from the Sundance Canyon Road is a pleasant forest path, easy walking most of the way, but the route is of little scenic interest. You do get tantalizing glimpses of the great pyramidal high peak on the Sundance Range, and at the pass there is a small meadow from where you see the north end of the Goat Range.

It was from this valley that Earle Birney made the first ascent of the Sundance Range, a climb which he told me was the model for *The Finger* in his superb narrative poem *David*. He and Norman Sanson had planned the attempt, but when they awoke in their bivouac tent, the older man didn't feel like going on. Birney climbed the peak alone. When he returned, elated with success, he encountered stoney doubt. "The old bugger wouldn't believe I got to the top. I was just a teenage kid."

The doubting persists. Look in *The Climber's Guide*, and you won't find Birney's name. Three decades later, a party reached the summit, and finding no evidence that anyone had preceded them, claimed the first ascent. However, lightning strikes may have destroyed any cairns that were left behind by Earle and others (Leonard Leacock made the second ascent soon after Birney).

You can cycle or walk to the trailhead.

Trail At the start, the grade is steep for about 15 minutes. After this, the route to the pass is easy. Beyond the summit, there are several steep hills down to the Spray River Fireroad.

In early summer, the first trickle of water (Giardia warning) isn't found until you've hiked almost an hour. The first substantial stream is south of the pass.

A goat trail bisects the path not far from the Spray River Road.

Trail Section	km from	time out	return time
Cave and Basin		↓	175 min*
Sulphur—Brewster Cr. Jct.	2.8	13 min*	168 min*
Trailhead	3.4	16 min*	165 min
Sundance Pass	11.0	132 min	67 min
Spray River Road	15.4	188 min	↑

* Cycling time

SUNDANCE CANYON

~ Short loop through canyon ~

Distance 10.1 km (6.3 mi) circuit from Cave & Basin
Height Gain 190 m (625')
Hiking Time 54 min*

Trailhead Park near the Cave and Basin (at the west end of Cave Avenue, south of the Bow River Bridge in Banff) and walk or cycle to the end of the Sundance Road, 4.0 km. The trail begins at the bridge to your left. Map page 12.

Options You can also take the Marsh and Discovery trails at the Cave & Basin. In addition, you can hike to Sundance Pass.

≈ The trail up the streambed gives good views of the canyon. If you continue the circuit and return down the forest trail, you get better mountain views, but most people agree the canyon trail is more interesting.

James White states that Stoney Indians used to meet upon the plateau above the falls of the canyon and perform sacred rites during their Sundance fete, hence the name for the canyon.

Trail From the trailhead, cross the creek, and climb steeply to a second bridge. Here the grade lessens. At the highest point, the route enters the pine forest and leads to the brow of the hill, returning to the valley floor west of the canyon.

Trail Section	km from	time out	return time
Cave & Basin		↓	54 min*
Trailhead	4.0	21 min*	38 min
Top of Canyon	4.9	28 min	28 min
Trailhead	6.1	38 min	21 min*
Cave & Basin	10.1	54 min*	↑

* cycling time

North peak of Goat Range from Sundance Pass

FATIGUE PASS

~ **Remote Pass** ~

Distance	**10.9 km (6.8 mi) from Bw 10**
Height Gain	**830 m (2,715')**
Hiking Time	**3 hr 22 min**
	2 hr 37 min return

Trailhead Brewster Creek Campground (Bw 10), 12.6 km via Brewster Creek Fire Road (10.1 km via the horse trail shortcut) from the Healy Creek parking area on the Sunshine Access Road. To reach Campground Bw 10, you can cycle the Fire Road (1 hr 35 min; 1 hr 4 min return); if you are hiking, take the Horse Shortcut Trail (2 hr 10 min; 1 hr 55 min return). See pages 158—159. Map pages 12 and 14.

Options You can continue to Citadel Pass and link with the trail to Sunshine Meadows.

≈ This trail is used primarily by equestrians, and few of them go all the way to the pass. It is unlikely to become popular with hikers. Eight fords, the remoteness and distance of the route and its limited attractions will discourage most people. You are in trees most of the way, and some parts of the trail are overgrown. Sections are faint or muddy. Only near the pass, do you get modest views.

You can go on to Citadel Pass, but the way is poorly marked.

Bring a pair of sneakers. You ford Brewster Creek once, Fatigue Creek six times, plus one major tributary stream. In 1992, four crossings of Fatigue Creek and the tributary stream had improvised (usually a single log) bridging near the ford; the first of these (three logs), proved treacherously slippery even when dry.

In 1992, I encountered a black bear near Fatigue Pass.

Pika

Trail From the campground, descend a hill and ford Brewster Creek. Go upstream, bending south to enter the valley of Fatigue Creek. You stay low near the creek for a kilometre beyond the last ford. You then commence a steep climb and cross two avalanche slopes. From the second opening, if you look back, you see in the distance to Mt. Louis and the three peaks of Mt. Edith beneath Mt. Brewster.

Proceed to a small meadow. On the far side is a precipitation gauge, a remote location for this instrument. You then re-enter forest before reaching another meadow below steep slopes leading to the pass. Here, equestrians have gone up the bank to a scenic knoll, making it appear that the trail ends at this point. Instead, you must cross the stream to the right.

The trail has vague sections ahead. Skirt right of the two ponds in the meadow, then proceed up the centre of the valley a short distance to where the path bends right. You have to force your way through 20 m of thick brush which has overgrown the trail, then watch for a low cairn where you turn left to cross the final steep hillside.

Fatigue Pass is marked only by a Mt. Assiniboine Park boundary sign. The Banff Park sign is located on the ridge you cross if you go on to Citadel Pass, 100 m higher than the actual pass.

Trail Section	km from	time out	return time
Campground Bw 10		↓	157 min
Brewster Creek ford	0.2	2 min	155 min
Fatigue Creek, first ford	0.9	13 min	143 min
Fatigue Creek, last ford	5.0	82 min	83 min
Fatigue Pass	10.9	202 min	↑

CITADEL PASS

The route from Fatigue Pass to Citadel Pass takes you in a bee line from just east of Fatigue Pass, over two connected hills, to a low flattened ridge of Fatigue Mountain where the Banff Park sign for Fatigue Pass is located.

If you go directly across the watershed, you enter a gully which takes you below and south of Citadel Pass. And if you go first to the provincial sign at Fatigue Pass, you miss the small cairns which help mark the bee line route.

Aim for the low crest (2450 m, 8,040') of a ridge of Fatigue Mountain which is in a direct line between the two passes. Your only guide is a band of small cairns pointing to a saddle beneath the ridge. Two white rocks on a giant gray boulder mark this saddle. From there, follow a slight gully up the low ridge, watching for the park trail sign to your left.

Go left, parallel to the Citadel Pass sign, watching for a few small cairns which lead to where the trail becomes more obvious, switchbacking down the hillside, before running out. Where the trail disappears, you can see Citadel Pass below.

The following times assume you follow the way directly. Expect to take longer if you are unfamiliar with the route.

Trail Section	km from	time out	return time
Fatigue Pass		↓	39 min
Banff Park sign	0.8	16 min	28 min
Citadel Pass	2.1	38 min	↑

Ridge of Sundance Range from Allenby Pass

"The extraordinary paucity of local names, whether Cree or Assiniboine — even in the case of important streams and mountains — in this part of the region, leads me to believe that the Crees themselves had not very long possessed these mountains, which, it seems highly probable, at no very distant date, were frequented only by the Kootanies."

G. M. Dawson, *On the Canadian Rocky Mountains, Read before The British Association, Birmingham, 1886*

ALLENBY PASS from BREWSTER CREEK

~ **Historic route** (photos pp. 48, 137, 157) ~

Distance **30.7 km (19.1 mi) from Healy Creek parking area**
Height Gain **1085 m (3,565')**
Hiking Time **5 hr 28 min***
4 hr 9 min* return

Trailhead From the Trans-Canada Highway, take the Sunshine turnoff, 8.6 km (5.3 mi) west of Banff (west interchange), and drive 0.8 km to the parking area by Healy Creek on the left side of the road. Alternately, start at the Cave and Basin and follow the Sundance Canyon Road to the Allenby Pass junction and turn right. Map page 14.

Options You can make a side trip to Fatigue Pass. En route, you can stay at campground Bw 10 or Sundance Lodge or Halfway Lodge (reserve through Holiday on Horseback, Banff — see page 23). You can cross Allenby Pass to enter the Mt. Assiniboine area via the Bryant Creek or Og Pass trails.

≈ You are in trees most of the way. Some openings permit views of the Sundance Range and the boundary peaks. The most inspiring sight is Brewster Glacier seen near the warden cabin. At 9 km, you pass a group of hoodoos.

The road is good for cycling to Sundance Lodge. Beyond there, expect many rough sections; bring your bicycle repair kit. Except for several long steep hills, the grade is easy to Halfway Lodge. From there to the pass is steep.

Old cabin, Brewster Creek

Aggressive cyclists can reach the pass and return within a long day, but most bikers should plan to stay overnight. Many rash cyclists have been benighted in Brewster Creek Valley. Expect to share the trail with horse traffic.

Brewster Creek is named for James Irvine Brewster, who prior to 1882 logged this valley to provide railway ties for the CPR. After he moved, the family referred to him as *Bowden Jim Brewster* to distinguish him from his famous nephew of the same name who lived in Banff. Before 1950, the site was called *Brewster Pass*. Erling Strom used this route to his lodge at Mt. Assiniboine. In 1940, his young daughter Siri developed acute appendicitis and was carried to Banff on a stretcher along this route. During one trip from Banff, Strom saw 31 moose. In recent years, parasites have reduced the numbers of these magnificent animals.

Trail From Healy Creek, go 0.6 km to the first junction on your right. Hikers can make a right turn here and follow the Horse Shortcut trail, but cyclists should continue another 1.4 km to the old road up Brewster Creek. There is a stiff climb to where the two routes rejoin on the old road, 5.4 km from Sundance Lodge.

Just before the end of the road, and shortly before Sundance Lodge, a horse trail turns right to the corral on the other side of Brewster Creek. Keep ahead and go by the Lodge. The route now becomes a wide trail.

At 12.6 km you reach the junction to Fatigue Pass and Brewster Creek Campground (Bw 10) on your right. Almost 3 km farther, in an open area just before you cross Brewster Creek on a sturdy bridge, you pass the remains of a lean-to shack on your right. After a steady climb, you continue almost 6 km to a rockfall where you get your first good view of Brewster Glacier backed by a high peak on the Sundance Range.

A little farther brings you to a ford (minor in late August). A kilometre past the ford, you reach a disused corral fence shortly before the site of the warden's cabin, on your left.

The trail bends right (south) to enter a major side valley where Halfway Lodge is located.

After going by the Lodge, you cross a stream and begin the steady ascent to Allenby Pass. You soon rise above the heavy forest and climb through open trees to timberline. The Allenby Pass sign comes a minute before the summit.

Trail Section	km from	time out	return time
Trailhead, Healy Creek		↓	249 min*
Horse Shortcut, North Jct.	0.6	3 min*	246 min*
Brewster Creek Road Jct.	2.0	8 min*	239 min*
Horse Shortcut, South Jct.	5.7	44 min*	221 min*
Hoodoos	9.1	58 min*	197 min*
Sundance Lodge	11.1	73 min*	186 min*
Fatigue Pass Jct. & Bw 10	12.6	88 min*	172 min*
Bridge	15.5	115 min*	152 min*
Ford	21.5	176 min*	101 min*
Horse Gate	22.8	195 min*	89 min*
Halfway Lodge	26.6	240 min*	54 min**
Allenby Pass	30.7	328 min**	↑

* cycling time
** hiking time

SUNDANCE LODGE via HORSE SHORTCUT Trail

≈ The grade is moderate. This route is shorter than the road, but if you are cycling, the road is faster. The trail is narrow, steep and rough for bikes, and is heavily used by equestrians.

Trail Section	km from	time out	return time
Healy Creek Trailhead		↓	112 min
Horse Trail, north Jct.	0.6	8 min	104 min
Horse Trail, south Jct.	3.2	58 min	71 min
Sundance Lodge	8.7	132 min	↑

SUNDANCE CANYON from HEALY CREEK

~ Good bike route ~

Distance 5.1 km (3.2 mi)
Height Gain 30 m (100'); 15 m (50') return
Cycling Time 35 min
34 min return

≈ Most of the route is level and makes good cycling. It is also frequented by horse traffic. The route follows the old road from the former site of the Healy Creek Warden Cabin. You can start from Healy Creek or from The Cave and Basin (via the Sundance Canyon Road).

Trail Section	km from	time out	return time
Healy Creek		↓	34 min*
Horse tr. to Allenby Pass Jct.	0.6	8 min	26 min
Bike trail to Allenby Pass Jct.	2.0	17 min	16 min
Sundance Canyon Trail	5.1	35 min*	↑

* Cycling times

Mt. Sir Douglas, Mt. Turner, three unnamed peaks and Mt. Byng from Allenby Pass

CARROT CREEK to LAKE MINNEWANKA

~ Historic route, fords ~

Distance	**19.9 km (12.4 mi) to Lm 31**
Height Gain	**870 m (2,855'); 670 m (2,230') return**
Hiking Time	**5 hr 9 min**
	4 hr 48 min return

Trailhead Park at the Carrot Creek Parking Lot, 1.6 km west of East Park Gate. Because of the divided highway, the parking lot can be reached only by westbound traffic on the Trans-Canada Highway.

Alternately, start at Lm 31 campground at Lake Minnewanka. Map page 13.

Options You can backpack to Devil's Gap or to the north shore of Lake Minnewanka. Campground Lm 31 can be reached by boat. (Lake Minnewanka Tours, located at the Lake Minnewanka boat dock, offers taxi rides around the lake.) There is also a campground at Carrot Creek.

≈ In 1841 James Sinclair led a party of métis

Mts. Girouard and Inglismaldie, L. Minnewanka

from the Red River Colony to the Oregon Territory. They entered the Rockies at Devil's Gap, followed the south shore of Lake Minnewanka, then reached the Spray River by taking the pass above the site of Canmore. It is thought they crossed Carrot Creek Summit en route.

Sinclair's guide was a Cree named Maskapetoon. It seems ironic that a mountain they passed beneath is now named for Peechee, another native guide who led Sir George Simpson on the more distant north shore of Lake Minnewanka just a few weeks earlier.

Carrot Creek is notorious for its fords. My daughters were young (seven and nine years old) when my wife and I took them here in 1971. We counted the number of times we had to remove our footwear, and found there were 25 fords. A group of cadets went by, burdened with heavy packs. They were completing a route march from Lake Minnewanka, their teenage enthusiasm undiminished, despite their soaking boots.

In 1992, all but six of the crossings had crude bridges, and two of the six can be avoided. Several bridges require brief detours. An extra pair of sneakers would be handy for the fords.

The trail beside Lake Minnewanka climbs numerous hills, accounting for 275 m of the height gain for the trip.

Carrot Creek is probably named for the cow parsnip, the showiest of the Carrot Family of wildflowers which grow here. It seems appropriate to choose a plant name for a valley which lacks mountain views. Until you reach Lake Minnewanka, the forest allows only glimpses of canyon walls and the clear stream. There are outstanding viewpoints by the lake which I like best in morning with the sun on the Fairholme Range. You see this if you start at Lm 31.

Trail From the parking area, cross the animal control fence by the gate at the kiosk and follow the trail through open forest to Carrot Creek. After a brief swing back into the trees, you come to a cairn which marks where you should turn left for the bridge to avoid the first ford.

In 1992, all the fords were bridged except #5, #12, #13, #14, #18, and #19. The spans are improvised, and may be slippery, springy or underwater. The logs are subject to spring washouts, and should not be counted on. A sturdy pole is recommended for balance. Several bridges are out of sight at the ford, and you have to go a short way upstream or downstream to find them. I found #12 and #13 could be avoided by keeping left (facing upstream) and scrambling over an easy rock ledge near #13. In September, I could cross #18 by hopping rocks.

Shortly after the last ford, you pass left of the Carrot Creek campground and commence a long ascent to the summit.

Here, you begin the steep descent to Lake Minnewanka, following an unnamed creek which you cross nine times. Fortunately, the stream is much smaller than Carrot Creek and there are logs (though often slippery) at most of the fords. Portions of the trail are apt to be wet.

The path around the lake to Lm 31 stays well above the lake. You climb several hills and cross a few rocky streambeds.

Trail Section	km from	time out	return time
Parking lot		↓	288 min
Carrot Creek	2.1	27 min	263 min
First ford	2.6	34 min	256 min*
Last ford	7.6	114 min*	208 min
Campground Ca 9	8.0	121 min	201 min
Summit	10.5	169 min	164 min
Lake Minnewanka	14.0	226 min	83 min
Campground Lm 31	19.9	309 min	↑

* Time at fords assumes rapid crossings. Add 15 minutes for each ford if you change boots; add several minutes for crossing each slippery bridge with the assistance of a pole.

Outlier of Mt. Costigan from the south shore of Lake Minnewanka

"The place [Lake Minnewanka] was too distant for me to reach, as it is uphill, and the only path an old Indian trail, but an active young Englishman rode over during our visit and did his best, but never saw a fish of any kind." W. S. Caine, 1887, *A Trip Round the World*

Lake Minnewanka is Banff Park's largest lake, 36 kilometres long by 2 kilometres at its widest point. The maximum depth is 142 metres.

The earliest white visitors to the Banff area went this way. In August 1841, Sir George Simpson came here, following the north shore. A few weeks later James Sinclair led a party of métis by the south shore.

In 1847 the Rev. Robert Rundle camped several days at the lakeshore and was impressed. "This is the most interesting Lake I ever saw."

On July 1, before hiking to Devil's Gap, he carved his initials (RTR) and the date on a tree. If the tree survived the forest fires which devastated the area when the railway was built, it must have disappeared when Lake Minnewanka was raised 25 m by successive hydro dams.

The lake's names imply the supernatural. Stoney Indians called this *Dead Lake, Ghost Lake,* or *Wendigo* (Cannibal) *Lake*. Somehow this became rendered as *Devil's Lake*. (Early translators of Indian names often categorized any native spirit as evil.) A Stoney myth tells of a spirit-creature, half fish, half person which troubles the lake. Once, a group of women and children fishing in a canoe commenced chanting, which offended the spirit. The back of a fish appeared, from which a huge hand grabbed a singer. A companion cut at the arm which then clutched the victim tighter and lashed at the water, making the boat capsize. Only one of the party ever got to shore to tell the story. Since then, no Stoney would boat on the lake. Another Indian legend states that a man, looking at the lake from a high mountain, saw a fish as long as the lake, so he called the place *The Lake of the Evil Water-Spirit.*

Captain Jack Standly. By permission, Whyte Museum of the Canadian Rockies.

Simpson renamed it Peechee Lake (as he spelled his guide's name), noting this was where Piché lived. Six years later, Rundle referred to it as Wildcat Lake. *Lynx*, or *Wild Cat*, is the translation of the Cree name for Piché. Surveyor G. M. Dawson only read Simpson's account after he had already officially named it Devil's Lake. However, in 1888, George Stewart, the first Park Superintendent felt this name would hurt tourism, so he renamed it Minnewanka, Stoney for *Lake of the Water Spirit*.

Lake Minnewanka is a good place for fishing, and some giant specimens have been caught. In 1887 W. S. Caine reported a man who had "caught 77 trout, weighing 220 lbs. in a single day, trolling with a couple of hand-lines." No one has matched the 1899 record of 47 pounds by Dr. Seward Webb, though divers today report seeing fish which might weigh 60 pounds.

The fish aren't always as big as they seem. In 1891 botanist John Macoun boasted of the 28 pound trout his son had caught. Next day he was outdone by a man who showed them a 32 pound prize he had captured. Macoun's son became suspicious when he noticed the mouth of the fish was sewn; he found 10 pounds of stones hidden inside.

The first boathouse was constructed in 1889. Charles Astley and his brother Willoughby ran the concession for the CPR, offering a three hour boat trip aboard either *The Daughter of the Peaks* or *The Lady of the Lakes*, stern wheelers moored at the small cottage town called Minnewanka Landing. Next year Willoughby moved to Lake Louise to manage the new Chalet. The mountain above the Landing was named Mt. Astley for Charles. Although this name appeared on some old maps, it has never been officially accepted.

One of the early operators, Captain Jack Standly (or *Stanley* — both spellings were used), had a unique way of drumming up business by getting people to the boat dock. Shortly before a cruise was due to leave, he would appear on his bike, wearing a knee-length bathing suit. He would ride onto the ramp at high speed. As he sped to the wharf, he pretended he'd lost control, and flew off into the lake, still on his bicycle. By the time he got back to the ramp, towing his bike, a crowd was gathered near the boat — and the ticket office.

Minnewanka Landing is now under water. The lake has been dammed twice, first in 1912, and again in 1941, as an emergency war measure. The dams raised the lake 25 metres and lengthened it 8 kilometres.

Although Minnewanka was used for ice boating many years ago, hydro development now makes travel on the frozen lake dangerous. Water is drawn out under the ice all winter to meet the power needs of the dam. Even when surface ice is a metre thick, it is unstable because of hidden air pockets beneath. During spring melt, the level can drop 6 metres. Several people and animals have drowned, after falling through the ice on the lake.

ATTRACTIONS and FACILITIES

Cascade Pond Located 0.2 km from the Trans-Canada Highway junction, a short connecting road takes you to a lovely picnic facility with tables, kitchen shelters and washrooms. From Cascade Pond you get a good view of the waterfall which gives Cascade Mountain its name. Trails to Bankhead and Johnson Lake commence from this parking area.

National Cadet Camp This facility, located 0.4 km from the Trans-Canada Highway junction, was erected in 1948 as a tent camp for Canadian honours army cadets. During its first couple of years, until the nearby refuse dump was closed, the camp was frequented by black bears. In 1949 I watched a bruin get its first look at a mirror, hanging from a tree near the mess tent. It reared on its hind legs and swayed from side to side for a couple of minutes, trying to make sense of the reflection and to figure out where the other bear disappeared each time it peered around the glass.

Johnson Lake/Two Jack Lake Road Located 0.8 km from the Trans-Canada Highway junction, this is a shortcut to these sites which you can reach also by keeping ahead on the circuit.

Lower Bankhead This is the remains of the industrial section of Bankhead, a coal town built by the CPR in 1904. It is located 2.8 km from the Trans-Canada Highway junction. The mines became unprofitable; after a strike, they were shut down in 1922 and the site was abandoned.

Upper Bankhead Located 3.3 km from the Trans-Canada Highway junction, this was Bankhead's residential community. The town population was slightly larger than Banff's.

Lake Minnewanka Located 5.1 km from the Trans-Canada Highway junction, the parking area is reached by turning left. Minnewanka Tours, a concession stand, boat ramp, public washroom and picnic area are found here as are trails around Lake Minnewanka to Devil's Gap, Stewart Canyon, Aylmer Lookout and Aylmer Pass.

Lake Minnewanka Tours The Lake Minnewanka boat cruise is a guided tour of the lake. It takes 1.5 hours and is a spectacular way to see the lake and its surrounding mountains. Boat rentals and taxi rides are also available. Write Box 2189, Dept. B, Banff, Alberta, T0L 0CO, phone 403-762-3473, Fax 403-762-2800.

Two Jack Lake Picnic/Boat Landing Site Located 7.6 km from the Trans-Canada Highway junction, this gives access to a body of water now fed by Lake Minnewanka. The original Two Jack Lake was landlocked and fishing was good. In 1930, Henry Ness' father caught seven fish, one a 16 pound trout, in an hour.

Two Jack Main Campground Located 8.2 km from the Trans-Canada Highway junction, this campground is open late June to Labor Day.

Two Jack Lakeside Campground This is the site of the original campground, 8.7 km from the Trans-Canada Highway junction. Renovated in 1991-92, it is normally open from late May to Labor Day.

Johnson Lake Road Located 9.9 km from the Trans-Canada Highway junction, this road leads to a popular recreation site, 2.2 km distant. Fire pits, picnic tables and a pit toilet are among the amenities. Johnson Lake and Anthracite Hoodoos trails begin here. There are also picnic facilities near the start of the connector road.

Two Jack Overflow Campground Located 13.0 km from the Trans-Canada Highway junction, the site has pit toilets and is open in summer as needed.

Minnewanka Landing and Cascade Mountain, ca 1900. Whyte Museum of the Canadian Rockies.

FLYING SQUIRREL

"Bill Johnson and I were assigned to a remote warden cabin up the Cascade Fireroad. Bill wore a red flannel shirt; I didn't know it would run so I threw it in with his long johns when I washed the clothes. After that, he wore pink underwear for pajamas.

"One night we were awakened by a racquet. Bill said, 'There's a bear on the porch.'

"But this rattle came from the stove. The damper was shut off and it was wiggling. So I said, 'It's in the stovepipe.' Bill had a little black dog. He said, 'Just a minute. I'll get Jackie.'

"I'd just painted the cupboard white that day and the paint hadn't set. The stove door was aimed right at the cupboard. When we opened the stove door, Bill was holding Jackie in front of it.

"He said 'OK, turn the damper.' I didn't think Bill was going to let go of the dog, but in the stove, with all the ashes and soot went the dog. Then this little black streak came boiling out of there — shoo — right at me. You only had time to see his beady little eyes. It was a flying squirrel that got down the stovepipe. He hit the cupboard, that newly painted cupboard, and the dog was right behind, pawing at him — what a mess! Around and around the cabin they went, Bill, in his pink underwear, chasing them with the broom. I was helpless with laughter but did manage to throw open the cabin door to let squirrel and dog out.

"After that we never turned the damper on the stove without thinking of that darned flying squirrel."

Edited from Maryalice Stewart's interview with retired warden Ole Hermanrude.

Northern Flying Squirrel gliding. Photo, Cy Hampson.

Bighorn sheep

"I am not quite alone. I have a most wonderful clever dog, sixteen mice. They are all tame and know different tricks. Then I have a big snake, but he is most of the time asleep, but when he is awake I put him near the fire, and play music for him. He is very fond of music. His name is Satan, and he understands his name every time. Then I have the ugliest looking toad you can imagine, but I love him for his good natured character. Then I have a dayly visitor, a big ugly looking porkepine. He stays with me for hours. I have learnt him to shake hands....

"Well, it seems to me they all love me. I know that I love them all. I find them better friends as one does amongst people."

Conrad Kain, at a trapper's cabin, Simpson River, *Where the Clouds Can Go*

Minnewanka Landing ca 1890. Photo, S. A. Smyth. By permission, Whyte Museum of the Canadian Rockies.

"Although Astley Bros. had tents to let, the one which we occupied was a large marquee, which was kindly loaned to us by Mr. G. A. Stewart, Superintendent of the Rocky Mountains Park.... The spot where we camped was called Shakespeare Point, so christened by the Caroline Gage people, who camped there for a month last summer. It is a point running out into Devil's Lake, thickly wooded with fir trees. Close by a little mountain stream supplies pure drinking water.... Devil's Lake, or more properly Lake Minnewanka, is a long, narrow sheet of water."
Charles E. D. Wood, 1890, *Macleod Gazette, quoted in Alberta History, Summer, 1977*

Anthracite, ca 1887, looking to Mts. Astley and Aylmer. By permission Whyte Museum of the Canadian Rockies.

> "We visited the coal-mines of the Canadian Anthracite Company, close to the next station east from Banff. This mine only commenced working November, 1886; already there is an hotel, a store, and several houses; about 150 hands were employed, and I was told many more men would shortly be wanted." W. Henry Barneby, *The New Far West and the Old Far East*

Lake Minnewanka and Mounts Girouard and Inglismaldie (Gibraltar Rock shows below Inglismaldie) from Aylmer Pass trail, near Aylmer Creek

> "I heard of wonderful fish being caught in the Devil's Head Lake [Minnewanka].... I saw a man who had been there and caught 77 trout, weighing 220 lbs., in a single day, trolling with a couple of hand-lines and spoon-bait, and one trout weighing 43 lbs. was caught there last year with a piece of beef." W. S. Caine, reporting his 1887 visit, *A Trip Round the World*

Mount Aylmer and Lake Minnewanka from the slopes west of Saddle Peak

"The Indian legend of Lake Minnewanka runs thus: One of the first Indians who saw this lake did so by climbing to the top of one of the highest mountains which surrounded it. In the lake he saw an enormous fish, so large that from where he stood it looked the whole length of the lake, to which he therefore gave its present name, The Lake of the Evil Spirit."

Mrs. Algernon St. Maur (Duchess of Somerset), *Impressions of a Tenderfoot*

LAKE MINNEWANKA to DEVIL'S GAP

~ Largest lake in Banff Park ~

Distance	**30.0 km (18.6 mi) to Devil's Gap**
Height Gain	**185 m (600')**
Hiking Time	**6 hr 34 min**
	6 hr 34 min return

Trailhead Turn off the Trans-Canada Highway at the Banff (east) interchange, and follow the Lake Minnewanka Road 5.4 km (3.4 mi) to the Lake Minnewanka Parking Lot on the left. Walk to the gate which blocks the access road to the resort. Map p. 13.

Options You can hike or cycle. Five campsites along the lakeshore are available to backcountry users. These campsites can also be reached by boat. You can go to Devil's Gap or to Carrot Creek Pass. You can divert to trails up Stewart Canyon, Aylmer Pass or Aylmer Lookout.

Minnewanka Landing. By permission, Whyte Museum of the Canadian Rockies.

≈ The trail is rocky and hilly with one long steep climb just after Stewart Canyon. Hikers will find it unkind to their feet; cyclists should bring a repair kit. Bikers should also note the trail is narrow and follows several steep exposed hillsides. Near the east end of the lake there are several washouts.

Approaching the east end of the lake, you see rolling foothills ahead through a gap which is the shortest route from Banff to the prairies.

The trail's low elevation permits early and late season hiking. If you go before mid-July, check for ticks. Mountain sheep frequent the shore. A pair of bald eagles have been nesting in the valley for at least ten years.

In 1933, Leonard Leacock was charged by a grizzly on the shores of Lake Minnewanka.

"I was staying with Lug Hutton at Scotty Wright's cabin, half way around the lake. We were out gathering berries when Lug said to me, 'We've been out six weeks, and haven't seen a bear all this time'. I said, 'Well look up there.'

"On the hill above us was a grizzly with two cubs. I knew better, but I tried to get a picture. It seemed too good a chance to miss. Then the wind changed, she caught our scent and charged. We turned and ran. The bear was so close I could hear her panting. Finally, we turned off the trail and ran into the lake. The grizzly came to the shore, and growled. After she left, and we came out of the water, every stump by the shore looked to us like that bear."

Trail Keeping left at all intersections, follow the service road through the picnic area to the trail sign.

Head up Stewart Canyon and cross the Cascade River Bridge. Keep ahead where the Stewart Canyon Trail turns left. A switchback leads up the steep hill on Mt. Astley. At the top you overlook the site of Minnewanka Landing. Until it is hidden in August by the rising lake, you see a spring far below. After a long descent and many small hills, you cross Aylmer Creek. Just after the bridge, trails to Aylmer Pass and Aylmer Lookout intersect on the left; to your right is the path to Campsite Lm 8. Keep ahead.

The hilly trail stays close to the lake. Pass Campsite Lm 9 and Lm 11, then the warden cabin. Washouts become more frequent and serious as you continue to Lm 20, Lm 22 and the east end of Lake Minnewanka.

Take the north shore of First Ghost Lake to a ford and the Carrot Creek junction. After passing the south shores of Second and Third Ghost lakes, you enter the foothills and the Park Boundary at Devil's Gap.

Trail Section	km from	time out	return time
Boat concession gate		↓	394 min
Trailhead (end of picnic area)	0.6	9 min	385 min
Cascade River bridge	1.5	18 min	372 min
Stewart Canyon Jct.	1.7	20 min	374 min
Aylmer Pass Jct. (and Lm 8)	8.1	106 min	285 min
Lm 9	9.6	124 min	267 min
Lm 11	11.2	146 min	245 min
Warden Cabin	15.4	201 min	190 min
Lm 20	19.5	256 min	134 min
Lm 22	21.3	280 min	114 min
End of Lake Minnewanka	23.5	308 min	86 min
First Ghost Lake	24.4	320 min	74 min
Ford	25.6	336 min	57 min
Carrot Creek Trail Jct.	25.7	337 min	56 min
Devil's Gap, Park Boundary	30.0	394 min	↑

"I went to Lake Minnewanka.... Lovely flowers on its banks, especially red and yellow lilies."
Conrad Kain, 1909, *Where the Clouds Can Go*

STEWART CANYON

~ Cascade River ~

Distance	**2.8 km (1.7 mi)**
Height Gain	**20 m (60')**
Hiking Time	**37 min**
	36 min return

Trailhead Turn off the Trans-Canada Highway at the Banff (east) interchange, and follow the Lake Minnewanka Road 5.4 km (3.4 mi) to the Lake Minnewanka Parking Lot on the left. Walk to the gate which blocks the access road to the resort. Map p. 13.

Options You can continue upstream along the Cascade River by an old trail which is no longer maintained. The path deteriorates at a cliffband.

≈ Named for George Stewart, first superintendent of Canada's first National Park, the narrow canyon is shallow and pales in comparison to Johnston's Canyon or even Sundance Canyon. The main attraction is the Cascade River. Don't expect great mountain views.

The Duchess of Somerset and her husband visited the Canyon prior to 1890. Much of what she saw is now flooded over. Modern dams have raised Lake Minnewanka 25 metres.

"We ... walked over very rough ground covered with burnt timber, to a cañon which Connor ['the forester of the National Park'] said he had just discovered. We climbed over the large charred logs, which was not a very clean amusement, for a few hundred yards, and then entered the cañon, which I can better describe as a deep ravine, almost closing over our heads, with precipitous rocks on either side, not unlike the eerie places which are occasionally seen in some wild Highland glen. The shades of the big pine trees somewhat darkened the cañon, still we were able to admire the lovely mosses and lichens which grew in the richest profusion among the fallen timber.

"As it seemed to me probable that we might come across a bear, and as none of us had brought even a revolver, I declined to go further; for in such a place it would have been impossible to run away, for we could only go slowly over the windfalls, and a bear visited thus in his own stronghold might resent intrusion. On our way in, Connor had shown us a place where he had seen one only three weeks before."

You can continue upstream via an old trail which follows close to the riverbank. In 1991, there was little deadfall, so you should have little problem going as far as the cliffband where the trail gives out.

Trail From the access road gate go through the picnic area to the trail sign, keeping left.

You follow a bay of Lake Minnewanka which has flooded the first part of the canyon. It leads to the Cascade River Bridge. Shortly after the bridge, you reach the trail sign to Stewart Canyon. Turn left onto this path.

The route goes up the Cascade River, above an older trail which you may want to divert to when the scenery looks interesting. Where the path descends at a rough spring runoff creekbed, you reach the end of the maintained trail.

Trail Section	km from	time out	return time
Gate		↓	36 min
End of picnic area	0.6	9 min	27 min
Junction, Minnewanka Trail	1.7	20 min	16 min
End of maintained trail	2.8	37 min	↑

Lake Minnewanka, ca 1910. Gibraltar Rock and Mt. Inglismaldie on the right. Byron Harmon photo, Whyte Museum of the Canadian Rockies.

Mt. Astley from Aylmer Pass

Buttress of Mt. Costigan from Second Ghost Lake

Mount Inglismaldie, Sundance Range, Mount Howard Douglas and Cascade Mountain from Aylmer Lookout

"This valley, which was from two to three miles in width, contained four beautiful lakes, communicating with each other by small streams; and the fourth of the series, which was about fifteen miles by three, we named after Peechee, as being our guide's usual home. At this place he had expected to find his family; but Madame Peechee and the children had left their encampment, probably on account of a scarcity of game. What an idea of the loneliness and precariousness of savage life does this single glimpse of the biography of the Peechees suggest!"

Sir George Simpson, describing Lake Minnewanka, *Narrative of a Journey Round the World during the years 1841 and 1842*

AYLMER LOOKOUT

~ Best views of Banff Park's largest lake ~

Distance **3.9 km (2.4 mi) from Lm 8**
Height Gain **570 m (1,870')**
Hiking Time **1 hr 36 min**
53 min return

Trailhead Aylmer Pass Junction Campground (Lm 8) is the nearest starting place. Map page 13.

Options You can do this as a day hike from the Lake Minnewanka Parking Lot: add 8.4 km, 106 min and 90 m height gain. You can also hike to Aylmer Pass.

≈ This site offers the best view of Lake Minnewanka you can reach by trail. You see most of the lake, plus a superb panorama of mountains.

The grade is stiff. There is no water after you leave Aylmer Creek (Giardia warning), just west of Lm 8 Campground.

Mt. Aylmer is the highest mountain near Banff. Before the country went metric, is was known as the only 10,000 foot mountain you could see from town. In 1890 surveyor J. J. McArthur, who made the first ascent, named the mountain after his native town, Aylmer, Quebec, which was in turn named after Matthew, Fifth Lord Aylmer, Governor General of Canada, 1831-35. Pioneer outfitter Tom Wilson said McArthur named it for a descendant of Lord Aylmer: Fred Aylmer, who was born in Quebec and worked on the CPR surveys near Banff in 1883.

The Fire Tower, built in 1948, was 40 feet high. The Lookout and attendant's cabin were taken down in 1985; only the foundations remain today. From 1949 until 1965, Norman Titherington manned the lookout, retiring at age 71. For five months each summer, seven days a week he remained at his post.

His telescope was powerful enough for him to see people diving in the pool at the Cave and Basin on a clear day. He told me he had once seen a cougar beneath the Tower.

In Norman's sixth season, a grizzly visited the Lookout at night once a month. It went around the cabin, so close he could hear it sniffing. Then, with "great slurps and belches," it helped itself at the water barrel. Once, Titherington forgot he had left a canvas tied over the water to keep rodents out. Instead of knocking the barrel down the canyon, as Norman feared, the bear "complained loudly and to make sure I was awake scratched his rear end on the southeast corner of the verandah. Sauce pans and frying pans showered down onto the floor [inside the cabin]."

The attendant always placed a salt block near the Lookout, and this attracted flocks of mountain sheep. These mammals still frequent the site. If you do this hike before mid July, check yourself for ticks which are prolific here in early season.

Trail From the trail junction at the edge of the campground, you hike up a hillside, staying high above Aylmer Creek.

At the Aylmer Pass Junction, you turn right to climb the ridge above Aylmer Canyon. The grade soon eases; there are even some brief downhill sections below a rocky portion of the ridge. As you approach the crest of the ridge at the Lookout site, the views improve and the grade steepens considerably.

Trail Section	km from	time out	return time
Aylmer Pass Jct. (Lm 8)		↓	53 min
Aylmer Lookout Jct.	2.3	50 min	23 min
Aylmer Lookout	3.9	86 min	↑

AYLMER PASS

~ Stiff ascent to Park boundary ~

Distance **5.7 km (3.5 mi) from Lm 8**
Height Gain **755 m (2,475')**
Hiking Time **2 hr 2 min**
1 hr 19 min return

Trailhead Aylmer Pass Junction Campground (Lm 8) is the nearest starting place. Map page 13.

Options You can do this as a day hike from the Lake Minnewanka Parking Lot. You can also hike to Aylmer Lookout, only 1.6 km from the junction. You can backpack beyond the Pass, hiking down the Ghost River in Alberta's Ghost River Wilderness Area.

≈ To reach Aylmer Pass from Aylmer Creek, you climb for two hours on one of the steepest trails in Banff Park. Beyond the Lookout Junction, the trail is overgrown in numerous places. After Aylmer Creek (Giardia warning), there is no water until near the pass.

Sheep are commonly seen near the trail.

The open country near the pass displays a wide variety of wildflowers, including Indian paintbrush which in this high location displays a great variety of hues. The specimens I saw here one July rate among the most diverse and lovely I have seen in the Rockies.

A great mound of fallen rock encroaches the meadow at the pass.

Trail From the campground, you take the steep trail to the Lookout Junction. From here, the grade becomes even steeper as you ascend the narrow gap between Mt. Aylmer and Mt. Astley. At the pass, the trail is faint; watch for cairns.

Trail Section	km from	time out	return time
Boat Concession gate		↓	184 min
Lm 8 (Aylmer Pass Jct.)	8.4	106 min	79 min
Aylmer Lookout Jct.	10.7	156 min	49 min
Aylmer Pass	14.1	228 min	↑

CASCADE POND TRAILS

~ Cascade Mountain, Douglas firs ~

Trailhead Turn off the Trans-Canada Highway at the Banff (east) interchange, and follow the Lake Minnewanka Road 0.5 km (0.3 mi) and turn right to the Cascade Pond parking area. Map page 13.

JOHNSON LAKE from CASCADE POND

≈ The trail passes Douglas firs atop a scenic hillside dominated by Mts. Rundle and Cascade.

From Cascade Pond, you get a good view of the waterfall which gives Cascade Mountain its name. In winter, the frozen fall is a popular ice climbing route. In 1990, a young man fell 300 m from the top; miraculously, he survived.

Trail Go to the east side of the pond, near the low bridge over the stream, and turn east on the prominent path into the forest. Ascend a steep hill. Beneath the power lines, the Bankhead trail turns left (no sign). Keep ahead on the obvious path following the brow of the hill to a disused road. After a short distance, the road divides. Take the more prominent track to the right to the water tower, then to Johnson Lake.

Trail Section	km from	time out	return time
Cascade Pond		↓	31 min
Water Tower	3.5	28 min	6 min
Johnson Lake	4.6	32 min	↑

BANKHEAD from CASCADE POND

≈ The circuit trail passes a half dozen unmarked intersections where you can go astray if you don't have a good idea of the topography and your destination. There are plans to put up signs as far as Bankhead and Two Jack Lake Campground; until then, I do not recommend this route which offers little of interest to see on the way to a destination easily reached by car.

Trail From the Cascade Pond parking area, go north, following the west side of the grassy picnic area. As you approach the last picnic tables at the edge of the trees to the north, take the prominent gravel path which materializes, and leads into the forest. You pass to the north end of the Cadet Camp to an intersection. Turn right and cross first, the Two Jack Lake Road, then a road to a gravel pit. From here, the route follows the old railway grade to Bankhead.

Keep ahead at the interpretive trail and pass the coal train display. Where the main path swings left to the Briquette Town display, an old roadway turns off right. Follow this track to the bed of the Cascade River (now a mere stream) and cross the water, using the high rocks. (They may be slippery.)

On the other side of the stream, follow the roadway uphill. At the top of the hill, where a wide path intersects, make a sharp right turn. Follow the crest of the hill to the power lines. The route bends left into a pine forest which ends at a meadow where a hiker sign shows the way if you are coming from the opposite direction. Proceed through the meadow, and cross the Two Jack Lake Road, keeping east (left) of the Steep Grade road sign. Two small blazed trees show where to pick up the gravel path which angles right, down the steep hillside.

At the bottom of the hill, join a minor track beneath the power lines which you follow to the edge of a hill above Cascade Pond where the trail from Johnson Lake intersects from the left.

Turn right and follow a steep descent to the valley and Cascade Pond.

Trail Section	km from	time out	return time
Cascade Pond		↓	50 min
Two Jack Lake Road	1.0	5 min	45 min
Bankhead, Cascade River	2.9	20 min	30 min
Hiker sign, Two Jack Road	6.4	43 min	10 min
Cascade Pond	8.5	50 min	↑

Mount Astley from Aylmer Lookout

Mt. Astley from Aylmer Lookout

"Some barometer observations taken by Dr. Dawson in 1883, but which have only recently been worked out, show that this valley has a westerly inclination, and that the surface of Ghost River, at the point where it flows past the gap of the Devil's Lake valley on its way to the Bow, is considerably higher than the surface of the lake. This fact would seem to indicate that at some former period, Ghost River, after leaving the mountains, re-entered them again by this valley and joined the Bow at Banff. Its change of course, like that of most streams in the country which have suffered similar diversions, is probably due to a damming of its channel during the glacial period, and the necessity thus imposed upon it of seeking a discharge in a different direction."

R. G. McConnell, Devil's Gap area, *1886 Report on the Geological Structure of a Portion of the Rocky Mountains*

Cascade Mountain and Mount Astley from Lake Minnewanka near the warden cabin

"We encamped in a hollow sheltered by bushes, near the foot of *The Mountain where the Water falls*, — an isolated rocky mountain in no way remarkable, except that a small stream runs down its face and loses itself in a hole in the earth."
The Earl of Southesk, describing Cascade Mountain, 1859, *Saskatchewan and the Rocky Mountains*

~ Historic ghost town ~

Distance **1.1 km (0.7 mi)**
Height Gain **10 m (30')**
Hiking Time **20 min circuit**

Trailhead Turn off the Trans-Canada Highway at the Banff (east) interchange, and follow the Lake Minnewanka Road 3.1 km (1.9 mi) to the Lower Bankhead Parking Lot on the east (right) side of the road. Map Page 13.

Options C Level Cirque, Cascade Ponds and Johnson Lake are other short hikes nearby.

≈ Interpretive pamphlets can be found at the parking lot where the trail begins. Displays with historic photographs help you identify many important sites. If you leave the trail, partially hidden holes and loose debris among the ruins are hazards.

Henry Ness told me that after Bankhead was abandoned, discarded material was taken to an open area and burned. Fires penetrated to the slack which smouldered for four years. When Henry was a warden in 1932, one of his jobs was to put out these fires. He connected hoses to the old water supply from the small dam upstream of the War Memorial, and let the water soak the ground. It is fitting that the man hired for this job was born at Bankhead.

The house where Ness was born was in an area south of the briquette plant, some distance from most of the town's residences at Upper Bankhead. Because there were a dozen small homes here, the townspeople called the place *The Twelve Disciples*. Every spring, a caravan of gypsies camped in the football field nearby, back of the main slack heap. When his mother told him to behave or she would give him to the gypsies, Henry had a vivid image of her threat!

Chinese workers were hired to sort coal at the tipple. Dan McCowan writes that in 1921 the body of a Chinese worker, Yee Chow, was found near a snowbank in the big avalanche slope above town. Apparently he had been searching the slope for herbs, and was killed in a snowslide. He was the first, and only person buried in Bankhead's cemetery — for a while. Other townspeople were buried in Banff because no one wanted to be first in the new cemetery. Yee Chow's relatives also felt this way, and a few years later his body was disinterred and taken to China.

Before his death, Yee Chow visited the elderly town laundryman, Sam Sing, staying till a late hour. Because of this circumstance, Sing was accused of murdering Yee Chow. At the trial, the laundryman denied the charge (since he was not a Christian, he took the oath on a chicken instead of the Bible). For lack of evidence, he was acquitted, but soon after, in response to pressure from suspicious townsfolk, Sam Sing was deported. Someone started a rumor that he laid a curse on Bankhead when he left town, and that this is why the mine closed down a few weeks later, making Bankhead a ghost town.

The CPR, which owned the mines, designed Bankhead as a model community. It grew quickly to a population of 900, making it larger than Banff. After a strike in 1912, the town's fortunes began to decline. The CPR closed the mine following another strike in 1922. By order of the Parks Commissioner, all buildings were removed. Many of them were taken to Canmore and Banff. In 1925, the town ceased to exist.

Although you can walk through the displays in 20 minutes, allow extra time for browsing.

Trail The well marked interpretive trail loops around the industrial section of Bankhead below the parking lot.

Trail Section	km from	time out	return time
Parking lot		↓	20 min
Parking lot	1.1	20 min	↑

Bankhead, ca 1920. By permission, Glenbow Archives, Calgary, NA 705-5.

C LEVEL CIRQUE

~ Awesome cliffs of Cascade Mountain ~

Distance **3.9 km (2.4 mi)**
Height Gain **430 m (1,400')**
Hiking Time **1 hr 16 min**
56 min return

Trailhead Park at the Upper Bankhead Parking Lot, on the Minnewanka Road, 3.5 km north of the Trans-Canada Highway. Note: there are two trailheads here. The one you want is on the west side of the parking lot, behind the no-tenting sign. Map page 13.

Options The trail is short enough to permit you to do other hikes nearby, including the Lower Bankhead interpretive trail. You can hike to a higher (80 m) viewpoint by following the obvious steep trail on the northern edge of the cirque.

≈ This trail goes near several open vent shafts from the mines below. These shafts are fenced off, but the surrounding ground is unstable, and you should keep clear, since the timber supports for the old mine shaft are nearly a century old.

The name of the cirque derives from the C Level seam, highest of the coal seams mined at Bankhead. (Since the seam is folded, the term *level* is misleading.) The pond at the mouth of the cirque used to be called C Level Lake, a source of confusion to listeners who wondered how a lake on Cascade Mountain could reach *sea level*. Also, you had to explain how tiny this *lake* really is.

The cirque is at the base of a spectacular amphitheatre. Mountain sheep may be seen at the start of the trail. In 1949, I watched a small herd emerge from the cool passageway under the remains of the briquette plant at Lower Bankhead. Mountain goat sometimes appear on high ledges of Cascade Mountain. Marmots, pikas, and golden-mantled ground squirrels frequent the boulder-strewn cirque. Once, I saw a weasel in ermine coat here.

Trail The start of the trail follows old mine workings. At the C Level shaft, a branch leads right, to a giant slack heap from where there is a good panorama. The main trail continues uphill, past old mine workings, then turns abruptly left into dense forest to the cirque.

Trail Section	km from	time out	return time
Trailhead		↓	56 min
Junction, slack heap viewpoint	1.3	24 min	41 min
Sharp bend left	1.8	37 min	34 min
Viewpoint near C Level Pond	3.9	76 min	7 min
End of trail up old moraine	4.7	88 min	↑

Cascade Mountain from C Level Lake

Short-tailed weasel in ermine coat

Bankhead 1965

Giant pulley near Johnson Lake

"The coal cars were moved in and out of the mine with electric motors. As the cars come out and dumped their load the motor moved them back into the mine then waited at a switch for another motor coming out. On one particular morning the ingoing motor did not make the switch when the outcoming motor heaved in sight. The motorman could not avoid a crash and jumped in time to save himself as his motor crashed into the standing train of empties. There was quite a spill and the superintendent was much enraged as he viewed the crash. Turning on the pale motorman he shouted, 'You could have saved her if you had stayed with her.'

"'Excuse, sir,' replied the motorman, 'there are no heroes in our family. They all jump.'

"'Well,' shouted the super, 'you jump down to the office and get your time.'" James L. Mitchell, Bankhead, 1904, *Alberta History, Winter, 1985*

Mt. Rundle from Johnson Lake

"Back in Bankhead early in 1905 there was difficulty in withdrawing the money in deposit in the post office. While waiting for it, a section boss of an *extra gang* engaged me to fill in his number of men. He hired me at $2.25 a day which was satisfactory but some of the men resented a new man coming on as they expected one of them would be laid off.

Some time later ... our job was finished at Bankhead. We were given a day to wash and clean up and a number of us were ushered into the office and paid off. Not in money but a statement of days employed to be honoured at the CPR station at Banff....

After a few days the pay cheque did arrive in Banff but when I reached for mine it was made out for $1.75 per day. Angered I threw the cheque back and walked out. A clerk followed me to ask what was wrong. When I told him I had been hired for $2.25 a day he said that's all I would ever get. The others had accepted $1.75 and it was useless for one to ask for more. This later proved to be a fact. I swallowed my pride and accepted the cash."

James L. Mitchell, *Alberta History, Winter, 1985*

JOHNSON LAKE Trails

Trailhead Turn off the Trans-Canada Highway at the Banff (east) interchange, and go 1.1 km (0.7 mi) to the Two Jack Lake Road and turn right. Go 3.5 km (2.2 mi), turn right at the Johnson Lake Road, and drive 2.2 km (1.4 mi) to the Johnson Lake parking area at the end of the road. Map page 13.

Options The Anthracite Hoodoos Trail, Cascade Pond, and four ski trails start from the same parking area. One ski trail passes the oldest known tree in Alberta; another goes by artifacts from mining activities at Anthracite.

JOHNSON LAKE

~ Scenic recreation site ~

Distance **2.6 km (1.6 mi)**
Height Gain **10 m (30')**
Hiking Time **39 min circuit**

≈ Johnson Lake is a popular spot for picnicking, fishing and swimming. Bicycles are permitted; cyclists will find the ski trails, being longer and less crowded, are better suited to biking than the lakeshore trail.

On the south shore, 110 m from the lake, there is a cabin that Billy Carver lived in for 25 years. Most summers, Carver found work in coal mines in northern Alberta, but he spent his winters here. He became known as The Hermit of Anthracite. In December, 1937, two local boys knocked at his door and found Carver inside, desperately sick. They made a fire in the stove of the icy cabin and notified police who took him to hospital. Three months later, the aged miner was taken to an old men's home at Gleichen. The cabin is still in remarkably good shape.

The lake is a good place to observe wildlife: among the animals seen here are loons, geese, ospreys, kingfishers, beavers, and muskrats.

Trail From the gate at the parking lot, take the obvious trail around the lake. The following times assume you take a clockwise direction.

Trail Section	km from	time out	return time
Parking Lot (go north)		↓	39 min
East end of Lake	1.2	21 min	18 min
Hermit Cabin Jct.	1.5	25 min	14 min
Bridge, west end of lake	2.5	37 min	2 min
Parking Lot	2.6	39 min	↑

ANTHRACITE HOODOOS

~ Hoodoos, historic sites ~

Distance **5.7 km (3.5 mi) circuit via mine vent and giant pulley**
Height Loss **60 m (200')**
Hiking Time **1 hr 15 min circuit**

≈ This trail leads past a row of hoodoos. I found Franklin's lady slippers, round-leaved orchids, and bracted orchids growing beside the trail.

You also pass slack heaps and mine sites of Anthracite, an abandoned coal mining town.

It is said that hunters discovered the coal, but surveyors had already noted its presence. Rights to mine the seam were acquired in 1886. By 1887, 300 people lived in Anthracite.

But the venture was seldom profitable. Half the coal brought to the surface was unmarketable and the mine was shut down in 1888 and again in 1890. The lease was sold in 1891, but the new company fared no better. In 1897, a flood on the Cascade River destroyed most of the town and filled the mines, drowning mules

Anthracite, ca 1888. By permission, Whyte Museum of the Canadian Rockies.

and horses. The workers barely escaped. In 1900, the owners lost $17,000. By 1904 only 70 people remained at Anthracite. Because competing coal mines at Canmore, and later Bankhead, were profitable, the enterprise and the town were soon abandoned. Rediscovering a seam of anthracite coal in 1926, Frank Wheatley and his brother renewed activities, supplying Banff for 25 years. Wheatley had been a union leader at Bankhead; Henry Ness, who mined here for a month in 1936 was impressed with the safety features at his workings.

When the Minnewanka dam and the Two Jack Lake channel to the nearby water tower were constructed in 1941, water flooded Wheatley's mine. He was given permission to open a new seam west of the power house. Although this operation closed down in 1950, a Chinese greenhouse operated among the slack piles until 1958.

Mine entrances and vent shafts can be seen near the hillside. If you continue to ski trail #4, you pass near the remains of a giant wooden pulley which was used to operate a fan at the vent shaft of one of Wheatley's mines.

Anthracite's main street ran parallel to the railway and the present highway.

Trail From the parking lot, go across the bridge at the west end of Johnson Lake. Take the trail to your right which follows the stream downhill. Turn left at the animal control fence.

You follow the hillside below the hoodoos to a wet area where you are likely to see diminutive orchids in late June or early July. Where the hoodoos run out, you climb atop the hill and turn left to skiing trail #4. Turn right. After a few metres, the trail makes a sharp left turn (don't take the prominent animal path which continues ahead). After a short distance, you come to the giant wooden pulley.

Go ahead to trail #1 and turn left. Proceed to #3. You can turn left onto #3, which follows the power line to the parking lot, but a more attractive route is to stay on #1 until it intersects with #2 near the east end of Johnson Lake. Diverge to the Johnson Lake trail and take the north or south side to the parking lot.

Trail Section	km from	time out	return time
Parking Lot		↓	73 min
Turn right (after bridge)	0.2	2 min	72 min
Start of hill	2.2	29 min	45 min
Ski Trail #4 jct.	2.4	33 min	42 min
Ski Trail #1 jct.	2.7	37 min	38 min
Wooden pulley	3.0	42 min	33 min
Ski Trail #3 jct.	4.2	57 min	18 min
Ski Trail #2 jct.	4.3	58 min	16 min
Bridge via west lakeshore	5.6	74 min	1 min
Parking Lot	5.7	75 min	↑

OLDEST KNOWN TREE in ALBERTA

~ Ancient Douglas firs ~

Distance **1.0 km (0.6 mi)**
Height Gain **10 m (30')**
Hiking Time **15 min**

≈ If you follow the hillside above Anthracite (especially, if you go east), you will find much larger specimens of Douglas firs, but in 1984, forester L. R. Jozsa identified this as the oldest known tree in Alberta. It began growing about 1310 and was 182 years old when Columbus discovered America. It is situated on the edge of a dry grassy knoll atop a number of hoodoos. Being remote from dense forest and underbrush, it was protected from major forest fires. The dry site shielded it from most fungal agents which attack trees.

Trail From the parking lot, go across the bridge at the outlet of Johnson Lake. Keep ahead at the junction with the trail (left) under the power lines. You soon see a ski trail #1 sign. The path leads to a roadway which divides (the left option is easier), climbs a hill, then reunites. At the brow of the hill, the road turns left and the route divides. Take the roadway to the right (#4) and follow the brow of the hill 160 metres (a little past a fenced vent shaft — due to be filled in, so this landmark may soon be gone) to where a medium-sized Douglas fir can be seen rising from just below the brow of the hill on your right.

Trail Section	km from	time out	return time
Parking Lot		↓	14 min
Ski trail #4 Jct.	0.8	13 min	2 min
Ancient Tree	1.0	15 min	↑

Oldest known tree in Alberta

"The White Tower," Mount Louis from the middle peak of Mt. Edith, one of Leonard Leacock's greatest photographs, from the mountain he climbed most often. This picture was exhibited at the Brussels World Fair, 1958. Mount Louis was Lawrence Grassi's favorite climb.

"Fred Stephens had always protested that climbing peaks, for the mere sake of climbing them, was foolishness — only, if sheep or goats could be shot by so doing, there might be some use in taking the trouble to get to the top of a mountain. From the look of Mount Edith, Collie judged that some very good rock climbing would be required to ascend it; and he looked forward to experiencing all the pleasures of the initiated, when he should have Fred dangling on the end of an Alpine rope.... With due solemnity the bacon was cooked for the last time ... and to wash the supper down Collie had brought with him a bottle of Pommery. Fred, however, was not enthusiastic, or even polite, to the champagne, remarking that he had tasted far better cider in his native and beloved Montana."
J. Norman Collie, Preparations for the first ascent of Mt. Edith, Stutfield and Collie, *Climbs and Exploration in the Canadian Rockies*

Mt. Assiniboine, first visited by Robert Barrett in 1893 and first climbed by James Outram in 1901, viewed from the Nublet. Lakes Magog, Sunburst and Cerulean show in the valley. Mounts Terrapin and Magog are seen left of Assiniboine. Wedgwood Peak peeps over Sunburst Peak. An outlier of The Marshall shows on the right in the distance.

"In 1893 I guided R. L. Barrett of Chicago to the base of the Mt. [Assiniboine]. George Fear of Banff was cook on the trip & we were the first party to visit the Mt. — on the return trip we came by way of Vermilion Pass & visited Marble Canyon on the way which I had found in 1888 when with W. S. Drewry, D.L.S. So Mr. R. L. Barrett was the first tourist to see & visit both Mt. Assiniboine & Marble Canyon." Tom Wilson, *letter to J. B. Harkin, June 28, 1922*

Old Banff, 1885-86, at the site of the present Buffalo Paddock. By permission, Whyte Museum of the Canadian Rockies.

"It was pitched at the foot of some low aspen and spruce covered hills, looking out to the east on a grassy park of five or six acres on which our teams and the teams of half a dozen other parties, and cattle intended for speedy conversion into beef, were quietly grazing. This park opened out between opposing lines of mountains that rose 4000 feet above it; double ranges, the lower wooded at the base and then ribbed with long lines of spruce that struggle with the rocks and frost and snow for a bare living, the higher springing from and immediately behind them great masses of naked limestone contorted by primeval convulsions, polished and worn down by glacial action and atmospheric influences into every conceivable form. Every one of these multitudinous peaks is worthy of a separate description, and would be honoured with it again and again could it only be transported to the plains — say near Winnipeg."

Rev George M. Grant, describing Aylmer Park (Either Old Banff or Hillsdale), 1883, quoted in *Canada, An Historical Magazine, Autumn, 1973*

"Good old days on the trail and evenings around the Campfire, and when the coffee pot upset just as it was beginning to boil and the sugar and salt got wet, and sometimes the beans went sour and the bacon musty and the wind blew the smoke in your eyes, and the ashes and sparks on your blankets, and the butt of the biggest bough hit the small of your back, and the mosquitoes almost crowded you out of the tent, and you heard the horse bell getting fainter and fainter, and you knew dam well they would be five miles away in the morning — but just the same, O Lord, how I wish I could live them all over again." Tom Wilson, *CAJ, 1924*

PREHISTORY and RECENT NATIVES

Archaeological digs in what is now Banff Park (including sites near Vermilion Lakes) indicate toolmaking hunters entered the Rockies 11,500 years ago.

Natives played important roles in the earliest recorded events in the area. A métis named **Alexis Piché** guided Sir George Simpson's party, the first whites to see what is now Banff townsite. (People today know Piché the way Simpson spelled his name: *Peechee.*)

Maskapetoon, also called *Bras Croche* (Broken Arm), a Cree chief, led James Sinclair across the Rockies three times, twice via White Man Pass, and once by Kananaskis Pass.

Both native guides were murdered. In 1843, Piché was shot after a gambling dispute. Wesleyan missionary Robert Rundle was an unhappy witness to Piché's death; he was also indirectly involved in Maskapetoon's demise.

In his younger years, Maskapetoon had scalped his wife whom he suspected of infidelity — she survived and doubtless saw him forsake violence after Rundle converted him to Christianity. The old chief tried to practice the Wesleyan's call for reconciliation and in 1869 entered the camp of hostile Blackfeet to urge them to make peace. They shot him.

In 1841, after he reached the Columbia, Maskapetoon took a ride on a river steamer. John Flett, one of the settlers he guided, reports, "He would not leave the vessel till he had received a certificate that he had been on board of a ship which required neither sails nor paddles. With this paper he said he could go back to his people, and, although they would not believe him, yet they would give full credence to all that was written." *The Beaver, Spring 1971*

The Palliser Expedition hired a number of native guides, including a famous Stoney hunter whose name James Hector couldn't pronounce, so he called him Nimrod, after the Biblical hunter. The Stoney was later baptized by the name **Hector Nimrod**.

Another Stoney, **Edwin Hunter,** called *The Gold Seeker* took prospector Joe Healy to a mineral find at Copper Mountain. Walter Wilcox reports that soon after, Edwin dropped dead while describing a buffalo hunt. Fellow Stoneys suspected his sudden death was a punishment for showing the shiny rocks to a White.

William Twin, who lived for 97 years, remembered as a boy meeting James Hector near Lake Louise just after the famous accident which gave Kicking Horse Pass its name. William showed John Brewster Ya Ha Tinda; after John's death, he adopted the Brewster boys and guided them to unmapped sites like Mystic Lake. He was hired by the CPR to escort guests staying at the Lake Louise Chalet. The remarkable Stoney astounded the Whites when he tracked a missing man over Simpson Pass.

Not all Indians were friendly to the explorers. The Blackfeet were considered hostile. James Sinclair's 1854 party was raided near the mouth of the Kananaskis River. Botanist Eugène Bourgeau left the Palliser Expedition because of fear of the Blackfeet.

The Belgian Jesuit, Pierre De Smet got on well with the Indians he met, but was surprised at how the Stoneys prepared food in 1845.

The Stoney Twins, Joshua and William. By permission, Whyte Museum of the Canadian Rockies.

"If a bit of dried meat, or any other provision is in need of being cleansed, the dainty cook fills her mouth with water and spurts it with her whole force upon the fated object. A certain dish, which is considered a prime delicacy among the Indians, is prepared in a most singular manner.... The whole process belongs exclusively to the female department. They commence by rubbing their hands with grease, and collecting in them the blood of the animal, which they boil with water; finally they fill the kettle with fat and hashed meat. But — hashed with the teeth! Often half a dozen old women are occupied in this mincing operation for hours; mouthful after mouthful is masticated, and thus passes from the mouth into the cauldron, to compose the choice ragout of the Rocky Mountains. Add to this, by way of an exquisite dessert, an immense dish of crusts, composed of pulverized ants, grasshoppers and locusts, and that had been dried in the sun, and you may then be able to form some idea of Assiniboin luxury."

Mount Rundle, named for Rev. Robert Rundle who first visited the Banff area in 1844. Photo taken late afternoon from the Cory Pass trail.

"[Rundle] had with him a favorite cat which he had brought with him in the canoes from Edmonton, being afraid to leave her behind him, as there was some danger of her being eaten during his absence. This cat was the object of a good deal of amusement amongst the party, of great curiosity amongst the Indians, and of a good deal of anxiety and trouble to its kind master....

"No sooner had we mounted our rather skittish animals than the Indians crowded around, and Mr. Rundell, who was rather a favorite amongst them, came in for a large share of their attentions, which seemed to be rather annoying to his horse. His cat he had tied to the pummel of his saddle by a string, about four feet long, round her neck, and had her safely, as he thought, concealed in the breast of his capote. She, however, did not relish the plunging of the horse, and

Early morning mists (rare in Alberta's Rockies) fill the valley in this view of Mount Rundle taken near the same site shown on page 188. Sulphur Mountain, source of the hot springs which led to the creation of Banff Park, shows on the right.

made a spring out, utterly astonishing the Indians, who could not conceive where she had come from. The string brought her up against the horse's legs, which she immediately attacked. The horse now became furious, kicking violently, and at last threw Mr. Rundell over his head, but fortunately without much injury. All present were convulsed with laughter, to which the Indians added screeching and yelling as an accompaniment, rendering the whole scene indescribably ludicrous. Puss's life was saved by the string breaking." Paul Kane, *Wanderings of an Artist*.

John Rowand, who was present, adds, "When my friend was thrown God knows how far, he never thought of his danger, only calling out, 'I hope my poor cat is not killed'." *The Rundle Journals 1840-1848, ed Gerald M. Hutchinson and Hugh A. Dempsey*

EXPLORERS, EMIGRANTS, SPIES, MISSIONARIES

David Thompson and Duncan McGillivray entered the Bow Valley in 1800, climbing a ridge near Exshaw. Prior to 1930, the eastern boundary of Rocky Mountains Park (now named Banff Park) was just east of Exshaw.

In 1841, **Sir George Simpson** (ca 1790-1860) entered what is now Banff Park while on a journey which proved to be the first circumnavigation of the globe by a land route.

As Governor of Ruperts Land for the Hudson's Bay Company, Simpson virtually ruled half of Canada and was called *The Little Emperor*. He had intended to canoe the river system and cross the Rockies via Athabasca Pass, the usual Company route. **John Rowand**, (1787-1854) Chief Factor at Fort Edmonton, accom-panied him through western Canada. Rowand's native guides warned Simpson the Columbia River would be in full flood. Consequently, the Governor changed plans, crossing the mountains by a more southerly pass on horseback.

Sir George Simpson, ca 1860. By permission, Hudson's Bay Archives.

Simpson compiled a secret assessment of senior company employees in a *Character Book*, completed in 1832. The book was kept locked in his possession. Moreover, the entries were coded so if anyone else read them, he wouldn't know who was described; the code key was kept separate. No doubt this secrecy was because many of the comments were acrid, and Simpson had experienced bad feelings when some previous assessments, sent in confidence to the Company's officers in London, got back to the employees. Typical of Simpson's invective is his description of Colin Robertson as "A frothy trifling conceited man, who would starve in any other Country." Of Donald McKenzie he wrote, "He is one of the worst and most dangerous men I ever was acquainted with. My presence alone keeps him sober."

One of the few men to receive praise in the *Character Book* was John Rowand. "One of the most pushing bustling men in the service whose zeal and ambition in the discharge of his duty is unequaled, rendering him totally regardless of every personal comfort and indulgence. Warm hearted and friendly in an extraordinary degree.... Of a fiery disposition and as bold as a lion.... Has by his superior management realized more money for the concern than any three of his colleagues since the coalition; and altho' his education has been defective is a very clear headed clever fellow. Will not tell a lie ... but has sufficient address to evade the truth when it suits his purpose: full of drollery and humour and generally liked and respected by Indians servants and his own equals."

Rowand was in charge of the Saskatchewan District for the HBC. At Fort Edmonton he owned the biggest house west of Toronto (70x60' and 3 stories high) as well as the first refrigeration plant in Western Canada. His ice house held as many as 600 buffalo carcasses.

Simpson hired Alexis Piché "a half-breed native of the Kootonais country" and a "chief of the Mountain Crees," to guide him across the Rocky Mountains.

When he made the 1841 trip across the Rockies, Simpson was no longer the young man who used to race up and down the rivers to the company posts led by his piper. Nevertheless, with horse and cart, he covered fifty miles a day crossing the prairies fast enough to pass **James Sinclair** (ca 1806-1856) and his party of Red River métis settlers.

Sinclair was proud to call himself a half-breed (his maternal grandmother was Cree). He was also a graduate of the University of Edinburgh.

Simpson and Rowand warned the settlers they would be overtaken by winter. (There were 116 emigrants with 55 carts, horses, cattle and dogs.) Simpson arranged for them to use the Athabasca Pass water route instead of the more southerly route Sinclair wanted to take. However, Sinclair kept to his plans, abandoning the carts at Edmonton and going by horse across the Rockies. He was guided by a Cree chief, Maskapetoon, who felt snubbed when Simpson chose Piché as his guide, so he was eager to offer his services to Sinclair. The Cree was a celebrity who had been received by U. S. President Andrew Jackson in Washington, D. C.

Like his guide, Sinclair had traveled widely, and was a friend of Ulysses S. Grant, having assisted the future Civil War general and U. S. President in courting his wife.

Unlike Simpson, who followed the north and west shores of Lake Minnewanka, Sinclair took the east and south side. After turning east to cross the Bow River, he followed the Spray River to White Man Pass. Fur traders named the place after him, spelling it *St. Clair's Pass*. (Today, a pass farther west, which Maskapetoon called Red Rock Gorge, bears Sinclair's name.)

John Flett, one of the settlers, described the scene as they abandoned their carts and loaded the cattle before they entered the Rockies. "The oxen ... were unused to the mode of traveling, and, becoming frightened, a stampede ensued. Then what a sight — oxen bellowing, kicking, running; horses neighing, rearing, plunging; children squalling; women crying; men swearing, shouting and laughing; while the air seemed full of blankets, kettles, sacks of pots, pans and jerkied buffalo."

The journey was a memorable achievement. The emigrants took almost five months, traveled two thousand miles, avoided hostile Blackfeet, forded large rivers and crossed unknown mountain ranges. Three children were born en route, additionally encumbering the party. All the settlers arrived safely.

Sinclair's Red River emigrants represented a feeble effort by the Hudson's Bay Company to counteract the influx of Americans in the disputed Oregon Territory. Delays in granting land undermined the purpose of getting a loyal population and played into the hands of American agitators. In the end, the settlers championed the U. S. claim. Just before his death, like most of the people he led, Sinclair applied for U. S. citizenship.

In 1850, at Simpson's request, Sinclair made a second crossing of White Man Pass with Maskapetoon to investigate the condition of the HBC forts which had fallen into poor condition since the 1846 boundary settlement. In 1854, he led another party of emigrants, and remained to manage the fort at Walla Walla which the HBC retained under the boundary settlement.

Sinclair, who most of his life had espoused native causes, was shot dead by insurgent Indians while trying to help a white woman reach the safety of his fort.

When **Robert Terrill Rundle** (1811-96) arrived at the Hudson's Bay post at Fort Edmonton October 17, 1840, the local officials thought they were getting a resident Protestant chaplain. They didn't expect a missionary who would spend nine years traveling long distances on foot and horseback visiting encampments of Cree and Assiniboine Indians. Twice, Rundle went near what is now Banff townsite.

His success as a Wesleyan Missionary was noted a decade after he returned to England by both Palliser and Southesk who were surprised at the Christian deportment and accomplishments of natives who still remembered Rundle. In addition to religious instruction, Rundle taught the Indians syllabic writing and encouraged them to plant vegetables to supplement their traditional hunting and trapping. John Palliser, skeptical of the value of missionary work, was sufficiently impressed by the Indians' "reverence and enthusiasm" for this Methodist, to change the name of *Terrace Mountain* (Hector's choice) to *Mount Rundle*.

In 1859, when Southesk reached the prairies, short of food, he was looked after by Indians, and was surprised to find that on Sundays, the Stoneys sang hymns — in *Cree*. When Rundle came to Edmonton, he learned the language of the Cree, who had dominated western Canada since the first contact by the white man. His subsequent dealings were principally with the Stoneys, who had only recently come this far west. Consequently, he taught them hymns in the only native language he knew.

Forty years after Rundle left, the Duchess of Somerset recounted another example of Rundle's influence. "[Mr. Stewart] told me ... when he first arrived here everything was in a state of disorder, not a house in the place, and his party were in tents and not too well stocked with provisions. Under these circumstances it was deemed advisable not to encourage the Indians, who from time to time came round begging for food.... However, late one afternoon an Indian arrived with his squaw and papoose and a little boy; they had evidently come a long way, and when food was refused the small child began to cry, and the Indian gave him his pipe, which is supposed to allay the pangs of hunger. On seeing that they were really in need, Mr. Stewart ordered them a dish of food; before touching it they sat down, and closing their eyes, asked their grace. The sight of starving people not forgetful to thank their Father above for His mercies could not fail to impress any one who witnessed the scene."

James Sinclair ca 1850. By permission British Columbia Archives. BCARS HP 4107

The Stoneys' regard for Rundle is also demonstrated in myth: after he left them forever, they told a story of his coming. It is recorded in E. E. Clark's *Indian Legends of Canada*.

In 1844, Rundle made his first visit to the Rockies, setting up camp on the Bow River on November 8. The sight inspired him.

"So here I am at last in the Ry Mts. Fine pine brush here.... Heard noises, perhaps stones falling in the mountains, thro' deer passing. Weather not cold for the season.... It is now night & I am writing before the fire. Thought today ... of Sinai & the delivery of the law by

Henry J. Warre's 1845 watercolor of White Man Pass. By permission, National Archives of Canada, C 31269

"Sunday 27 July — We had a very cold night with hard frost and at [6:30] we commenced the ascent of the height of land up very steep scarp of about 1200 ft to a small lake and about a mile from this we found the waters running to the west but the view still impeded by the surrounding mountains which appear higher and more beautiful in shape as we advance. We took 4 1/2 hours to cross."

Henry J. Warre, White Man Pass, 1845, *Journal, Vol. I, National Archives of Canada*

Jehovah. What a fine place for such an event!" Next day he tried to ascend a summit, the first record of a mountaineering attempt near Banff.

"Am now climbing a mountain. Here are two veins, perhaps of spar, in the bed of rock where I am now sitting.... I became quite ill thro' fatigue &c. but was in good spirits when climbing, until I was very high up. I made two attempts to get up an elevation but could not succeed. Rocks very steep — felt very weak, so weak, that at last I was near fainting whilst passing over a projecting ledge or rock. What a moment of anxiety. I have some recollection of calling to the Almighty to assist me & praised be His name, my prayer was heard."

Since he would have been wearing leather-soled boots which would slip on the mountain slopes, it is small wonder Rundle was frightened and didn't make the summit. He climbed high enough to throw a stone over a cliff and hear it drop "thousands of feet below."

The return was even worse. "I descended to the next stage. It was presumptuous of me I know but I began again to see if I could not find a way to scale higher but I could not succeed so I now abandoned my design & commenced descending. I was not careful about the road & had great difficulty in descending. I was very weak from want of food, having left without breakfast, & began to feel afraid; ever & anon too I heard the moving stones which terrified me. How hard, too, to pass along the steep sloping sides sloping away to fearful descent. At length, however, I reached the bottom, but how was I to get to the encampment? I had lost the road."

He was away so long, his companions fired shots to help him find his way back to camp. He wrote, "Had *breakfast* about sunset."

In 1845, Rundle met the Jesuit priest Pierre De Smet at Rocky Mountain House. Rundle was always worried that his converts would succumb to the "snares of popery"; surprisingly, he got along well with De Smet, the rare note of anything but cordial relations coming when the two got into an argument on doctrine which Rundle said he won.

On June 28, 1847, Rundle camped at "Wildcat Lake." (Six years earlier, Sir George Simpson had named it *Peechee Lake* after his métis guide. *Wild Cat* or *Lynx*, was the Cree name for Peechee. Today, we call it Lake Minnewanka.)

"This is the most interesting Lake I ever saw. Fish are in it; one kind very fine, salmon or trout.... The water has at times a beautiful appearance, in part of it owing to something about light. Does it not look green?

"... The lake is several miles in length, embedded in the mountains which rise in grandeur. The water at times has the most beautiful appearance....

"In this neighborhood lies buried a half-caste girl ... whom I trust to meet in my Father's house above. I baptized her at Rocky Mountain House.... She took great delight in religion and once when prayers were held in her father's tent and she was unable to sit up without assistance, she was held in her father's arms so she could take part. She died in the mountains where there was not sufficient depth of soil to bury her, so her remains were brought to this part. Passing near her tomb caused peculiar emotions of hallowed pleasure in my mind."

The place seems an appropriate location for a grave. Before Simpson changed the lake's name, it was called Dead Lake which later became Ghost or Devil's Lake. (The current Cree name is more neutral: Minnewanka, meaning *lake of the water spirit*. It was applied by Park Superintendent George Stewart).

Rundle carved his initials (RTR) and the date (July 1, 1847) on a tree near the lake. It is unlikely the tree survived the forest fires which devastated the area about the time of the construction of the railway, or the raising of the lake (25 m) for hydro dams. The missionary followed the shore to the Dead (now, Ghost) River where he left the mountains.

The Rev. Robert Rundle. By permission, Whyte Museum of the Canadian Rockies.

Life in Western Canada had its dangers. Rundle was thrown from his horse while protecting his cat; he broke an arm in another fall. Sled dogs had him down, and almost killed him before help arrived. He had a lucky escape from a prairie fire. When he fell through ice on a prairie lake, he narrowly averted drowning by clinging to a buffalo corpse.

Rundle left Canada, worn out with injuries. He hoped to return to the Stoneys. Wesleyan Methodists in England turned over the ministry to the Canadian church, and missionaries from England, perhaps, were no longer wanted.

Lt. **Henry J. Warre** (1819-98) was the first man known to paint in the Rockies (earlier Indian pictographs were done by unknown

Henry J. Warre's sketch of camp at the base of Mt. Rundle (near the site of Canmore), looking to Cascade Mountain. By permission, National Archives of Canada, C-1618.

artists). In 1845 he and Lt. Mervin Vavasour crossed White Man Pass on a secret mission to investigate the possibilities of defending the Oregon country against U. S. claims.

American president Polk was claiming all the West from parallel 42, the northern boundary of Spanish territory, to parallel 54° 40', the southern boundary of Russian territory. Britain's rights to the Columbia River drainage and north were countered by Polk's rallying cry: "Fifty-four, forty or fight!"

Warre and Vavasour were to assess the problems of sending British troops, and to estimate the numbers of American and Canadian citizens in the area. While pretending they were tourists, hunting and fishing, the pair were instructed to use the route "lately passed by [Sinclair's] emigrant families from Red River Settlement." Warre kept a discreet journal of his activities and observations on the trip.

The lieutenants crossed the mountains on horseback, leaving Edmonton with 60 ponies. By the time they reached Fort Colville on the Columbia River, only 27 horses survived. "The steepness of the mountain passes, the want of proper nourishment, the fearful falls that some of these animals sustained, rolling in some instances many hundred feet into the foaming torrent beneath, combined to cause this great loss. The scenery was grand in the extreme; similar in form to the Alps of Switzerland, you felt that you were in the midst of desolation: no habitations, save those of the wild Indians, were within hundreds of miles; but few civilized beings had ever even viewed this."

Next year, Warre and Vavasour returned via Athabasca Pass. They stated that transporting troops "over such impracticable Mountains would appear to Us quite infeasible." Ironically, by the time they submitted their report, the issue had been settled, Britain agreeing to fix the border at the 49th parallel.

Warre was an amateur artist. He made sketches and watercolors of the scenery (and the forts) along the route. A book of his lithographs, *Sketches in North America and the Oregon Territory* was published in 1848. He went on to a distinguished career in the Imperial army, including service at Sebastapool in the Crimean War. He was knighted and attained the rank of general.

Warre and Vavasour were led through the Rockies by **Peter Skene Ogden** (1794-1854), chief factor of the Hudson's Bay Company.

In his notorious *Character Book*, Simpson gave Ogden equivocal words of praise and condemnation: "A keen, sharp off hand fellow of superior abilities to most of his colleagues, very hardy and active and not sparing of his personal labour.... His ambition knows no bounds and his conduct and actions are not influenced or governed by any good or honourable principle. In fact, I consider him one of the most unprincipled Men in the Indian Country, who would soon get into habits of dissipation.... A man likely to be exceedingly troublesome if advanced ... but his services have been so conspicuous for several years past, that I think he has strong claims to advancement."

Apparently Simpson's opinion changed, for after Ogden's death, he wrote, "Our regard for each other had been the growth of years, on my side increasing as I became more & more intimately acquainted with his character and worth."

After crossing White Man Pass heading west, Warre and Vavasour met **Father Pierre-Jean De Smet** (1801-73) who was heading east. The parties met at Pend d'Oreille Lake near the Columbia River and crossed paths again next May when, on their return trips, they traveled over Athabasca Pass.

A Belgian Jesuit, De Smet, was a man of wealth and education who devoted himself to missionary work in western America. He crossed the Canadian Rockies in an unsuccessful attempt to reach the Blackfoot Indians whom he hoped to convert and persuade to live in peace with the native tribes of Oregon.

Because he was overweight, friends were skeptical he could withstand the hardships of the trip, but De Smet had been strong and athletic since youth (childhood friends used to call him *Samson*). Traveling the narrow twisting mountain paths on horseback proved a problem for the heavy man.

"I have a little word of advice to give all who wish to visit these latitudes. At the entrance of each thick forest, one should render himself as slender, as short and as contracted as possible, imitating ... an intoxicated cavalier, but with skill and presence of mind. I mean to say, he should know how to balance himself — cling to the saddle in every form, to avoid the numerous branches that intercept his passage, ever ready to tear him into pieces, and flay his face and hands. Notwithstanding these precautions, it is rare to escape without paying tribute in some manner to the ungracious forest. I one day found myself in a singular and critical position: in attempting to pass under a tree that inclined across the path, I perceived a small branch in the form of a hook, which threatened me. The first impulse was to extend myself upon the neck of my horse. Unavailing precaution! It caught me by the collar of my surtout, the horse still continuing his pace. Behold me suspended in the air — struggling like a fish at the end of a hook. Several respectable pieces of my coat floated, in all probability, a long time in the forest, as an undeniable proof of my having paid toll in passing through it. A crushed and torn hat — an eye black and blue — two deep scratches on the cheek, would in a civilized country, have given me the appearance rather of a bully issuing from the Black Forest, than of a missionary."

Not only was he tough and stoical, he was determined. When warned he couldn't make the return trip — via Athabasca Pass — because of his girth, he fasted for 30 days.

De Smet was good humored about his corpulence. He wrote his niece, "If ever you build a new house, give the door of my chamber six inches extra width." He added, "Uncle Pierre ... has a mouth ... which hardly ever opens save to laugh or to make others laugh".

Everyone seemed to like the Jesuit, including Rundle who usually railed against "popery." When the two met at Rocky Mountain House, the Methodist had nothing but kind words for the priest.

In 1864, during the worst hostilities with the Sioux, De Smet was permitted entry to Sitting Bull's camp. General D. S. Stanley notes, "I could give you only an imperfect idea of the privations and dangers of this journey, unless you were acquainted with the great plains and the Indian character, which is naturally inclined to vengeance. Father De Smet, alone of the entire white race, could penetrate to these cruel savages and return safe and sound. One of the chiefs, in speaking to him while he was in the hostile camp, told him, 'If it had been any other man than you, Black-robe, this day would have been his last....'

"He is the only man for whom I have ever seen Indians evince a real affection. They say, in their simple and open language, that he is the only white man who has not a forked tongue; that is, who never lies to them. The reception that they gave him in the hostile camp was enthusiastic and magnificent. They came twenty miles to meet him, and the principal chiefs, riding beside him, conducted him to the camp in great triumph. This camp comprised more than 500 lodges, which, at the ratio of six persons to the lodge, gave a total of 3,000 Indians. During his visit, which lasted three days, the principal chiefs, Black Moon and

Rev. Pierre-Jean De Smet, S. J.

Sitting Bull, who had been redoubtable adversaries of the whites for the last four years of the war, watched constantly over the safety of the missionary; they slept beside him at night, lest some Indian might seek to avenge upon his person the death of some kinsman killed by the whites. During the day time, multitudes of children flocked to his lodge, and the mothers brought him their new babies that he might lay his hands on them and bless them.

"In the gathering of the Indians the head chiefs promised to put an end to the war. Sitting Bull declared that he had been the most mortal enemy of the whites, and had fought them by every means in his power; but now that the Black-robe had come to utter the words of peace, he renounced warfare and would never again lift his hand against the whites."

As he ascended White Man Pass, religious images came to the priest's mind. "Projecting mountains rise like holy towers where man might commune with the sky — terrible precipices hang in fragments overhead....

"After much fatigue, labor and admiration, on the 15th [September, 1845] we traversed the high lands separating the waters of Oregon from those of the south branch of the Saskatchewan.... The Christian's standard, the cross, has been reared at the source of these two rivers: may it be a sign of salvation and peace to all the scattered and itinerant tribes east and west of these gigantic and lurid mountains.

"On the cypress which serves for constructing the cross, the eagle, emblem of the Indian warrior, perches himself. The huntsman aims — the noble bird lies prostrate, and even in his fall, seems to retain his kingly pride....

"We breakfasted on the bank of a limpid lake at the base of the Cross of Peace."

De Smet was torn between his desire to convert the Blackfeet and his fear of them resulting from tales of their savagery. He met, instead, a band of friendly *Assiniboins of the Forest* who were suffering from disease. He feared their dogs — with good reason. One of them crept into his tent and devoured the fur lining of his riding breeches, a pair of shoes, and the collar (leather or fur) of his cassock. "I have little charity for these poor brutes."

Although in his journal, Rundle describes meeting the Jesuit, De Smet makes no mention of the Methodist missionary, unless he is the unnamed Calvinist of the following story.

"Now if you want something about Indians to fill a corner with, here is an anecdote, not altogether savage.... Among the converted Indians on the Canadian frontier there was once a certain Jean Baptiste....

"Jean Baptiste it appears had done a little thieving in his time, and when he was converted the Black-robe enjoined upon him to restore two dollars to the Calvinist minister of the neighborhood. Jean Baptiste accordingly presented himself before the minister, and the following dialogue ensued:

"'Well, what do you want?' said the preacher to the native.

"'Me, one time, rob you. Black-robe tell me, *Jean Baptiste, you give the money back*.'

"'What money is that?' inquired the reverend.

"'Two dollar. Me, bad Indian, rob you; now, me good Indian, got water on forehead — me, heap child Great Spirit — here your money.'

"'All right — don't steal any more — good bye, Jean Baptiste.'

Banff, ca 1890. Photo from the collection of Henry Ness.

"'Ah — good bye no good; me want something else.'

"'What do you want?'

"'Me want receipt.'

"'A receipt! What do you want a receipt for? Did the Black-robe tell you to ask for one?' said the surprised minister.

"'Black-robe say nothing. Jean Baptiste (pointing to himself) want receipt.'

"'But why do you want a receipt? You stole the money, and you have given it back; that is all there is about it.'

"'That not all about it; listen. You old — me young; you die first — after while, me die. Understand?'

"'No, I don't. What is it you mean?'

"'Listen — me mean heap. Me go heaven after while, go knock on gate. Great Chief Saint Peter come open — say,

"'Hello, Jean Baptiste, what you want?'

"'Me want come in Great Spirit's lodge.'

"'How about your sins, Jean Baptiste:'

"'Black-robe forgive sins all right.'

"'How about that two dollar you stole from minister? You give him back? You show me your receipt!'

"Now then, poor Jean Baptiste, poor old Indian, got no receipt; have to run all over hell to find you!"

Thirteen years after De Smet reached the Bow River, **James Hector** (1834-1907), deputy leader and expedition doctor for the Palliser Expedition, followed the valley past the site of Banff to Vermilion Pass. He detoured three miles out of his way to see Bow Falls. Next year, 1859, he again explored the Bow River. He named Cascade Mountain (a translation of the Stoney Indian name), Castle Mountain, and Mt. Ball. Years later, he told Mary Schäffer Warren he had ascended Cascade Mountain.

The Palliser Report was pessimistic about the agricultural potential of the southern prairies. In 1879, botanist **John Macoun** (1831-

1920) went up the Bow River as far as the *Point of Rocks* from where he saw the Cascade River. Macoun's more optimistic reports on south-western Canada prompted the government to abandon plans to push the CPR through the more northerly Yellowhead Pass route. His daughter Clara married surveyor A. O. Wheeler.

THE CANADIAN PACIFIC RAILWAY

The railway reached the site of Banff in 1883, opening the area to tourism. Surveyors had given the name *Aylmer Park* to what is now the Buffalo Paddock. (CPR surveyor Fred Aylmer said it looked like an English park.) A station was built at Aylmer Park; for a few weeks it was known simply as Siding 29, then it was named Banff. It soon boasted two general stores, a lumber yard, butcher shop, hotel and saloon (selling home-made whiskey). After the present Banff station was built, the old siding continued in use until 1888 (photo, p. 186). For a few years, there were two Banffs; the station handier to the Banff Springs Hotel prevailed.

For almost thirty years, the railway was the only means of reaching Banff, and it continued to be a major means of visitor transport until about 1960 when high operating costs and competing highways made passenger traffic by rail unprofitable.

The CPR influenced the development of the Banff area in other ways. The company erected the Banff Springs Hotel and the first boathouse at Lake Minnewanka. Backcountry lodges at Mt. Assiniboine and Shadow Lake as well as many of the present trails were built by the CPR. Free passes were issued to bring founding members of the Alpine Club of Canada from diverse places to Winnipeg to establish the organization. In addition, The Trail Riders of the Canadian Rockies and The Skyline Hikers were created by the railway company.

Since the CPR allowed children to ride free, when Edward Whymper sent a young eagle from Banff to the Vancouver aviary, he told the station agent the bird should travel free of charge because it was under five years old.

Eleanor Luxton reports an unintentional gaff, when Sir John A. Macdonald's wife was traveling to Banff. Superintendent Niblock wired a request to have a bouquet of flowers presented to Lady Macdonald. By the time the message reached Banff, the key words were misspelled, and when she arrived, the great lady was given a bag of flour by the dutiful station agent.

THE SURVEYORS

As the railway opened up the Rockies, The Geological Survey of Canada began mapping the area. **G. M. Dawson** (a dwarfish hunchback who became Canada's most renowned surveyor), **R. G. McConnell**, **J. J. McArthur** and **A. O. Wheeler** are the best known men who worked extensively in the Banff area.

THE HOT SPRINGS

David McDougall was taken to the Middle Springs and the Cave and Basin site in the early 1870's. He said the Stoney Indians brought their sick to the Springs. They told him it was their peace grounds.

The first attempt to explore and exploit the Cave came on August 7, 1883 when three railway workers, **William** and **Tom McCardell** and **Frank McCabe** entered the cave, using a pole to descend a hole in the roof. They built a shack on the site and registered a claim to the springs. A lawyer from Ottawa persuaded McCabe to sell him the rights and to forge McCardell's signature. The Government of Canada became involved in the ensuing legal dispute and appropriated the site for Canada's first national park, awarding the main claimants financial compensation.

William McCardell settled in Anthracite. McCabe left town. He never saw a penny of the $1,500 the slick-talking lawyer had promised. Perhaps the experience made him suspicious. Years later, he set a burglar alarm at his cabin near Fort Steele, balancing a nine foot saw over the entrance so it would crash down when the door was opened. After a few hours of sleep, he headed outside in the dark to answer a call of nature. The trap worked perfectly: McCabe spent two months in hospital.

For several years, access to the Cave was by a tree ladder. Many distinguished people (including Sir John A Macdonald, his wife, and the Prince of Wales) used this hazardous method of entering the Cave.

William McCardell. By permission, Whyte Museum of the Canadian Rockies.

Bill Peyto. Photo, Walter Wilcox, The Rockies of Canada.

In 1887, a tunnel was blasted to the Cave, causing the temperature inside to drop. (McCardell had found it so hot, he removed most of his clothes.)

The Upper Hot Springs were also developed, Dr. Brett piped hot sulphur water to his hotel which he named The Sanitarium, and people called Banff *Sulphur City*. The hot waters provided relief to people suffering from complaints such as rheumatism. On nearby trees, crutches were hung with testimonials such as "I had to be carried up to the springs.... I had not walked for two years, and every movement was an agony. In three weeks I walked down to Banff, and in five I ran a foot race. Praise God!" Soon, extravagant claims were made for afflictions from eczema to syphilis.

OUTFITTERS

Tom Wilson, a packer for the CPR survey, became Banff's first outfitter. Although his greatest discovery trips (Lake Louise, Emerald Lake) date back to 1882, it was 1893 when he guided R. L. Barrett to Mt. Assiniboine. After this last major exploration trip, Tom became so much in demand that he spent most of his time in Banff running the business, hiring younger men to lead the trips. Most of the famous guides in the early days got started with him.

Tom became a public relations man, lecturing at the CPR hotels in Banff and Lake Louise. His ready wit was demonstrated when he thanked the Trail Riders for honoring him with a plaque. "Only once before did I ever make an impromptu speech — it was short, and this will also be short. The first occasion was when a cayuse stamped upon my foot. You can imagine what I said."

Tom's best known protégé was **Bill Peyto**, who set up his own business in 1901. Walter Wilcox who often hired him, considered Peyto "one of the most conscientious and experienced men with horses I have ever known." Curiously, some years later, Peyto named one of his horses *Wilcox*.

Although Peyto may have been great with horses, Henry Ness called him "one of the worst men with an axe I've ever seen."

Tom Wilson and Jim Brewster. By permission of the Whyte Museum of the Canadian Rockies.

Samuel Allen. Photo, AAJ, 1941. By permission, Whyte Museum of the Canadian Rockies.

Peyto's eccentricity is legendary. Once he loosed a trapped lynx in a Banff bar, watching with interest as other patrons fled. The feline was then donated to Banff's zoo.

Peyto joined the warden service in 1913. He had a quick temper, as Henry Ness witnessed about 1927 at a camp near Redearth Pass. An eager young assistant, Walter Childs, saddled a yellow horse named Snake for the older warden. Snake bucked Peyto off. The furious warden, who always packed a nickel-plated pistol, accused his helper of putting a bur under the saddle. "If I thought you'd done that on purpose, I'd shoot you dead where you stand."

Ness was astounded that anyone could suspect Childs' intentions. "He was not the stereotype of a rough, tough, cursing warden; he always wanted to be pleasing others."

The **Brewster brothers, Jim and Bill**, entered the guiding business in 1899. **Jim** expanded into transportation, and his younger brother **Pat** took over the outfitting in 1926. One of Bill's grandsons, **Bud Brewster** —

with his children — carries on the guiding tradition of the family.

When King George VI and his Queen visited Banff in 1939, Jim Brewster drove them around town and accompanied them up Tunnel Mountain. The monarch asked to see Jim's hunting trophies, so the royal couple were brought, unexpectedly, to Jim's home. The story that Jim announced the arrival to his wife with the words, "Dell, we got company!" may be apocryphal, but there is no doubt the visit took her by surprise. Jim commented, "I may forget a lot of things about the royal visit but never my wife's face when we walked in the door."

MOUNTAIN CLIMBERS

Many of the first visitors to the Banff area came in hopes of making first ascents in the Rockies. **Robert Barrett** (1871-1969), guided by Tom Wilson, made the first recorded visit to Mt. Assiniboine in 1893. Barrett agreed with Wilson that the climb "was not a one boy job."

Barrett was a wealthy Harvard student who in his long life (he lived almost 98 years) pursued his enthusiasm for geography and the mountains in numerous expeditions to remote areas around the world. Geoffrey Martin wrote, "He shunned life in settled places, was deliriously happy when perched on a mountain top, and in particular enjoyed exercising there vigorously at dawn and dusk."

Walter Wilcox. Photo, American Alpine Journal, 1944.

In 1894, **Samuel Allen** (1874-1945) reconnoitered Mt. Assiniboine with Yule Carryer. Next April, Barrett wrote Wilson to arrange another trip, if he could find two others to share the expenses. "I have one man sure, but the third, an expert climber, I am not sure of." The one man was **James Porter** (1871-1939). The third, probably Allen, was demonstrating early signs of schizophrenia and alienating even close friends. At the last moment, **Walter Wilcox** (1869-1949), Allen's former companion at Lake Louise, persuaded Wilson to let him take Allen's place. The three men climbed minor peaks in the area, but the great achievement was the reconnaissance of Mt. Assiniboine by Barrett, Wilcox and outfitter Bill Peyto. In two days, they circled the great massif, a distance of 51 miles by Wilcox's estimate. En route, they met Allen, an encounter which must have been awkward for both Wilcox and Allen.

Left out of Barrett's plans, Allen made his own arrangements, taking Dr. Howard Smith. Allen and Smith headed south from Ferro Pass and reached a low summit from which they saw the southwest face of Assiniboine. Allen says little else about this trip which lasted a month. After 1895 Allen never returned to the Rockies.

Robert Lemoyne Barrett. Photo, courtesy, Harvard University Archives.

His father forbade further trips, and soon after, the young man was confined to an asylum. Probably he was ordered not to complete the published account of his 1895 trip to Mount Assiniboine. One manifestation of his mental illness was an obsession to climb great mountains (including Mt. Everest). All these early trips to Assiniboine went via Ferro Pass.

In 1899, Wilcox returned to Assiniboine with **Henry G. Bryant** (1859-1932) and Louis J. Steele, pioneering a new route via Citadel Pass and Og Lake. When Wilcox was forced to

Henry G. Bryant. Photo, American Alpine Journal, 1944.

go back for some gear he lost near Citadel Pass, Bryant and Steele tried to climb Assiniboine, getting to about 10,000'. Attempting to beat an approaching storm on the descent, they survived a frightening fall.

The party left the area via the creek which now bears Bryant's name and the Spray Lakes.

A founding member, and later, president of the American Alpine Club, Bryant had unsuccessfully attempted Mt. St. Elias in 1897, the same year the Duke of Abruzzi made the first ascent, but by a different route. On his return, Bryant went aboard the Duke's ship to congratulate him. He found Abruzzi "so disfigured by venomous bites as to be totally unrecognizable." The famous Italian climber told him, "Mr. Bryant, I have conquaired ze Mt. St. Elias, but ze mosquitoes, zay have conquaired Me!"

In 1901, **James Outram** (1864-1925), with two Swiss guides, made the first ascent of Mt. Assiniboine. He boasted, "The date of September 3 is now a marked one in [Mt. Assiniboine's] calendar." After reading another account Outram wrote, in which he pointed out how quickly he travelled, Edward Whymper, no modest man himself, was outraged: "It would have been better if someone else had said it."

Possibly Whymper was upset that Outram, who was his guest, had stolen his outfitter, Bill Peyto. Or perhaps as the first man to scale *The Matterhorn*, Whymper felt a need to put down a rival who had made the pioneer ascent of *The Matterhorn of the Rockies*.

An Anglican curate who came to Canada in 1900 for his health, Outram was a superb alpinist, but with an ego. In 1920, he held the record for first ascents in the Rockies, and no doubt this was on his mind when he proposed that we name our highest mountains for the greatest climbers.

One of his outfitters, Jimmy Simpson, held this candid assessment of the great mountaineer: "Outram ... wanted all the glory himself. His guide, Kaufmann, was just help. He mellowed later in life when he came into the title of Sir."

Sir James Outram. By permission, Whyte Museum of the Canadian Rockies.

Ever since **Conrad Kain** led the first ascent of Mt. Louis in 1916, that mountain has been a touchstone for climbing excellence. With its vertical strata, the mountain seems unscaleable. Kain told his client, "Ye gods, Mr. MacCarthy, just look at that; they never will believe we climbed it."

The man most closely associated with Mt. Louis is **Lawrence Grassi**. Born in Falmenta, near Torino, Italy, Andrea Lorenzo Grassi (1890-1980), was one of the greatest mountain guides of his time. He was also the finest trail builder the Canadian Rockies has seen. Generous and unassuming, he was admired and loved by all who knew him.

After he moved to Canada in 1912, he Anglicized his name to Lawrence. Grassi spoke with a strong accent, though most of us who have a stereotyped image of how Italians speak, would not have identified his northern dialect. He never added extra vowel sounds at the end of his words; he would say "Shteep r-r-rock," with a fierce burr. You had to listen to him carefully, because he spoke in a soft voice.

There is ample testimony of the high regard he earned. After Grassi's eyesight faded, Bill Cherak, who read him his mail, found letters from famous people around the world.

The modest guide has been praised in Canada's House of Commons. In 1938, Dr. J. S. Woodsworth proposed naming Grassi Lakes (near Canmore) in his honor. As recorded in *Hansard*, his speech ends, "The world needs Grassis ... men who will seek new paths; make the rough places smooth; bridge the chasms that now prevent human progress; point the way to higher levels and loftier achievements."

Late in life, Grassi received the Alberta Achievement Award.

In 1916, the young Italian moved to Canmore to work in the coal mines. Within a few years, his mountaineering proficiency was famous. The Swiss guides at Lake Louise were jealous of his renown, though he did not really compete with them, and he never charged a client a fee. Yet he matched the Swiss in climbing skill, and surpassed them in customer relations. Where the Swiss were formal, he was down to earth.

Ken Boucher told me "Grassi was the last person you'd think of as a climber. He wore braces to hold up his trousers, and never wore proper climbing boots; he used old miner's boots with hobnails."

Bob Hind wrote, "During his last few years of guiding, Lawrence ... climbed in ordinary rubber boots such as farmers wear. This did not impair his ability since he ascended Hungabee in this unconventional footgear." Peter Vallance said Grassi went up one part of Mt. Inglismaldie in stocking feet.

Yamnuska was a favorite solo climb. He pioneered many routes there. But the mountain closest to his heart was Mt. Louis. He climbed it "Jusht thir-rty-two times," he told me. Peter Vallance was amazed at Grassi's detailed knowledge of the route. As they were climbing down the chimney, at one point Peter couldn't find anything to grab. The guide shouted from above to reach into the crack, beside his knee. Sure enough, there was a good hold.

Once, he made trips up Louis on successive days, the second ascent to retrieve an iceaxe his companion had left on the summit. Tim Auger put Grassi's achievement in perspective. "At the time, this route was the world standard of rock climbing, as difficult as anything people were doing in Europe." When Auger visited him in the Canmore lodge, Grassi was blinded by cataracts. Yet he described in detail the route on the lowest of the Three Sisters which Tim could see, but for the aged man was only a dark blur. Later, when he made the climb, Tim found Grassi's description precise.

Lawrence's nonchalance on steep cliffs was legendary. Sidney Vallance mentioned that on the broad summit of the Tower of Castle Mountain, his guide walked to the sheer cliff, and with his legs dangling over the abyss, ate lunch. His assurance on difficult places helped put companions at ease. "I was nervous when we did the face of Cascade, but just watching Lawrence ahead made me feel confident," said Lud Kamenka.

If you examine *The Climber's Guide*, you will find Grassi's name listed for many first ascents. "But," Lud Kamenka told me, "no one will ever know how many climbs he made. He often did solo routes which have never been recorded, including many first ascents. When we went up Mt. Charles Stewart, I rushed to the cairn to put my name inside. But I couldn't get Lawrence to sign. He said, 'I know I climbed it. That's enough.'"

Grassi was always disappointed he didn't climb Mt. Waddington in 1936. His companions never realized he was an accomplished guide, so he had no say in the route the party attempted. Stan Larsen said that after he returned, Grassi told Lizzie Rummel "They wouldn't listen to common sense."

In 1926, when he was only thirty-six, he was made a Life Member of the Alpine Club of Canada, a rare appointment in those days. That year, Dr. Williams fractured his ankle near the summit of Mt. Bastion in the Tonquin. Grassi carried the much larger man on his back for two miles down the steep mountain, across a glacier and moraine to a rescue party. At the 1932 ACC camp, Lawrence climbed Mt. Sir Donald five times on successive days. Because the clients were usually slow, he got only a few hours sleep each night.

If necessary, he could travel fast. Bill Cherak told me that one November — when the days are short — he hiked from Canmore to Mt. Assiniboine, climbed the mountain, walked to Banff via Citadel Pass, and back to Canmore via Goat Creek. It took him four days to make the climb and to backpack 135 km (84 miles)!

Grassi learned to ski late in life. He glided with the poles between his legs and managed very well despite this unusual technique.

"Everyone who knew him spoke not only of his superb climbing ability, but of his immense strength," adds Bob Hind. "Wherever he worked

Lawrence Grassi, 1914. From the collection of Bill Cherak.

Lawrence Grassi on Mt. Charles Stewart. Photo, Sidney Vallance, from the library of the Skyline Hikers.

one can see huge stones that he moved single-handed to construct steps, bridges or pavement.

"Lawrence was at Glacier Camp in 1932, where he took a party of Camp boys [Hind plus Ken and Hugh Boucher] over the Asulkan Pass to set up a fly camp above the Geikie Glacier. Most people think of Grassi as a miner, but before he came to Canada he was a lumberjack and his skill with an axe was great. When the fly camp was set up, he cut a six inch tree some way up the mountain. Two blows with the axe and he pushed the tree over, lopped off the branches and grabbing one end of the 25 foot long trunk, came bounding down the mountain. After the tent was up he moved a five hundred pound stone, the size of a kitchen range — the three of us together couldn't budge it — to a suitable place to set the cook's stove.

"Once, at Fay Hut, Lawrence showed up with a huge load including a ten gallon can of paint. He had left another can part way up the final hill which we went down and fetched. That was the only time I ever heard him admit he was a little tired. Because of the lead content, the paint cans would have weighed about a hundred pounds each. In addition, he was packing his personal gear."

Eventually Grassi overdid it, hurt his back, and had to give up climbing.

Grassi is unmatched for the quality and quantity of his trail work. No one has detailed all the paths he built. His first trails were near Canmore, beside the Bow River, and to the lakes which now bear his name.

Beneath the south end of Mt. Rundle, these two clear blue tarns used to be called Twin Lakes. In 1925 , with the help of other miners, he constructed a trail to the site, starting at the back of his small house where he always left a bucket of walking sticks he had fashioned for hikers. At the upper lake, he dug three cave-like shelters, made a fire pit, and built benches. These shelters, now partly filled by debris from the road to Spray Lakes, can still be seen.

The trail from Grassi's cabin passed a sulphur spring where he dug a swimming hole, six feet down at the deep end. He trenched the effluent a mile to the Bow River so it wouldn't pollute the town's drinking water. Beside the pool, he fashioned picnic tables and benches. At the time, Canmore was part of Rocky Mountains Park; when authorities in Banff found out what he'd done, they made him fill in the pool.

His best known trail work was done at Lake O'Hara, many of his paths built on early visits.

Lud Kamenka noted, "For many years the Canmore mines operated only three days every two weeks, Wednesday one week, and Tuesday and Thursday the alternate week. On days off, Lake O'Hara was Grassi's favorite spot. He made trails there in the 30's. Lake McArthur and Odaray Plateau were two of them."

When Chief Warden Jim Sime asked Grassi to take over the newly built warden cabin at O'Hara in 1956, he was delighted. "When I brought him his first pay cheque, he was as surprised as if it were Christmas. He didn't expect to be paid. He had been asked to give visitors advice and information. Grassi was picked because of his familiarity with the trails and the mountain routes. But he took it on himself to work on the trails, making new routes and improving existing ones.

"When I saw what he was doing, I suggested he use dynamite. He told me 'No, it would ruin the serenity of this place.'"

Single-handed, Grassi built the lakeshore trail, for the most part following George Link's path. But where Link's route crawls over rocks, he made a way around them; where Link went in a straight line through trees, he followed the shoreline. Other routes, such as Oesa and McArthur, he widened to standard width. Link was startled when he first saw Grassi hoist his huge wheelbarrow on his back and carry it up the switchbacks when he worked on the Lake Oesa trail. He moved rocks weighing more than half a ton. Tim Auger noted that Grassi came from a community in Italy where even the clotheslines were made from rock, so stone-work was in his blood.

He had to give up the Lake O'Hara job in 1960 after park officials found out he was over 65.

When he stayed at the Banff ACC Clubhouse, he was always busy building steps, railings, benches, and a trail to a viewpoint which club members still call Grassi's Lookout. In 1933 he made the trail to Mt. Louis.

While working at Skoki in 1947, he started a trail to Merlin Lake but he didn't have time to finish it. Jeanette Manry, who managed Skoki Lodge, said his trail was supposed to stay high.

Presumably he planned to build steps up the cliffs like he did at Lake Oesa, or to engineer a catwalk as he had done on a cliffside on Pigeon Mountain. (He showed Don Gardner this trail he made for the Youth Hostel Association to link Canmore to Jumping Pound and Bragg Creek. When the Trans-Canada Highway was constructed on the west side of the Bow River, much of the route was wiped out.)

Grassi was long ahead of his time in his feeling of respect for the country. When he looked after the Elizabeth Parker Hut, he would pack firewood for miles, rather than cut nearby trees, which grow slowly at that high elevation. Yet, Jim Sime overheard a club member thoughtlessly criticize the condition of the hut. Lawrence said nothing, but he was deeply hurt. "He never showed it, but he had a thin skin."

Grassi enjoyed the mountains more than any other man according to Ken Boucher. Lud Kamenka called him a true naturalist. "He knew all the flowers and animals."

When Grassi didn't show up in Calgary for an eye examination, Joe Clitheroe asked what happened. He explained, "When I got to Ghost Dam, I looked back, and those mountains looked so far away, I had to go back."

His friends tolerated his enthusiasm with affection. "He brought his slides to my father's house at Minnewanka Landing," Peter Vallance, told me. "And he showed them all! It went on for three hours! We tried to keep our eyes open, but everyone was nodding off."

It bothered Grassi that some climbers didn't share his love for the mountains. He told me, "A lot of them are only in it for the glory. When they can no longer do the big peaks, they won't come back."

Jean Gill summed up Grassi's character in a word: unassuming.

When a young man was killed on a solo climb of Mt. Grotto, Grassi went up, recovered the body, and brought it down for burial. No one asked him to take on this kind of unpleasant job. He never did it for pay.

When Ken and Mary Betts took Grassi to Jasper, he wouldn't go into the motel with them, insisting on camping out. Nor could they get him to share their meals. "He was happy to open a can of stew instead of eating steak. He hated to bother anyone."

People who knew him only in his old age were surprised at the condition of his home. As his eyesight faded, his house grew black with dust from his coal stove. He loved wine and the odd glass of whisky. When Ken Betts and Keir MacGougan visited, they always brought him a bottle of rye. Grassi would bring out three blackened glasses. "You didn't ask for a towel to clean them because the towel was dirtier than the glasses," said MacGougan.

When people took food to him, he would protest, saying he had lots. "I got some stew. You want some?" Frightened by the clouds of dust in his shack, the guests always declined.

Grassi didn't claim the old age pension. "I've got enough. Why should the government look after me?" he said. It took Sidney Vallance a couple of years to persuade him to accept it.

He would give Bill Cherak's children a dollar for doing chores like taking clothes to the Laundromat. A dollar was a lot of money to him; he would caution them, "Don't tell your father I paid you."

No doubt Grassi's character was molded in his youth. Bill Cherak told me an early harrowing experience which shows his sensitivity, his desire to please, and his moral values.

When he was a child in Italy, he saw where a woman had left a small bar of soap near the stream where the village women did their laundry. He knew his mother had no soap that day, so he took it home to her. She dragged him by the ear to the stream and made him give it back to the person who had left it. But that wasn't his worst memory.

Lawrence Grassi on unidentified summit (probably Mount Louis). Photo courtesy Mary Betts.

Lawrence Grassi, about 70. Photo from the collection of Bob Hind.

"As we went through the streets, my mother denounced my crime to everyone we passed, saying, 'This is my son, the thief.'"

Grassi ended the story, "You know, since that day, I never stole."

He lived simply; his house had neither telephone nor indoor plumbing.

When Steve Cherak, who had sold him his house in 1926, offered to put up new wallpaper, Grassi always said no, he was satisfied with what was already there.

Dr. K. MacGougan, who operated on his cataracts, turned the tables on the man who never accepted pay for guiding. This predated Health Care. When MacGougan refused to take payment, Grassi became upset. Eventually, he presented the specialist with a lovely piece of quartz crystal he had collected. Although the operation was successful, his sight soon degenerated (incurably) to shadow vision because of his deficient bachelor's diet.

After going without teeth for years, gumming his food, Grassi finally got a false store-bought set which he wore for company. But when he walked to the Skyline Hiker's Spray River camp in 1943, he was toothless. Sidney Vallance asked what happened. Grassi grinned: he'd got them stained chewing tobacco (he wore out a spitoon from the habit); when he tried to clean them in boiling water, they warped.

Stan Larsen called Grassi "the happiest, sanest, and politest bachelor. He liked women, and some friends urged him to marry, once suggesting he ask Lizzie Rummel. He answered, 'I got nothing to offer her. I'm an old man.'" He loved music and had many records, especially opera.

Lud Kamenka said, "He was the kind of man who would never hurt you; probably he would do you good. Once, he saw crystals above Bow Lake and was especially pleased with a giant piece he found. He was on the lookout for a mate to make bookends. Taking friends to the site, he found another big one. After he got back to his car, he set it on the running board. While he had his lunch, it was taken. As these *friends* drove away, I could see he was upset. It wasn't in his nature to say anything to them. If they'd asked him, he would have given it gladly, but it bothered him that they just took it."

Grassi had a wry sense of humor. In 1935 when Social Credit came to power in Alberta with promises of money handouts, Lawrence snorted, "You don't get nothing for nothing."

In Grassi's old age, Bill Cherak's son took his washing. Once, his dark mine underwear came back shrunk. The old man teased him, "Wait till you get married. I'll tell your wife you don't know how to wash clothes!"

To the end, this unassuming guide hated to be a bother. The day he died, he said to his friend Bill Cherak, who was at his bedside, "I'm sorry, Bill."

TWO BANFF PIONEERS

Among early residents of Banff, the man most associated with hiking is **Norman Sanson** who is credited with walking 20,000 miles of trails. He joined the Alpine Club of Canada in 1913. Twenty years later, he became a founding member and first president of the Skyline Hikers.

Sanson (1862-1949) was put in charge of the Banff Museum when it opened in 1896, a post he held for 35 years. He collected specimens from the mountains nearby. Despite his lack of formal training, he was consulted by world authorities on natural history. In 1903, the present Banff Museum was built.

Sanson was appointed Banff meteorologist in 1896. That year, with George Paris, he ascended the north peak of Sulphur Mountain on snowshoes from the Cave and Basin. The two men returned to the Middle Hot Springs, sliding down much of the way. Norman chose the summit for a weather observatory which was built in 1903. On his winter trips up to this lofty station, Sanson sometimes left bitterly cold temperatures in the valley and climbed to Chinook-warmed upper currents.

At first, Sanson visited the observatory every week, then every second week. The townspeople kept count. On July 1, 1931, the old man prepared to make his thousandth official ascent. For the occasion, friends organized a sunrise breakfast atop Sulphur Mountain, catered by the Banff Springs Hotel staff. Among the procession of townspeople who went with him to the summit, to celebrate the occasion was his friend Harry Leacock.

Sanson often visited the Leacock residence. Fred Leacock told me, "Sanson had a metronome voice which made you want to go to sleep." Being a bachelor, the meteorologist never worried how late he stayed, to the consternation of Fred's parents. Finally, Harry Leacock solved the problem of getting his friend to leave at a reasonable hour by purchasing a

Norman Sanson taking meteorological readings on Sulphur Mountain, ca 1925. Photo, Dan McCowan, by permission, Whyte Museum of the Canadian Rockies.

record of *God Save the King*, which he played when it got late. Fred recalled, "The first time Dad played it, the patriotic guest leapt to attention for the national anthem. After it was over, he said to Dad, 'They usually play that at the end of things.' Dad replied, 'That's right.' Sanson took the hint. He got so used to it, at eleven o'clock he would look at his watch and say to Dad, 'Time for the record.'"

Although a great hiker, Sanson had no experience with cars. Fred Leacock remembers his father driving Norman to Massive, so he could collect specimens from the Redearth Fireroad while Harry and Fred fished the Bow. When Sanson returned to the auto, he curled up in the back seat. The Leacocks didn't see him when they looked inside late in the day. So they went back to the Bow where they could watch the bridge for him as they continued to try their luck in the river. Long after it grew dark, they checked the vehicle again, and saw him. "Why didn't you blow the horn?" Harry blurted in vexation. "I'd have blown the horn, if I knew where to find it," the sheepish passenger replied.

In 1931, his last year as weatherman, Sanson led the King and Queen of Siam up Sulphur. Eight years later, King George VI asked the old man to accompany him up Tunnel Mountain.

Sanson ascended Sulphur at age 83 to observe a solar eclipse. A year before his death, the summit where the observatory stands was named Sanson Peak in his honour.

A devout Anglican as well as an enthusiastic climber, Sanson chose the epitaph inscribed on his tombstone: "Gone higher."

Another Banff pioneer closely associated with hiking is **Leonard, *Doc*, Leacock** (1904-1992). Whereas most early mountain travelers went on horseback, he usually walked.

Doc always said his birth came as such a surprise, he didn't speak for months. In 1908, when Leonard was four years old, the Leacocks arrived in Banff.

Harry Leacock had fought in the Boer War with fellow Englishman Sid Unwin. Harry planned to emigrate to South Africa, but Sid, who had moved to Banff, urged him to come to Canada. He invited the Leacocks to use his house. On the night of June 7, they arrived in Banff in pouring rain and met Unwin on the station platform. Sid was catching the train to Lake Louise to join Billy Warren guiding Mary Schäffer on her famous expedition to Maligne Lake. Sid pointed up Muskrat Street, "It's the last house on the right." The new arrivals trudged up the darkened street, wondering how they would know when they reached the last house. "When Dad was halfway up Tunnel Mountain, he knew we had passed it."

Life in early Banff was primitive. There was no electricity; water had to be carried half a block from Woodworth's well. The bathroom, in the back yard, had a half moon over the door.

In Doc's memory, the great event for every child in Banff was *The Christmas Tree*, held annually in Brewster's Hall. Mrs. Jack made sure every child received a present. Louis Hill, the town fireman, played Santa. Once, this celebration had to be cancelled because of an epidemic. So Hill went to each home in Banff to give the children their gifts. How could he foresee the hospitality of the townsfolk? At every house, parents insisted he have a drink before going back into the cold. Sometimes he was given tea. Other households plied him with stronger cheer to keep him warm as he made his

Leonard Leacock (right) and the author on Mt. Rundle, 1951. Photo, Leonard Leacock.

rounds. Since no one had expected him to play the Santa part for so long in an evening, no fly was designed into the Santa suit. It was always stuffed to give him the appropriate girth, then sewn up. By the time he reached the Leacock house, Louis was in agony from the accumulated fluids. To provide the necessary relief, he was stretched out on the kitchen table where Harry Leacock cut an appropriate opening. Harry referred to this operation as the first Caesarean Section ever performed on a man.

In 1924, Leonard moved to Calgary where he taught music at Mount Royal College for 63 years. From 1940-44 he served as Dean of Boys. Often he administered first aid at sports functions and in the residence. The boys began calling him *Doc*, a name which stuck.

A highlight of his creative career came when his orchestral tone poem *The Lonely Lake* was performed in Sweden. Another thrill came when he was asked to accompany the great Danish heldentenor Lauritz Melchior at a school benefit. When Doc saw the hall's old upright instrument, he protested, "Mr. Melchior, they won't hear the piano." The giant singer assured him, "Don't worry, they'll hear me."

Doc never lost his love of the mountains, returning to Banff each summer. In 1932 he went from Gleichen to Jasper on horseback, walking back to Banff after his pony got sick and died. The next year, he went to Castleguard Meadows. In 1935, he ran a hiking camp at Shadow Lake. Cartoonist Stew Cameron, who had shared the 1932 and 1933 trips, looked after the horses which supplied Leacock's Shadow Lake camp. Doc spent a summer at Castleguard Meadows working for Pat Brewster who had set up a string of camps from Banff to The Ice Fields, a venture devastated by the Depression. Only one party got as far as Doc's campsite.

Louis Hill, town fireman and Santa when Leonard Leacock was young, and Harry Leacock on Sulphur Mountain, celebrating Norman Sanson's thousandth ascent. Whyte Museum of the Canadian Rockies.

Leonard Leacock at his studio, Mount Royal College, 1953

Often, Doc did trips on his own. In 1950, he took Cy Harris's dog up Mt. Edith. On the way down, the pooch became frightened on a low cliff, and Leacock had to jump off the ledge holding it in his arms. Otherwise, the animal had no problems — but it didn't forget the experience. A few days later, Leacock met Harris on Banff Avenue. Cy asked where he had taken his pet. Hearing of the climb, Harris chuckled,

"Well that explains it. The dog won't leave the house. He hasn't been outside for two days!"

Doc got his adventurous nature from his father, a veteran of the Boer War, World War I, and World War II! In 1939, when Harry came to Calgary to join up, the medical officer recognized the Leacock name and asked him if he was acquainted with the man who taught music at Mount Royal College. Harry, who was twenty years overage, told the officer, "Yes, I know him very well. Leonard is my older brother." Perhaps, because his son went prematurely bald, Harry got away with it, serving overseas for two years before they discovered his true age. Doc tried to enlist but was rejected because of flat feet and a murmuring heart, disabilities which never slowed him on mountain trails.

Doc shared his love for hiking, introducing hundreds of his students and young friends like me to the Rockies.

Leacock was an outstanding amateur photographer who had photographs displayed at the Brussels World Fair, and published in prestigious magazines.

In 1986, Leonard Leacock was inducted into the Order of Canada.

THE AUTOMOBILE

Annie Staple was Rocky Mountains Park's first gate keeper. She began in 1916, when the park's eastern boundary was Exshaw. This was the first year cars entered the park, and since there were no facilities, she set up a table and tent near the road. On her first day, a visitor, suspicious of this casual arrangement, went to the RCMP in Banff and accused her of pocketing the fees. Her husband died in 1919, leaving her with a small family to raise on her earnings. Before she retired in 1948, the park gate moved to Carrot Creek, then to its present location.

When Annie Staple began her job, driving from Calgary to Banff was an all day trip;

View south from Pharaoh Peak, showing Scarab and Mummy lakes. Photo, Leonard Leacock.

everyone knew her. Today's highway allows fast access to the area; six lanes whisk you through the gate Mrs. Staple used to tend.

CANADIAN PARKS SERVICE

George Stewart surveyed the ten square mile area reserved for Canada's first national park in 1885. In addition he laid out Banff townsite and named the streets. When he was appointed the first park superintendent, January 1, 1887, he also served as town planner, supervisor of development, Justice of the Peace, and arbiter between government and townspeople. On June 3, 1887, the Reserve was enlarged (at Stewart's instigation) to 260 square miles and named Rocky Mountains Park. Perhaps his numerous duties were too much for Stewart. In 1897, he was relieved of his position because of an illegal land sale. It may have been no coincidence that he was fired after an election brought in a new government. Many decisions affecting national parks have been motivated by politics.

Stewart was concerned about forest fires, which were devastating in the early days of

Rocky Mountains Park Gate, Exshaw, ca 1925. Photo, Annie Staple, courtesy Canadian Parks Service.

wood-burning locomotives. He planned to flood old marshes and turn them into fire breaks.

One of Banff's first Fire Wardens was **Charlie Phillips**. In 1915, he obtained for the Park the first portable fire pump in North America. The apparatus was tried out at Castle Mountain Internment camp. Two men or a horse carried the 143 pound pump which could move 20 gallons of water per minute through 1,500 feet of hose. Hoses brought water from a lake or river to the pump and from there to the fire. Where water had to be raised more than 172 vertical feet, several pumps could be used.

The success of fire suppression eventually raised concerns that too much protection was unhealthy for the forests, and in 1983, Banff Park began to set controlled forest fires.

Ole Hermanrude is one of the many colorful wardens who worked near Banff, serving as Healy Creek district warden from 1951-1966. Among his accomplishments, he rerouted trails, like Allenby Pass, above the muddy valley floors.

Ole's pride in his district cabins was tested by a pack rat. "One fall warden Hugh Jennings and I were at Egypt Lake Cabin to cut and skid the yearly wood supply of firewood. Upon reaching the cabin I had bragged that this was one cabin that pack rats could not get into.

"We went to bed that night with few worries and slept like logs, that is until something landed on my forehead with four wet cold feet which violently shattered all hopes for a peaceful slumber. When I shone the flashlight around I discovered a fuzzy-faced pack rat sitting there on my pillow wiggling his whiskers at me.

"Hugh reacted with, 'This is one cabin pack rats can't get into,' and broke into throws of laughter that only Hugh was capable of. I didn't realize until then that he actually laughed backwards. "Aah, aah, aah!' rather than the normal 'Ha, ha, ha!' like most people. After opening the door, the chase of the year was on, behind

Superintendent George Stewart and his family at his house in Banff. By permission, Whyte Museum of the Canadian Rockies.

Banff's first fire engine. From the collection of Jim Sime.

everything, over and under everything in the cabin, including Hugh. My bare feet were getting colder as my temper was rising and the backward laughter continued until at last the rat made it safely out. After finding and repairing the hole beside the window frame we finally got back to sleep. The next day I saw the rat in the woodpile. I still hear that backward laugh of a good friend whenever I think of pack rats or of cutting wood."

Bill Vroom remembers Ole for his one liners, such as, "I'll never forget the time I passed out of grade 3. I was so excited, I forgot to shave." He used to describe the old lift at Sunshine, which snapped you forward with a jolt, as, "The only ski tow in the world with a jerk on every line."

THE ALPINE CLUB OF CANADA

Robin C. (Bob) Hind has a distinguished mountaineering record, and a history of generous service to the Alpine Club of Canada.

Bob's peers will tell you that he is among the finest climbers Canada ever produced. In 1932, he got a job at the ACC Rogers Pass camp. Here he made his first climbs with two other camp boys, Ken and Hugh Boucher.

Hind has kept detailed records of all his climbs: 276 significant summits, 21 of them first ascents. This tally doesn't include some of his toughest routes because they were short

Bob Hind, after climbing Mt. Robson, 1936. Photo, Sterling Hendricks, from the collection of Bob Hind. Bob's face is marked from the crampons of Hendricks who fell on the ascent.

(rock faces he did when his electrical engineering job took him to Britain), or easy climbs like 9,000' Nub Peak. To appreciate his achievements, you must remember Bob was away from the Rockies for eight years on war service and at work in England. Also, our mountains weren't so easily approached when he was in his prime. Backpacking to Clemenceau took him three days; today, you can go in an hour by helicopter.

Jim Tarrant says Hind is a great navigator; in a white-out, when nobody else could find the way, he stayed on the route. Returning from Mt. Alberta, he brought them out within fifty yards of where they had hung their sneakers at the Sunwapta River ford. On the descent, where many other climbers have trouble finding the route down because the mountain looks different, Bob never has a problem.

Bob is a responsible leader. Tarrant calls him a "sensible climber," not one who will continue to the summit at all costs. Pacing himself to his party, he believes in traveling at a rate you can keep up all day. He would start the climb slowly, then gain momentum. If the trip demanded it, he might drive people to keep them going, but he always brought his group back together.

He could move fast if he were with a strong party. Ken Boucher remembers them climbing Mt. Edith and driving back to Calgary to play tennis at 2:00. Ken also recalls a trip up Victoria from Wiwaxy Gap which Bob led. Edward Feuz saw them from the summit, and said he thought it was the police coming up after him. Before Bob climbed Biddle, a friend told them he would watch for him on the summit at 2:00; Bob was back by 12:30! Returning from Mt. Assiniboine, with Rex Gibson setting a fast pace, two Americans in the party noticed Gibson eased the pace as they ascended Og Mountain (as a shortcut), and whispered hopefully, "He's slowing down." Before the day was over, they covered 35 miles!

Bob has climbed most of the peaks near Mt. Assiniboine (many of them several times): Assiniboine, Eon, Sturdee, Wedgwood, Towers, Terrapin, Magog, Brussilof, in addition to the easy ones: Wonder and Nub. He also did a high traverse over the Assiniboine—Sturdee col to Aurora Creek. The club's R. C. Hind Hut at Mt. Assiniboine is named in his honour.

Among his memorable trips was the long route to Mt. Clemenceau. "It was new country for me, a trip of exploration." Bob rates the NW ridge of Sir Donald, Mt. Tupper and his solo of Mt. Louis as his most enjoyable climbs. Another highlight was scaling Dungeon Peak in the Tonquin, a long difficult first ascent, made after several strong parties, one led by a Swiss guide, had failed. "I like the Tonquin. It's good rock," he told me. Bob compares climbing with other athletic endeavors. "You are pitting yourself against something challenging which you try to overcome." He doesn't condone *hardware climbing*. Although he carried aids for safety, he says if you can't do the climb on your own ability, you shouldn't be trying it. He adds, "Climbing is not really hard; you just need a bit of courage."

Bob's stoicism was demonstrated when he was injured on Mt. Marpole. The accident happened at 11:00 am August 30, 1947. He had ascended a cliff and sat on a huge boulder to belay his fiancée, Peggy. She slipped, and as Bob took the strain on the rope the boulder slid off the ledge as if it were on rollers, carrying him over the cliff. He fell 20 to 30 feet, and rolled down the scree, stopping before another small cliff. Bob looked at his leg and saw the foot splayed at right angles, the bone protruding from the skin at the ankle. With the broken foot flapping loose, he rappelled down the 30 foot cliff to a safe ledge where another climber straightened his leg and strapped it to his ice-axe. Wheelbarrow fashion, Bob descended about 500 feet, on his hands and good leg while another man supported his broken limb. As he waited for help, he watched a small pond far below turn pink with his blood. Two climbers brought a toboggan from the Stanley Mitchell Hut, where Bob was carried, arriving at 7:30 pm. All this time, Bob had nothing to deaden the pain.

Peggy had rushed ahead to Twin Falls Chalet to phone for a doctor, getting there just as the staff were leaving for the day. The doctor who came from Field tried to splint the leg, but didn't do it right on his first try, and the leg snapped back. Bob said this hurt a lot more than the first time when the non-professional straightened it. The doctor wouldn't administer any pain killer, fearing if he were sedated, Hind might fall off the horse he had to ride to the road at Takakkaw Falls. They reached the Falls at 12:30 am and Bob was driven to Calgary, arriving at 7:30 am.

His injury on Marpole inhibited climbing for two years, but he was determined to overcome the impediment. After climbing Mt. Bowlen with the ankle wobbling, he had the joint fused (at 5° off from normal to allow him to climb). The operation left him with one leg shorter than the other and an ankle he couldn't bend. Because his heel came up when he bent his knee, skiing was difficult, but Bob managed it by placing most of his weight on his good leg.

A small, wiry man, in his prime Bob had remarkable strength and could do one arm push-ups with ease. Now, at age 82, his climbing days are over, but he still goes to the Rockies to hike. He has a deep love of the mountains, though he has seen them too often in dangerous conditions to get lyrical over them.

Although Bob is taciturn, he is great company, with a keen wit and lots of self assurance. He is not one to mince words. If you do something silly, he will tell you. He has strong opinions, such as the responsibilities of the trip leader and is critical of guides who leave the party behind to get back early for tea.

Bob Hind receiving an award from Bill Goodrich, ACC Camp, 1953. Photo, Barbara Richardson, from the collection of Bob Hind.

Bob has a fund of memories from his mountain experiences, such as Major Longstaff, brother of the renowned English mountaineer, who brought his own bathtub to every ACC camp. Once, he brought a sewing machine and sail making equipment. He also took liquor to camp, something unheard of just after World War II. Other campers whispered, perhaps with envy, "He drinks, you know." Bob also remembers climbing Brussilof with an excessively slow Englishman in the party. On the descent, they had to shelter under a rock in a violent thunderstorm. This woke up the Brit. "When we started moving again, I had to slow him down so the others could keep up."

When Rudolph Aemmer was climbing Assiniboine, he dropped his pipe. He shouted, "Grab it, grab it." The climbers below, hearing the clattering brier, and misunderstanding his words, dodged, shouting the warning to those below, "Rock, rock." To his dismay, Rudolph

Bob Hind climbing Martin's Peak, 1954. Photo, Len Chatwin, from the collection of Bob Hind.

saw them rushing out of the way of his precious pipe. (Bob retrieved it on the way down.)

During the war, when Bob was in the navy, Major Rex Gibson tried to get him transferred to help train the Lovat Scouts for mountain warfare. Gibson received a telegraphed reply from headquarters, "The army doesn't need any help from the navy."

Teaching is in his blood, as Bob's thirty years work with Wolf Cubs show. Ken Boucher says Bob is rigid about using proper technique for safety and gets upset if you don't keep the proper tension on the rope. Bruce Fraser says Bob stresses "climbing quietly"; if you take the time to place your feet carefully, you reduce the chance of causing accidents by knocking down loose rocks, and you'll be a lot better climber.

Bob has been a staunch supporter of the ACC. He started climbing when working for the club as camp boy. He has served the organization as chairman of the hut committee, the climbing committee, and Chairman of the Calgary Section. He led climbs at every camp and participated in work crews at club huts.

Once when he was repairing the electrical wiring at the Clubhouse, an English member made a sarcastic comment behind Bob's back, "There goes the patriarch of the club." Little did he know how prophetic this was. Bob was awarded the Silver Rope in 1935, made an Honorary Member in 1969, and awarded a service badge in 1971. He became club Vice President (1954-55), and President (1964-65). In 1990, he was made Honorary President.

After he climbed Mt. Brussels (the difficult peak Frank Smythe couldn't climb), Bob got a standing ovation at the Fryatt Creek camp in 1960, the only time participants remember this reaction at any ACC camp. He was 50 years old when he did it.

THE SKYLINE HIKERS & THE TRAIL RIDERS OF THE CANADIAN ROCKIES

In 1924 The Skyline Trail Riders of the Canadian Rockies were organized by John Murray Gibbon, author and head of publicity for the CPR. Nine years later, Gibbon added a sister association, The Skyline Trail Hikers. Both groups were sponsored by the CPR until 1961.

A guest of the 1931 camp of the Trail Riders was Prajadhipok (1893-1941), King of Siam. His grandfather was King Mongkut (Rama IV), the protagonist in Anna Leonowens' book, *Anna and the King of Siam* which Rogers and Hammerstein turned into a musical, *The King and I*. His father, Prince Chulalongkorn, was the eldest son in Anna's story. Prajadhipok succeeded his half brother who died without heir in 1925. He ruled Siam as Rama VII from 1925-35. His absolute monarchy ended in 1935 when he abdicated in favor of his son.

The first president of the Skyline Hikers was Norman Sanson who is credited with over 20,000 miles of hiking. When he retired as Banff meteorologist at age 69, his hiking time up Sulphur Mountain was less than two hours.

John Murray Gibbon, 1924. By permission, Glenbow Archives, Calgary, NA 1263-1.

INDEX

Names of trails are printed boldface. Page listings for trail descriptions and main entries are boldface and come before other page entries.

Mount Assiniboine and Lake Magog ca 1900. Photo, George and Mary M. Vaux, Alpina Americana. Compare with page 44 for glacier recession.

"The experiences we had together are a fund of delightful reminiscence for the years to come, when the now willing feet will have to be content to travel nearer and smoother paths." Mrs. Algernon St. Maur (Duchess of Somerset), *Impressions of a Tenderfoot*